The Sac and Fox Indians

THE CIVILIZATION OF THE AMERICAN INDIAN SERIES

The Sac and Fox Indians

By WILLIAM T. HAGAN

NORMAN
UNIVERSITY OF OKLAHOMA PRESS

LIBRARY OF CONGRESS CATALOG
CARD NUMBER: 58-6851
ISBN: 978-0-8061-2138-3

The Sac and Fox Indians is volume 48 in The Civilization of
the American Indian Series.

To April

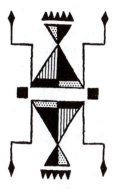

Preface

THE HISTORY of the Sac and Fox Indians is a case study of the results of the clash of two civilizations. The Sacs' and Foxes' experience was not unique in most respects. The Osages, the Iowas, the Winnebagos, and scores of other tribes were confronted with comparable problems, with usually the same miserable results.

Unfortunately, the tendency has been to ignore in the history of the Sacs and Foxes all but those bloody events of 1832. There were important events leading up to the Black Hawk War, including a significant role in the War of 1812 and a tragic history following 1832. This is an attempt to bring the entire story into better perspective.

Although the Sac and Fox Indians are currently regarded as one tribe, I have chosen to consider them as two tribes throughout the book, in preference to arbitrarily selecting a date at which the two tribes may be said to have become one.

My debt to those who have assisted and inspired me along the way is considerable. Professor William B. Hesseltine supervised my early research and urged me to continue my work. Professor Carl Sutton read a draft of the manuscript and made suggestions concerning style. Dorothy Rideout, Margaret Nichols, and Mary Pennal not only shared in the typing but frequently challenged my mode of expression.

The staffs of several libraries and institutions were uniformly co-operative. These include North Texas State College, the University of Wisconsin, the Illinois Historical Library, the State Historical Society of Wisconsin, the Kansas Historical Society, the Chicago Historical Society, the Missouri Historical Society, the Oklahoma Historical Society, the Dallas Public Library, the Library of Congress, and the National Archives.

Clifford L. Lord, Alice Smith, and Josephine Harper of the State Historical Society of Wisconsin not only provided assistance and encouragement, but also furnished working quarters in the early stages of the manuscript. North Texas State College, by special research grants, aided me in completing the project.

To Chief Emory Foster, Sadie Feder, Horace Wakilli, and other Sacs and Foxes I am indebted for an insight to the current Sac and Fox status in Oklahoma. Robert K. Thomas, a happy combination of anthropologist and Cherokee Indian, shared generously with me his unrivaled knowledge of the modern Sacs and Foxes and introduced me to many members of the tribes.

Raymond H. Bitney, assistant area director for the Bureau of Indian Affairs at Anadarko, Oklahoma, and Robert Grover, in charge of the agency office at Shawnee, Oklahoma, briefed me on the government policy towards the Sacs and Foxes.

The *Missouri Historical Review* has granted me permission to reprint material it first published.

Finally, I must acknowledge the continuous and indispensable aid of my wife, Charlotte Nix Hagan, in all phases of the preparation of the manuscript.

William T. Hagan

Fredonia, New York

Contents

Illustrations

The Sac and Fox Indians

MAPS

The Sac and Fox Indians

1. The Sacs and Foxes of the Mississippi Valley

IN THE spring of 1800, as Sacs and Foxes on the upper Mississippi deliberated in council, William Henry Harrison, delegate from Northwest Territory, rose in Congress Hall to introduce a bill. The young legislator proposed that Congress divide Northwest Territory into two political units, and a few weeks later President John Adams signed the bill creating Indiana Territory. To serve as governor, Adams chose well-qualified Delegate Harrison. The stalwart twenty-seven-year-old Harrison had served his apprenticeship in the regular army under that taskmaster Anthony Wayne. After resigning his army commission, Harrison became secretary of Northwest Territory in July, 1798. From this office the voters of the territory had sent him to Congress.

From his new capital at Post Vincennes, Harrison surveyed a domain which extended from the Ohio River on the south to the Canadian border, and from what is now the western boundary of the state of Ohio to the Mississippi. Inhabiting this vast region was a scanty population of about 5,500 whites, most of them of mixed French and Indian blood. Using canoes, keels, mackinaws, and flatboats to navigate the rivers of the area, on land the infrequent traveler followed the paths trodden by the buffalo and Indians.

Although they were not included in the census returns of 1800, the population of Indiana Territory included many thousands of Indians. In the summer of 1795, Harrison had been present when Wayne negotiated the Treaty of Greenville with tribes from this area, and as aide to the General he assumed the duty of seeing the provisions of the treaty carried into effect. This training stood Harrison in good stead as governor, for the activities of the traders, the naturally belligerent proclivities of the Indians, and the encroachment of white settlers upon Indian lands brought inevitable clashes between the two contending civilizations under his jurisdiction.

Not so closely in contact with the advancing line of settlement as many of the other Indian nations in the territory of Indiana, the Sac and Fox tribes afforded Harrison many unhappy moments. Residing in several villages scattered along the banks of the Mississippi from around the mouth of the Des Moines River to the French settlement at Prairie du Chien, these Indians, on the grounds that they had never entered into treaty relations with the United States, refused to negotiate with the governor of Indiana Territory.[1] True, they had not signed the Treaty of Greenville, but at Fort Harmar in January, 1789, two Sacs signed the treaty which Governor Arthur St. Clair of Northwest Territory concluded with representatives of several tribes. Article XIV of that treaty specifically mentioned the Sacs as being received into the "friendship and protection" of the United States on an equal basis with the other tribes.[2]

The role of the Sacs and Foxes in the Old Northwest made some settlement with them a necessity. Brave and warlike, they

[1] Harrison to the Secretary of War, July 15, 1801, in *Messages and Papers of William Henry Harrison* (ed. by Logan Esarey), I, 25–31.
[2] The text of any treaty cited in this study may be found in Charles J. Kappler (ed.), *Indian Affairs: Laws and Treaties*.

4

had dispossessed the Illinois Indians who formerly inhabited their area. Originally, their home had been to the north—the Sacs in the upper Michigan peninsula and the Foxes on the south shore of Lake Superior. Midway in the seventeenth century, Iroquois and French pressure drove the Sacs south to the area around Green Bay. Previously, the Chippewas had eased the Foxes out of their lands on the shore of Lake Superior, and the latter had gradually moved south until they occupied land around Lake Winnebago and along the Fox River.

In the early eighteenth century an attack by the French drove the Sacs and Foxes into the close confederation which marked their relationship until the middle of the next century. When the French sought to punish the Foxes for interfering with their traders, the Foxes sought refuge in the midst of the Sacs. The latter, though friendly to the French, refused to surrender the culprits, and the French vented their wrath upon both tribes. This attack forced the now allied tribes to migrate again, and they jointly attacked the Illinois Indians, whose land they coveted.

By the time Governor Harrison entered upon his duties at Post Vincennes, the Sacs were living in one large village and several small ones on the Mississippi, between the mouth of the Des Moines and the mouth of the Rock. The Foxes were scattered in several villages, from the mouth of Rock River north along the banks of the Mississippi to Prairie du Chien. The largest Sac village, Saukenuk, was the wonder of all who visited it. Occupied by the majority of the Sac nation, in 1817 it contained probably one hundred lodges, and its chiefs could muster one thousand warriors. The location, on a point of land between Rock River and the Mississippi, was an enviable one. The rushing waters at the rapids of the Rock and of the Mississippi teemed with fish. Extensive stands of bluegrass around the village furnished ample pasturage for the horses. On the fertile prairie which ran parallel to the Mississippi,

5

the women of Saukenuk and an adjoining Fox village tilled several hundred acres of corn.

Besides raising enough corn to allow for a surplus to be sold to the traders, the women cultivated pumpkins, beans, and squash. From the bluff which rose out of the prairie bordering the Mississippi gushed several springs of clear, sparkling water. Rock Island and the surrounding country provided in abundance berries, apples, plums, and nuts to enhance the diet of the Sacs and Foxes. In exile, Black Hawk remembered, "We always had plenty—our children never cried with hunger, nor our people were never in want."

One or more families lived in each of Saukenuk's hundred lodges. Occupied only in the summer, the lodges were not constructed for warmth. Forty to sixty feet long and about twenty feet wide, they were simply furnished frames of upright posts covered with white elm bark. Running the length of each side of the lodge was a long bench covered with bark, upon which the women spread blankets and skins. The Indians left the area between the benches open for fires and food preparation. There was no opening for a chimney, and the smoke escaped either through the roof or out the doors. Sometimes fences, consisting of poles over which melon vines trailed, enclosed individual lodges. The entire village gave an impression of neatness and good order unusual among Indian habitations.

The Sacs and Foxes, particularly the Sacs, reflected this pride in appearance. Both nations were of Algonquian stock and had the culture of the eastern Woodland Indians modified by practices adopted from Plains tribes. Although they were so closely allied as to be treated as one nation, they retained definite tribal characteristics. Noted for their fighting ability and the relative efficiency of their political administration, the Sacs were respected throughout the upper Mississippi valley. Well developed physically and tastefully attired in breechclout and beaded moccasins, his scalp lock treated with vermillion and yellow, his face streaked with red, blue, and yellow, a string of wampum or bear's claws around his neck with ear bobs to match, the young Sac brave was an imposing sight.

His counterpart among the Foxes was equally impressive in appearance, although the Foxes did not enjoy the prestige accorded the Sacs. Their smaller number, perhaps 1,600 compared to 4,800 for the Sacs in 1804, was not the only explanation. While the Sacs were noted for their political organization, the Foxes were relatively deficient in this respect. Moreover, among an improvident people the Foxes were noted for improvidence and for their addiction to the white man's firewater. In the confederation the Foxes followed the lead of the Sacs.[3]

At best, government among the Sacs and Foxes was a slack harness for a primitive people. In each tribe, authority for enforcing the simple rules of its society nominally resided in the civil chiefs and a council composed of the chiefs and adult males. The posts of civil chief, of which there were several, one being accorded first rank, were hereditary. Despite the respect accorded the office in matters of social and ceremonial significance, the actual political control exercised by the chief depended largely upon his own personality. If he were wise in council and brave in the incessant warfare, the civil chief might exert considerable authority. If he displayed no such qualities, he found himself with little voice in tribal affairs. But even the influential chief found it expedient to bow to the wishes of the tribal council, which, in the final analysis, wielded what authority there was among the Sacs and Foxes.[4]

In addition to civil chiefs, the tribes distinguished outstanding braves, who were themselves the elite of the warriors, by granting them the title of war chief. They retained the title

[3] Thomas Forsyth to Thomas L. McKenney, August 28, 1824; Forsyth to Lewis Cass, May 12, 1822; both in Indian Office Files. Photostatic copies are in the possession of the State Historical Society of Wisconsin (hereafter, the term "Photostat WHS" will be used).

[4] Thomas Forsyth to William Clark, January 5, 1827, in Draper MSS. (State Historical Society of Wisconsin), 9T2-3.

only so long as they maintained their reputation for valor and resourcefulness. Actual leadership of a war party rested with any individual who could attract sufficient followers for such an expedition. A record of successful campaigning was a valuable asset in recruiting men for a war party against the current enemy, but dreams and visions likewise played an important role.

Ma-ka-tai-me-she-kia-kiak, or Black Sparrow Hawk, a Sac brave and war chief of about thirty summers when Harrison became governor of Indiana Territory, was typical of his class. The descendant of a chief, he was of medium but strong build. His sharp, dark hazel eyes, unshielded by eyebrows, peered over a Roman nose. His generous mouth overhung a slightly receding, sharp chin. Only a scalp lock adorned his otherwise shaven head. Not unpleasant, his features, with his light yellow complexion, had a slight Chinese cast.

Several children graced the lodge of Black Hawk, as he was commonly known, and Asshewequa, or Singing Bird, his attractive and devoted wife. Although polygamy was common among the Sacs and Foxes, Black Hawk remained faithful to Singing Bird. More typical of his tribe was the Sac's love of war. At the age of fifteen he had wounded an enemy and won the right to paint, wear feathers, and be called a brave. In the succeeding years Black Hawk led or was a member of many war parties which left Saukenuk in search of enemy scalps.

Whenever he wished to lead a war party, Black Hawk followed the customs of the tribe and prayed and fasted in order to communicate with the Great Spirit and receive some omen to rally others to his side. Since so much emphasis in the Sac and Fox society was placed upon skill and valor in combat, the young Indians were ever ready for war. If Black Hawk, or some other ambitious brave, could announce that the Great Spirit had informed him of the location of a band of unsuspecting Sioux, Osages, or Menominees and had assured him success, he had no difficulty recruiting his force. Individually, those who wished to join him would visit Black Hawk in a lodge which he had erected apart from the others and agree to place themselves under his leadership for the projected expedition. This was all that was necessary to loose a war party whose deeds might provoke retaliation and a general conflagration. Older and wiser heads might attempt to dissuade Black Hawk, but they were not often successful.

Like many primitive peoples the tribesmen displayed considerably more order in their social organization. Each family among the Sacs and Foxes belonged to one of the dozen or more great gens, or groups. Membership in the gens, which bore such names as Bear, Buffalo, Sturgeon, and Thunder, was hereditary. Important for the transmission of property, which had to be hereditary within gens, the groupings also had religious significance, and most of the ceremonials employed the concept.

Nonreligious in content but equally important in the social organization of the Sacs and Foxes was a division of the male population of each tribe into two orders. Like all other parents, Black Hawk and Singing Bird daubed with black or white paint the face of each of their sons at birth, thus enrolling him in one or the other of the orders. Distinguished by their face paint, the youths teamed with others of their order in the tribal games and vied in feats of daring and stratagem in war.[5]

The close social organization of the Sacs and Foxes helped the tribes maintain their unity despite a weak political structure and a migratory mode of life which led Black Hawk and his fellows to occupy their villages only between hunting trips. Normally, in the spring following their winter hunt, the Sacs returned to Saukenuk to plant their crops and deal with the traders. On arrival at the village, Black Hawk would repair his lodge and open the cache which he had left the previous fall.

[5] Sol Tax, "The Social Organization of the Fox Indians," Fred Eggan (ed.), *Social Anthropology of North American Tribes*, 243–44; Major Morrill Marston to Rev. Jedediah Morse, November, 1820, in Draper MSS., 1T58; Forsyth comments on this in Draper MSS., 9T6.

For days he and his family gorged themselves on the bark-packaged contents. The dried corn, squashes, beans, and crab apples, present so sparingly in their diet during the difficult winter months, had been carefully concealed in their hole by a covering of sod which blended with the rest of the prairie.

Having satisfied their immediate cravings, the Indians then turned to other occupations. Black Hawk and the other warriors traded, negotiated with their agent, and relaxed in long convivial sessions marked by smoking, boasting, and drinking liquor donated by the traders.

While Black Hawk and the other men were thus pleasantly engaged, Singing Bird took her hoe and joined the women and children in the fields. Planting in the same hills year after year made it unnecessary to clear new ground—by far the most difficult task of the farmer on virgin land. Three or four cultivations with a hoe sufficed, and after repairing the flimsy fences of poles, Singing Bird could join Black Hawk in the ceremonial feasts and dances which regularly occurred after the planting.

Following the feasting and dancing, the tribe once again dispersed. Black Hawk and the hunters departed for the boundless prairies west of Council Bluffs to stalk the elk and buffalo and the occasional party of Osages or other hostile bands also following the grazing herds. Singing Bird and the children fished and gathered bark for bags and flag reeds, from which the women wove the mats used in making their winter lodges. Or they might go up the Mississippi to the lead region to mine and smelt ore. The Foxes, who occupied the sites of some of the richest lead veins on the Mississippi, were particularly active in the production of the metal. Their annual output of three thousand to four thousand pounds of smelted metal went to the traders.

After a month or six weeks of these activities the hunters, lead miners, fishermen, and reed and bark gatherers reassembled at the village to share their various products and indulge in a riot of feasts, dances, and games. With plenty of food available for all, feast followed feast. As the fresh corn and other garden products became available, the Indians gorged themselves. Dysentery frequently resulted, and every year saw several deaths attributable to this ailment.

In addition to feasting, the Indians raced horses and played ball. With hundreds of excited warriors participating, the ball games on the open prairie were particularly spectacular. The ancestors of modern lacrosse, the games were played on a field perhaps two or three hundred yards long. In crucial games between bands or villages, warriors armed with rackets and fortified by fasting and ceremonials could turn the vigorous sport into a modified form of mayhem. Spectators and participants alike gambled heavily, wagering guns, horses, blankets, and other property on the outcome of the games and races. Infrequently, intertribal games and races provided occasions for great celebration.

Ball games and horse racing came to an end when the crops were in. A tribal council then convened to allot hunting areas for the coming winter and to fix a date for the Indians to leave the village. Caches dug, and corn, beans, and other garden products dried and buried for use the following spring, Black Hawk and his family were ready to depart.

Early in September the crier circulated through the village announcing the date of departure. In the last hours the Indians busily loaded canoes, prepared packs, and drew on credit from the traders the arms, ammunition, traps, and other items necessary for the long winter. On the chosen day the old men and the women and children slipped down the Rock in canoes and the able-bodied men turned their horses toward the hunting grounds.

Reassembling at their allotted area, the various bands of one or more families each settled down for uninterrupted hunting until the season of severe cold arrived. Then they congregated in the vicinity of the establishments of their traders, these hardy individuals having followed them to the hunting grounds. Attempting only a little hunting and trapping, the Indians waited out the worst of the winter snug in their winter lodges of mats and skins.

When the melting snows and mild breezes heralded the approach of spring, the encampments once more hummed with activity. Black Hawk joined one of the parties leaving to trap beaver, raccoon, and muskrats. With the others who remained behind, Singing Bird and the children prepared to go into sugar camp, a pleasant stop in the tribal itinerary. However, it was not of long duration, and the tribe soon reassembled at a rendezvous on the Mississippi to return to the village, settle with their trader, and begin the cycle again.

Over a period of a century and a half the Indians had become completely dependent upon the white trader.[6] Although Black Hawk, like any other Sac or Fox hunter, would have hotly denied the term, he was essentially a hireling of the fur companies. For the warrior, independence was a thing of the past. Without the articles supplied by the trader he could not have existed. Arms, ammunition, traps, cooking utensils, knives, blankets—all were obtained by Black Hawk and his fellows in return for their peltries. The tobacco he smoked and frequently the pipe in which he smoked it, the paint which adorned his face, and the wampum which he used as jewelry as well as a medium of exchange, came from the indispensable trader.

Over the years the Sacs and Foxes had dealt with French, Spanish, English, and American traders. Following the War of 1812 the Americans gradually supplanted their competitors, as John Jacob Astor's American Fur Company profited by Congress' exclusion of foreigners from the Indian trade.

Most of the transactions between the Indians and the traders involved credit. The improvident Indians seemed incapable of operating on any other basis. This situation satisfied the trader, as it gave him a hold on the hunter and helped insure

6 Thomas Forsyth to Lewis Cass, October 24, 1831, Photostat WHS.

that furs came to his post instead of that of his competitor. Although the debts stimulated the diligent Indians, the shiftless were consoled by the certainty of receiving credit for the next hunt, whether or not they had cleared their old account.

In 1806, Lewis and Clark estimated that the Sacs and Foxes, reputed to be the best hunters on the Mississippi and Missouri, brought $10,000 worth of furs annually to their traders.[7] By 1831 the trade had increased until Farnham and Davenport, the agents of the American Fur Company at Rock Island, who had practically a monopoly on the tribe's trade, could report that each year they invested capital ranging from $33,000 to $60,000. In the seven years preceding 1831 their total credits amounted to $137,000; $53,500 was still uncollected in 1831.[8]

Normally, Indian traders considered doubtful a debt not paid the first year. They termed desperate one unpaid for two years.[9] To be sure, there was one successful method employed whenever possible to collect old debts. This was to have them written into treaties. Thus, annuities might be applied on the debts, or the government might assume them in partial consideration for a land cession. Living for the moment, the Indians were more concerned with obtaining traps and powder for the next hunt than with the disposition of their land twenty years in the future. Each fall the Sacs and Foxes went into debt outfitting for the winter hunt and added to that debt by small purchases throughout the winter.

Under the prevailing credit terms the Indians could amass a considerable debt quite simply. In the late 1820's, Farnham and Davenport were marking up 25 to 50 per cent on such principal items of trade as blankets, and more on such minor items as brooches, playing cards, and mirrors. These same ar-

[7] *American State Papers: Indian Affairs*, I, 711.

[8] Russell Farnham and George Davenport to the Secretary of War, November 22, 1831, Photostat WHS.

[9] Henry R. Schoolcraft to Lewis Cass, October 24, 1831, L. F. Stock Transcripts in the possession of the State Historical Society of Wisconsin (hereafter cited as Stock Transcripts).

ticles, when sold to the Sacs and Foxes for cash, were marked up only 12.5 to 25 per cent. Nor was this the only source of profit. When the Sac and Fox hunters brought in their beaver, muskrat, raccoon, deer, and other skins, which constituted the principal part of their trade goods, Farnham and Davenport credited them with an arbitrary valuation on the furs, estimated to be 25 to 50 per cent below the St. Louis rate. Canoes, maple sugar, and meat were purchased at similar discounts.

Despite this apparently more than comfortable margin, the traders rarely became rich at the expense of Black Hawk and his fellows, although their parent firm, which supplied the trade goods and marketed the furs, frequently did. Farnham and Davenport had heavy expenses. When the Indians visited their posts, they expected and received rations. In times of famine, which were alarmingly frequent among the Indians, this became a serious drain. Also, traders found it politic to humor visiting hunters and their families with small gifts of tobacco, needles, thread, and flints.

Although Black Hawk did not realize the actual role he played for the American Fur Company, he did realize the importance of the trader in his way of life. A relationship had developed between the two parties which had no counterpart among other white-Indian relationships. Frequently taking wives from among the sisters or daughters of influential braves or chiefs, the traders enjoyed the unrivaled confidence of their customers. The Indians consulted them on their relations with other whites and with the United States government. Although members of war parties had an unsavory record for indiscriminate murder, no Sac or Fox ever separated one of his traders from his hair.

As a rival to the trader for influence with the Indians, the United States relied upon the Indian agent. Depending upon the experience and ability that he brought to his position, the agent could be a real asset to the tribe to which he was assigned and an able representative of his nation's interests, or an extremely ineffectual link between the two diverse peoples. Political appointees though they might be, the agents on the frontier of the Old Northwest during this period, with few exceptions, performed their functions in a reasonably efficient manner.

The role of mediator between Indians and whites was no sinecure. It required an individual with the wisdom of Solomon to resolve the multitude of intratribal, intertribal, and white-Indian conflicts which occurred. Year by year the line of settlement encroached upon the Sac and Fox hunting grounds and increased the possibility of clashes. Both Indians and whites appealed to the agent for justice. The complaints of the whites usually dealt with stolen livestock and dismantled fences, forced levies of food and drink, and, occasionally, beatings and scalpings. From the Sacs and Foxes came tales of trade frauds, invasion of hunting grounds, stolen horses, and, occasionally, beatings and murders.

Presumably, the treaties between the United States and the Indians provided for an equitable settlement of grievances. Courts dealt with the guilty parties, whether white or Indian, and compensated for property damage. In practice this system exhibited many weaknesses, such as the Indians' reluctance to testify in court. A general prejudice against red men made it unlikely that a jury of frontiersmen would find a white man guilty, and guilty Indians were difficult to apprehend. However, it is apparent that the white claimant fared much better than his red counterpart. The law of the white man did not prove to be an adequate fence around the property and rights of the Indian.

Governor Harrison, as the first governor of Indiana Territory, had ample opportunity to experience the difficulties and embarrassments which were the lot of any government administrator on the frontier. The resourceful young governor solved the problems arising out of Indian-white relations in a manner which endeared him to his white constituents if not to his red children.

2. The Treaty of 1804

IN FEBRUARY of 1803, President Thomas Jefferson instructed Governor Harrison regarding his position as agent for the Indian affairs of Indiana Territory. President Jefferson was particularly concerned with cultivating friendly relations with the Indians. But his humanitarianism did not blind him to the advantages of negotiating with them as long as they retained great areas of fertile land for which Western voters hungered. In the trading houses the United States was currently maintaining for the benefit of the Indians, Jefferson saw a means of separating the savages from land which the whites might more profitably use. In order to facilitate the transfer of Indian lands to the United States, the President advocated encouraging the influential chiefs to go into debt, "because we observe that when these debts get beyond what the individuals can pay, they become willing to lop them off by a cession of lands."[1] Although the Sacs and Foxes did not as yet have a factory among them, Harrison hoped to remedy that deficiency.

Shortly after arriving in Vincennes, Governor Harrison be-

[1] Moses Dawson, *A Historical Narrative of the Civil and Military Service of Major General William H. Harrison*, 36.

came interested in negotiating a treaty with the Sacs to include them in the general Indian agreement covered by the Treaty of Greenville. Previously, Sacs, choosing to ignore the St. Clair treaty of 1789, had refused to talk with him until they concluded with the United States a treaty placing them on an equal footing with the other tribes under its protection. The possibility that they might be holding several whites as prisoners heightened Harrison's desire to negotiate with them.

In February, 1802, the young governor proposed to the Secretary of War a treaty with the Potawatomi, Miami, Eel River, Wea, Kickapoo, Sac, and Kaskaskia tribes, to draw permanent boundaries between them and the United States. At the same time he recommended that the Secretary include the Sacs in the Treaty of Greenville. As an inducement, Harrison advised that an annuity of $500 be granted to the tribe, although he emphasized that the Indians themselves were "extremely desirous" that a treaty be negotiated.

Secretary of War Henry Dearborn gave Harrison permission to negotiate and grant the Sacs the annuity, "if their conduct and disposition shall appear to deserve it." At Secretary Dearborn's suggestion, Harrison intended to require contributions from the Piankashaws, Kickapoos, and Kaskaskias to make up a part of the projected annuity. Fortunately for those tribes, the Sacs did not appear for the council at Vincennes in 1802. Lack of a treaty-defined relationship between the Sacs and the United States would plague the Governor for two more years. During this period, Jefferson purchased the vast Louisiana Territory, embracing the Sac hunting grounds. This accentuated the need for a treaty between that tribe and the United States.

In the spring of 1804 a party of Sac warriors attacked a band of Osages, a tribe with which they frequently contested hunting grounds. On their way to St. Louis in a boat belonging to a fur-trading firm of that city, some of the Osages were killed and others were taken prisoner. Captain Amos Stoddard, acting governor of the District of Louisiana, commented indignantly that the Sacs lacked the proper respect for the United States. In an effort to obtain the Osages taken prisoner by the Sacs, the tall, Connecticut-born officer held a council with a deputation of the latter and their allies, the Foxes.

In their speeches at the council the Indians protested against the whites' occupation of their lands and, as on several previous occasions, asked that the United States establish a factory among them. Although he did not know why, Stoddard also learned that the British were inviting the Sacs and Foxes and other tribes to a meeting in Canada.

By 1803 the Sacs and Foxes practice of visiting British posts in Canada, alarming to frontier inhabitants, was well established. During the Revolution the Sacs and Foxes had aided the British against the colonists, and the friendly relations between the two tribes and the British had continued.

In 1798 and again in 1799 parties of Sacs and Foxes visited Canada. In 1799 they said they merely wished to prove their fidelity to the British government. A king's official at Amherstburg complained that the Sacs and Foxes remained a month and consumed considerable quantities of provisions which might have been better expended on tribes nearer the Canadian border. Nevertheless, these visits stirred the suspicions of the Americans. Other incidents on the frontier reminded them of the hold the British maintained on the two tribes through the traders operating out of Canada.

In March of 1804, when Captain Meriwether Lewis and Lieutenant William Clark were preparing to embark upon their famous expedition to the Pacific, Lewis had sent a message to the Sacs and Foxes. Unable to read it, the Indians asked a British trader to interpret it for them. The trader did so, in a vein unfavorable to the United States. To correct the false impression, at the council he held with them Stoddard had his own interpreter read the message to the Sacs and Foxes.

Before Captain Stoddard could inform Secretary Dearborn

of the council, Dearborn authorized Governor Harrison to negotiate with the Sacs. "It may not be improper," he advised the Governor, "to procure from the Sacs, such cessions on both sides of the Illinois, as may entitle them to an annual compensation of five or six hundred dollars; they ought to relinquish all pretensions to any land on the southern side of the Illinois, and a considerable tract on the other side."[2]

The Governor's prompt invitation to the Sacs to treat with the United States arrived when their hostilities with the Osages made them and the Foxes particularly anxious to come to terms with the Americans. The Osages were on excellent terms with the United States, and the other tribes considered them favorites of the Long Knives. By stopping war parties of Indians from east of the Mississippi bound to attack the Osages, United States troops strengthened this supposition.

One element of the Sacs and Foxes strongly impressed by these facts, desired to reach an agreement with the Americans in order to gain equality with the Osages. The galling news that a party of their enemies had recently left St. Louis loaded with presents and "puffed up with ideas of their great superiority" drove one Sac faction to direct action. Reasoning that fear of the Osages induced the Americans to be generous with that tribe and that nothing was to be gained by a pacific attitude, some of the young Sacs went on the warpath.[3]

The reaction on the part of the whites was not the one the Indians had anticipated. Investigating the news of an attack on the settlements on Cuivre River, a few miles north of St. Louis, the leader of a party of Americans found "three persons murdered in a most barbarous manner, with their scalps taken off." Fearful that this attack presaged a general war, the settlers fled the area or feverishly prepared to defend themselves. To add to their fears, rumors spread that the Sacs were holding

[2] Secretary of War to Harrison, June 27, 1804, in *American State Papers: Indian Affairs*, I, 695.

[3] James Bruff to James Wilkinson, November 5, 1804, in Clarence Edwin Carter (ed.), *The Territorial Papers of the United States*, XIII, 76–80.

war talks with the Potawatomis and that Sac warriors were trailing the American flag from the tails of their horses.

From their partially completed stockade fort the frightened Americans remaining on Cuivre River hurried desperate appeals to Major James Bruff at St. Louis for arms, ammunition, and reinforcements. Outraged at the audacity of the Indians, some of the settlers wished to retaliate on their villages nearest St. Louis. "It was with difficulty, and upon promises of ample justice" that Bruff dissuaded the irate settlers.

In the Sac towns nearest the settlements panic prevailed. The warriors had brought the scalps of their white victims and thrown them tauntingly at the feet of their chiefs. Fearful of reprisal, the Indians began to abandon their towns. Two chiefs, hoping to avert hostilities, ventured to St. Louis under the protection of a French trader. They freely admitted that four of their tribe had committed the murders. However, to Major Bruff's demands for the surrender of the warriors, they gave evasive replies and pleaded inability to control their young men.

Releasing the two Sacs to return to the lower towns they represented, Major Bruff dispatched by them a strongly worded demand for the surrender of the guilty warriors. Alarmed, Bruff warned his superior officer, the colorful adventurer General James Wilkinson, that "there is but one opinion here— that is—unless those Murderers are demanded; given up and examples made of them; our Frontier will be continually harrassed by Murders and Robberies."

While a few miles north of St. Louis settlers were doing sentry duty in anticipation of a savage onslaught, in holiday attire the carefree townsmen enthusiastically welcomed Governor Harrison when he arrived in the city on October 12. Accepting the invitation of the wealthy landowner and fur trader Auguste Chouteau, Harrison settled himself in the finest mansion in the bustling little community of almost two hundred houses. Civil affairs had first priority on the Governor's attention, and he busied himself in organizing the administration of the District of Louisiana, which Congress had attached to Indiana Territory for administrative purposes. Aided by Judge John Griffin, Harrison quickly drew up a civil code and reorganized the courts and the local militia in time to receive a deputation of Sacs and Foxes just arrived in St. Louis with one of the warriors involved in the Cuivre River killings.[4]

The surrender of the one warrior forced Harrison to take a stand on the guilty Sac. On the assumption that an Indian in the guardhouse was worth three on the prairie. Harrison offered to pardon the other murderers if they would testify against the one in custody. The Governor even considered releasing the one prisoner on the technicality that the crime had been committed while Spanish law was in effect and specified a defunct court to deal with it. Well aware of how this would be received by local inhabitants, Major Bruff protested vigorously against this interpretation. Therefore, the Governor contented himself with imprisoning the one culprit at hand and then applying to the President for the warrior's pardon.

Recognizing the psychological moment, Harrison broached the subject of a treaty and pressed the delegation for a land cession. Although Secretary Dearborn had not mentioned the Foxes in his instructions, the close relationship between them and the Sacs made a joint treaty feasible, if not essential. The chiefs were in an amenable mood. Harrison had distributed over $2,000 worth of finery among them, and they were undoubtedly anxious to get their host's mind off the unfortunate incident on Cuivre River. Major Bruff described them as willing "to make a treaty that wou'd shelter them from their natural enemies—the Osages, now consider'd by them as under the protection of the U. States; and without hesitation, offered to cede an immense tract of country containing much valuable lead & other minerals."

4 James Bruff to James Wilkinson, November 5, 1804, in *ibid.*, XIII, 76–80. I have depended almost entirely on this account of the treaty.

The tribal councils had instructed the members of the delegation to "pay" for the persons killed. "Wiping away the tears" of the deceased ones' relatives by a payment in money or goods was standard Indian practice. However, the chiefs were certainly not authorized to cede the entire area the unscrupulous Harrison secured for the United States. Not until the chiefs returned from St. Louis wearing fine coats and medals did the other Sacs and Foxes learn of the sale of their lands.[5]

In their defense, according to Black Hawk, the Indian delegates reported that on their arrival in St. Louis they met with the proper officials and asked for the release of the Sac prisoner the tribe was surrendering. With Harrison agreeing to release the prisoner only in return for a land cession, they signed a treaty ceding a tract on the west side of the Mississippi and another on the Illinois side opposite the Two Rivers. Then the Americans released the prisoner and shot him when he was only a few feet from his friends. This was all the chiefs could remember of the negotiations. Their fellow tribesmen suspected that they were intoxicated most of the time they were in St. Louis.

Actually, the prisoner was shot, but not as Black Hawk described. Harrison had applied for a pardon for the Indian, and in February, 1805, Jefferson granted it. The President felt, as the Secretary of War expressed it, "that we ought to commence our intercourse with the Indians in Louisiana, in such a manner as to show not only our regard for justice, but our benevolent and tender feelings for the unhappy."[6] Unfortunately, the warrior tired of the close confinement before the pardon could reach him. In a prison break he received a load of buckshot in the head.[7]

It fell to the lot of General James Wilkinson, a pompous,

---

[5] *Life of Black Hawk*, (ed. by Milo Milton Quaife), 89.

[6] Secretary of War to Harrison, February 12, 1805, Letter Books of the Secretary of War, National Archives. (National Archives will hereafter appear as NA.)

[7] Harrison to the Secretary of War, May 27, 1805, in *Messages and Papers*, I, 134.

egotistical intriguer, to explain this regrettable incident to the Sacs and Foxes. Newly appointed governor of Louisiana Territory, he arrived in St. Louis from Kaskaskia on July 1, 1805, after a trip marked by "much pain and fatigue from an impetuous current, a burning Sun and myriads of musquetoes." The travel-weary general found 150 Sacs and Foxes waiting to speak with him.

In a council held with them the Governor explained the circumstances of the warrior's death and produced the president's pardon. For the benefit of the credulous Indians the sly Wilkinson interpreted the late arrival of the pardon as a manifestation of the "will of the great Spirit that he should Suffer for Spilling the Blood of his White Bretheren, without Provocation." Asking the young brother of the dead warrior to step forward, the Governor presented him with the pardon. Wilkinson admonished the youth to "receive and carefully preserve it, in remembrance of his Brother and as a warning against Bad Deeds." Overwhelmed by the attention he, a mere youth, was receiving, the brother accepted the letter with "Evedent Marks of Pleasure."

Before the council closed, the tribesmen expressed "deep regret and much discontent" with the treaty negotiated the previous autumn. They had been anxious to "oblige" the United States, the spokesman for the tribes stated, but never having sold any land previously, they were ignorant of its true value. He concluded dolefully that "we have given away a great Country to Governor Harrison for a little thing."

Although "we made a bad bargain and the Chiefs who made it are all dead," declared the Indian, "yet the bargain Stands, for we never take back what we have given." He added an appeal which moved Wilkinson by its humility: "We hope our Great Father will consider our Situation, for we are very Poor, and that he will allow us Something in addition, to what Governor Harrison had promised us." To Secretary of War Dearborn, who had originally suggested the cession, Wilkinson advised an adjustment in favor of the Sacs and Foxes. As he indicated, a "douceur" at this time would help "to Secure the Confidence of these Nations."[8]

The treaty occasioned by the surrender of the warrior to the Americans was an infinitely greater tragedy to the Sacs and Foxes than his subsequent death. Although the United States received the tribes into its protection, the Indians paid dearly for it. In return for an annuity of $600 for the Sacs and $400 for the Foxes, to be paid in goods, and presents worth $2,234.50 which Harrison distributed at the time of the treaty negotiations, the chiefs ceded to the United States all their nations' claims to land on the east side of the Mississippi and a segment of their hunting grounds on the west side of that river. Included was the area of the present state of Illinois north and west of the Illinois River, a slice of southern Wisconsin, and a small section of the state of Missouri.

Article VII of the treaty provided that the Indians might continue to live and hunt upon the land "as long as the lands which are now ceded to the United States remain their property." This article was responsible for much of the trouble that ensued in later years. Lulled into a false sense of security, the Indians disclaiming the treaty pointed to their subsequent occupation and use of the land as evidence that the land had not been sold.

Other articles of the treaty were more conducive to peaceful relations between the Indians and the United States. They provided for the settlement of disputes and a mutual respect of territorial holdings. That the Sacs and Foxes might benefit from the United States factory system, the Americans provided that factories should be established among them.

Harrison was careful to include an article calling for a cessation of hostilities between the Sacs and Foxes and the Osages. This did not please the Sacs and Foxes, who were

8 James Wilkinson to the Secretary of War, July 27, 1805, in Carter, *Territorial Papers*, XIII, 164–72.

more interested in canceling the advantage the Osages had enjoyed in the hostilities than in peace. To insure that this and the other articles should be observed, the United States negotiators secured permission of the tribes to erect a fort at Prairie du Chien. An additional article, included in the treaty at the behest of Harrison's host, Auguste Chouteau, who had large property holdings, provided that grants under the Spanish regime should not be invalidated by the cession.

In presenting this treaty to the Senate, President Jefferson excused Harrison's liberal interpretation of his orders on the grounds that the Sacs and Foxes generally acted as one nation and had come forward together. He spoke warmly of the advantages to be derived from the treaty, particularly the opportunity it offered to strengthen American control of the Indian trade on the Mississippi, as the British traders in that region were showing scant respect for the authority of the new republic. The treaty, to which was affixed the marks of Layauvois, Pashepaho (the Giger), Quashquame (Jumping Fish), Outchequaka (Sun Fish), and Hashequarhiqua (the Bear), pleased the senators if it did not meet the approval of the members of the tribal councils. The dignitaries in Washington ratified it January 25, 1805.

The land hunger of the Americans, the temporary embarrassment of the Sacs and Foxes, and the stupidity or venality of the Indian negotiators set the stage for years of mutual hate and distrust. Wise leaders among the tribesmen might labor to reconcile their people to the loss, and intelligent and sympathetic American officials might attempt to aid the tribesmen in every way possible—short of annulling the treaty—but in 1832, bloody scalps and smoke rising from burning cabins and Indian villages would testify to their failure.

3. Discord and Distrust

INAUSPICIOUSLY launched by the Treaty of 1804, relations between the Sacs and Foxes and the United States continued to be marked by discord and distrust. As was always to be the case, American officials on the frontier had difficulty translating into action the lofty sentiments expressed freely in Washington. "Our system," President Jefferson had told Governor Harrison in 1803, "is to live in perpetual peace with the Indians, to cultivate an affectionate attachment from them, by every thing just and liberal which we can do for them within the bounds of reason, and by giving them effectual protection against wrongs from our own people."[1]

At the time Harrison induced the Sacs and Foxes to sign the treaty at St. Louis, Indian affairs in Louisiana Territory rested in the hands of the territorial governor. Assisting him were an agent and two interpreters. In July, 1804, Pierre Chouteau, half brother of Auguste, had been appointed Indian agent for Upper Louisiana, and the Secretary of War directed him to be "particularly attentive to our friends the Osage nation"—the enemies of the Sacs and Foxes. The appointment was approved by General James Wilkinson, the intriguing first

1 Dawson, *Harrison*, 36.

26

governor of Louisiana Territory. The new agent had played a leading role in the life of St. Louis and had had wide experience in Indian affairs. For eight years prior to 1802 he and Auguste had had a monopoly of the Osage trade. As interpreters to assist Chouteau in the discharge of his duties as agent, the Secretary of War appointed two local residents, Noel Mongrain and Nicholas Boilvin. Hopefully, the Secretary ordered Chouteau to keep the tribes at peace and gradually to introduce them to the arts of civilization. A year later, to help implement this policy, William Ewing was appointed instructor in agriculture. In May, 1805, he, an assistant, and an interpreter established a post adjacent to a Sac village near the mouth of the Des Moines.[2] There Lieutenant Zebulon Montgomery Pike, ascending the Mississippi that summer with a small detachment, found him.

Governor Wilkinson had sent the slender, blue-eyed Lieutenant to search out the headwaters of the Mississippi and to report on the Indians living along the great river. Wilkinson had also directed the young officer to locate possible sites and obtain the consent of the Indians concerned for the erection of two military and trading posts.

On August 20 the small party reached the foot of the Lower Rapids of the Mississippi, at the mouth of the Des Moines River. Here Ewing, an interpreter, and nineteen Sacs from the villages in the vicinity met them to assist Pike in passing the rapids. In accord with Wilkinson's orders to "spare no pains to conciliate the Indians and to attach them to the United States," Pike held a council with the chiefs from the neighborhood. Distributing gifts of tobacco and knives among them, he treated the Indians to a little whiskey and explained the object of his trip. To his inquiries about a site for the factory promised them in the Treaty of 1804, the chiefs replied that

[2] Secretary of War to William H. Harrison, March 8, 1805, Letter Books of the Secretary of War, NA; Pierre Chouteau to William H. Harrison, May 22, 1805, in *Messages and Papers*, I, 128–30.

they represented only a small part of the nation and were unable to decide alone. They did provide Pike with a young Indian to accompany him and explain his mission to other Sacs and Foxes along his route.

Not until they passed the mouth of Rock River did the young Lieutenant and his men see their first Fox village. The friendly and co-operative Foxes impressed Pike quite favorably. By furnishing them food and moccasins when they happened on his village, one Fox chief aided two of Pike's men, left by accident at the Lower Rapids, to rejoin the expedition.

While the Americans were proceeding up the Mississippi beyond the Fox villages, Jefferson was ordering Governor Harrison to join Wilkinson in an attempt to end the continued strife between the Osages and the Sacs and Foxes, supported by other tribes east of the Mississippi.[3] On receipt of these orders the governors dispatched messengers to the tribes concerned. By September the representatives of the tribes began to gather in St. Louis, but General Wilkinson was apprehensive.

Considering the magnitude of the problems confronting the officials concerned with Indian affairs, Wilkinson was justifiably pessimistic. Since the council he had held with the Sacs and Foxes in July, in which they discussed the questions of the pardon for the dead warrior and the treaty, the General had heard reports from Pike and others which forecast trouble.

As the weeks passed, the nervous general learned nothing to reassure him. The Sacs appeared for the conference, but, even while their delegation was in St. Louis, they had a war party out against the Osages. Wilkinson had no doubt that the Sacs had employed every means during the previous six months to effect an alliance among the tribes for an attack on the settlements. He found small comfort in their failure to accomplish this; "the disposition still remains," he wrote Secretary Dearborn. In the smallness of their annuity and "the excitements

3 Dawson. *Harrison*, 68.

of the British Traders," the General found much of the source
of their discontent. Indeed, the goods comprising the first annuity payment were so unwisely selected and arrived in such
poor condition that Wilkinson and Harrison decided to sell
them for what they would bring and purchase more suitable
goods from St. Louis merchants.

Despite the disadvantages under which they labored, Harrison and Wilkinson managed to bring to some agreement the
Indians present in St. Louis for the council. On October 18,
1805, representatives of the Delawares, Miamis, Potawatomis,
Kickapoos, Sacs, Foxes, Kaskaskias, Sioux of the Des Moines
River, Iowas, and Osages signed a treaty of peace. During the
negotiations the commissioners sternly warned against any
more scalping parties' crossing the Mississippi. To provide
some means of arbitrating disputes, the authors of the treaty
stipulated that if members of a tribe injured those of another
and refused satisfaction to the injured, the latter should apply
to the superintendent of Indian affairs for redress.

For what they could make of it, "James Wilkinson Governor
of the Territory of Louisiana, Superintendent of Indian Affairs
for Said Territory, and Brigadier General Commanding the
Army of the United States," and "William Henry Harrison
Governor of the Indiana Territory, Superintendent of Indian
Affairs for the same and Commissioner Plenipotentiary for
Treating with the Indian Tribes North West of the Ohio" had
their treaty. It probably meant about as much to Quas Qua Me,
Voi Pa Naha, and Cha He Ca Ha Qua, who signed for the
Sacs and Foxes, as did the titles of the commissioners.

But the commissioners themselves were not at all at ease.
Reporting to the Secretary of War following the signing of
the treaty, they expressed the fear that the Mississippi Indians
were "inimically disposed towards the United States" and
would "embrace the earliest occasion, to strike our frontiers."
In the estimation of Harrison and Wilkinson, only the display
of armed force near Prairie du Chien would suffice to check

the Indians. If military force would not be available to overawe the savages, perhaps a visit to Washington would do the job. In February, 1805, as part of the program conceived by Jefferson to improve relations between the United States and the Louisiana Indians, the Secretary of War had authorized Governor Harrison to permit a deputation of them to visit Washington.[4]

An unexpectedly large number of Indians assembled in St. Louis to make the trip. Captain Lewis and Lieutenant Clark had sent nearly fifty tribal chieftains to be forwarded to Washington. Chouteau suggested that Sac and Fox chiefs should make the trip. Harrison agreed with the agent and further expanded the proposed delegation to include a few of the Sioux.

In October, Captain Stoddard, acting governor of Upper Louisiana until Harrison took over, finally set out for Washington with a contingent that had been limited in size by Indian illness and the desire of Wilkinson to economize. He, however, did not let his economy cripple his diplomacy. Although he had trimmed the number of chiefs from the eleven nations to twenty-six, and at one time had hoped to limit it to twenty, the Sac and Fox chiefs comprised one-third of the group leaving St. Louis. He included such a relatively large number from those tribes "in consideration of our very delicate standing with those Nations."[5]

Suppressing their feuds, Oto, Missouri, Pawnee, Kansas, and Osage tribesmen from the Missouri River and the great plains beyond joined with their inveterate enemies the Sac, Fox, Iowa, Kickapoo, Potawatomi, and Miami chiefs in the excursion. Traveling by horse to Louisville, up the Ohio in boats, and then overland by carriage from Wheeling to Washington, the chiefs arrived in the capital about the first of the year.

4 Secretary of War to Harrison, February 12, 1805, Letter Books of the Secretary of War, NA.

5 Wilkinson to the Secretary of War, October 22, 1805, in Carter, *Territorial Papers*, XIII, 243–44.

In the course of their visit, Jefferson received the Sac and Fox and Potawatomi chiefs with appropriate ceremony.

"Our nation is numerous and strong; but we wish to be just to all: and particularly to be kind and useful to all our red children," the President informed the assembled chiefs. He assured them that as rapidly as possible the United States would establish factories among them to supply them with goods in exchange for their peltries. "We want no profit in that business," declared the President. Then, turning to the problem of intertribal wars, Jefferson spoke glowingly of peace. Referring to the United States, he stated, "My children, we are strong, we are numerous as the Stars in the Heavens, and we are all gunmen, yet we live in peace and friendship with all Nations."[6]

That they might see for themselves the advantages of peaceful relations with the Americans, Jefferson invited the chiefs to make a conducted tour of Baltimore, Philadelphia, and New York. While the Sacs and Foxes were considering the offer and mulling over the beauties of a state of peace as expounded by a man who had at one time advised a little rebellion now and then, their fellow tribesmen back on the frontier were jauntily lifting not only Indian but white scalps as well.

Jefferson had good cause to lecture the Sacs and Foxes. Reports from the frontier told of renewed attacks on the Osages and even on isolated white settlements. The treaty negotiated by Harrison and Wilkinson had not inhibited the red men. Perhaps the commissioners had been correct in suggesting that a garrison near Prairie du Chien would be necessary to protect the settlements. It was Harrison's frank opinion that only the presence of the troops Wilkinson brought to the area prevented a war with the Sacs. "Greater exertions have been made in the course of the present year to poison the Minds of the Indians and to make the United States obnoxious to them than at any

6 Stock Transcripts. Stock dated the talk "about January, 1804," but it undoubtedly occurred during the visit of the Indians in the winter of 1805–1806.

former period," he warned Jefferson. The frontiersmen credited British agents with undermining American influence among the Indians.

The winter and spring of 1805–1806 brought no relief to officials on the frontier. War parties continued to leave the Sac towns and search out the Osages along the Missouri. Frequently, warriors, finding no Osages, lifted white scalps because they did not wish to return to their villages empty handed and risk the taunts and jibes of their fellows. This may explain the fate of three whites hunting in November on a branch of the Missouri, about sixty miles from the little settlement of St. Charles. They encountered a party of Sacs, and the warriors killed two and wounded one of the Americans. The settlers also accused the Sacs of killing a man at a salt works 70 miles above Portage des Sioux and attacking another salt works operated by a son of Daniel Boone about 150 miles up the Missouri.

Fearing that these incidents might precipitate general war, Governor Wilkinson took steps to end them. Early in December, 1805, the Governor assembled in St. Louis a delegation of Sacs. Warning them that if they persisted in their wrongdoing he would prevent traders from entering their country and they would not receive "a blanket, a gun or a charge of Powder," Wilkinson demanded in the name of their "great Father the President of the United States and of the Seventeen-fires" that the Sacs deliver to him within "three moons" the warriors who had "Spilt the blood of the White Men." He also called for any Osage prisoner among them. The Governor closed with an ominous reference to the "misfortunes which have overwhelmed your red brethren towards the rising of the Sun," and might befall the Sacs if they refused to comply.[7]

Not content with this warning in council, Wilkinson ordered

[7] Wilkinson to the Secretary of War, December 10, 1805; Wilkinson to Chiefs of the Sac Nation, December 10, 1805, both in Carter, *Territorial Papers,* XIII, 297–302.

an artillery officer, Captain James B. Many, to visit the Sacs with a "strong talk" and require the return of any Osage prisoners they might have. Like Lieutenant Pike, he was also to look for a site for a fort near the mouth of the Wisconsin River. Convinced that the Sacs, Foxes, and Iowas were ready for war and that the Canadian and St. Louis traders were responsible, the Governor recommended to the Secretary of War that he interdict their trade for the next season, "to preserve tranquility and save blood."

In the spring of 1806 the experiences of Captain Many on his mission to the Sacs and of Lieutenant Pike on his return from the headwaters of the Mississippi confirmed the reports of the hostile attitude of those Indians. Captain Many had first visited Prairie du Chien and examined the area for a site for a fort. Accompanied by a few Menominees and Winnebagos, he then descended the river with his small detachment and visited the great Sac village near the mouth of Rock River. Although he had been warned that the Indians at Saukenuk were drunk, the foolhardy Captain had gone anyway, and the Sacs soon made him regret his decision.

Screaming epithets at the "bloody Americans" who had killed this man's brother and that one's father, the intoxicated warriors jostled the officer and his men. Highly alarmed, Captain Many managed to withdraw his troops from the village and crossed the river. Carrying pistols concealed under their blankets, a number of Sacs followed the soldiers. Refusing to discuss the issue of Osage prisoners, the Sacs demanded to know why Many wore a plume in his hat. The plume, the Indians declared, was a mark of warlike intentions. In defiance they promptly placed some plumes in their scalp locks.[8]

At this critical juncture, Lieutenant Pike and his detachment arrived on the scene. An attack on the whites now would be a more expensive affair, and, although the Sacs persuaded

[8] *The Expeditions of Zebulon Montgomery Pike* (ed. by Elliot Coues), I, 210.

the Menominees and Winnebagos accompanying Many that the whites would poison them if they went to St. Louis, the troops were permitted to proceed downstream with their scalps intact. Safe in St. Louis, Pike reported to Wilkinson that he and Many regretted that their orders did not permit them to punish the "scoundrels, as by a *coup de main* we might easily have carried the village." Captain Many attributed the hostile demonstration to the machinations of agents of the British Northwest Company and the "extreme discontent" of the Indians with the Treaty of 1804, which they said "a few contemptible fellows" had negotiated.[9]

Even as Captain Many was alerting his detachment to repulse a possible Sac attack, officials in Washington were moving to strengthen the position of the United States among the Indians of the Mississippi. In April of 1806 the Secretary of War appointed Nicholas Boilvin as Indian agent at the Sac village at the Lower Rapids of the Mississippi. Boilvin, who was also to visit other Sac and Iowa towns occasionally, was eminently suited for the position. A Canadian by birth, he had moved to the Illinois country as a lad of thirteen. Shortly after the Americans occupied Louisiana, he entered government employ as an interpreter under Pierre Chouteau.

The appointment was certainly opportune, as the activities of William Ewing, the only official agent to the Sacs, were discreditable. In the autumn of 1805, Wilkinson complained that the agriculturist was causing unnecessary expense by frequently sending to St. Louis for small articles. This complaint came as a shock to Secretary Dearborn. That gentleman had difficulty recalling that such an individual as Ewing existed. In October, 1805, only seven months after he had appointed him, Dearborn inquired piquantly of Wilkinson, "Pray who is Mr. Ewing, who resides on the River Le Moin?" The Governor

---

[9] James B. Many to Wilkinson, May 20, 1806, in Carter, *Territorial Papers*, XIII, 512–13.

hastened to enlighten him. "Utterly unqualified," "a wretched example," and "a young man of innocence, levity & simplicity —without experience or observation," blazed Wilkinson's description of the hapless Ewing. Nevertheless, the latter continued to occupy his position. It remained for William Clark, brigadier general of the militia of the District of Louisiana and a veteran of the most celebrated exploring expedition in his country's history, to clear up any remaining doubts the Secretary may have entertained about the agriculturist.

In March, 1807, the President appointed Clark agent for all tribes except the Osages. A tall, powerfully built redhead, General Clark combined the attributes of a Virginia gentleman with the bluff directness of a frontiersman. Four years service in a frontier army and the expedition to the Pacific Coast with Lewis had qualified him to judge a man of Ewing's caliber. Clark had not been in office four months before he drew up charges against the agriculturist. He accused Ewing of unauthorized purchases in the name of the government and of trading for the Indians' guns with whiskey and then reselling them at a considerable profit to the warriors, who had to have them or starve. To buy trinkets for the Indian woman he had taken to enliven his lonely outpost, Ewing had sold government corn to traders and employed on his private projects men in the pay of the government.

Although William Ewing had proved to be an unfortunate choice, Pierre Chouteau, Clark, and Boilvin were excellent ones. They were needed as a counterpoise to Robert Dickson, the British trader at Prairie du Chien. In the immediate years that followed, the necessity of combating British intrigue among the Indians of the Northwest became a major responsibility of William Clark and his subordinates.

The first two years of official relations between the Sacs and Foxes and the United States had not been harmonious. Despite several councils in St. Louis, the new treaty of 1805, and a visit to Washington, the Sacs and Foxes had demonstrated on several occasions that the Treaty of 1804 had only aggravated their hostility toward the Long Knives. William Ewing had been a failure; it remained to be seen if General Clark and his other agents could solve the problem of how to bring about more amicable relations.

Keokuk

From a painting by J. O. Lewis at Prairie du Chien, 1825.
Chicago Historical Society.

Sacs and Foxes at St. Louis to see steamer off, April 10, 1833.

From a drawing by Karl Bodmer in Maximilian's *Travels* (1843).
Smithsonian Institution.

*George Catlin, who painted this tribal chieftain and his
horse in 1834, called him Chief Running Fox of the Sac
and Fox tribe.*

Poweshiek, a Fox chief.

From a painting by C. B. King, 1837, in Redwood Library, Newport, R. I. *Smithsonian Institution.*

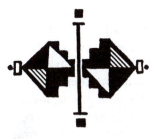

4. War Comes to the West

ETWEEN 1806 and 1812 the Indians viewed with dismay
the settlers pouring into the region between the Ohio and
the Mississippi rivers. Most of them found farms in Ohio,
but a sufficient number moved farther west to make it necessary that Congress organize Illinois Territory. Despite the
availability of fertile acres, the settlers were unhappy; they
had difficulty in disposing of their bountiful crops as England tightened her blockade of the Continent. Moreover, the
frontiersmen charged the British with agitating the Indians.
Governor Harrison's policy of exacting every acre possible
from the tribesmen had afforded the king's agents ample
troubled water in which to fish.

While the Sacs and Foxes were negotiating in Washington
and their fellow tribesmen were tomahawking Osages and an
occasional white on the frontier, a new prophet had arisen
among the Shawnees. A brother of the accomplished chief
Tecumseh, the Prophet joined him in an effort to organize
an Indian confederacy and expel the Long Knives. Both were
fluent, impassioned orators, Tecumseh providing the organizing skill while the Prophet was the intermediary with Heaven.

The Sacs and Foxes never constituted an important link in

the confederacy the Shawnees loosely knit together. They were too far removed from the center of the alliance, and they had no leaders comparable in ability to Tecumseh and the Prophet, although Black Hawk equaled them in distrust of the Long Knives. Nevertheless, Sac and Fox discontent with the Treaty of 1804 and their belief that the Americans unduly favored their old enemies the Osages made them fertile ground for Shawnee propaganda.

Although the Secretary of War was confident that Boilvin's agency would discourage any Sac hostility, Governor Harrison was not so sanguine. In August, 1806, the Governor warned Secretary Henry Dearborn that the tribes demonstrating a willingness to come to terms with the United States over boundaries were being "almost daily Solicited by the Kickapoos Sacs &c to join in a War against us."[1] The Sacs and Foxes were no friendlier than when Captain Many and Lieutenant Pike had visited them a few months earlier. However, the tribes did not effect the proposed alliance, and until late in the summer of 1807 the relations between the Sacs and Foxes and the Americans were relatively undisturbed by acts of violence or threats of war. Only the slaying of a Frenchman by a Sac in a drunken frolic at Portage des Sioux, a little settlement on the Mississippi, served to disturb the calm before the storm.[2]

By August of 1807 a new note was evident in the warnings flowing from the frontier in an increasing stream. The Indian agent at the village of Chicago reported that Indians in his vicinity favored war and were trying to stir up other tribes. Even as he wrote, they had a war chief among the Sacs trying to enlist that tribe's support. He concluded that "the tomo-

[1] Harrison to Jared Mansfield, August 8, 1806, in Carter, *Territorial Papers*, VII, 375–76.

[2] Nicholas Boilvin to the Secretary of War, June 16, 1807, Secretary of War, Letters Received, NA. This incident may be the origin of the legend that the Treaty of 1804 resulted from the visit to St. Louis of a delegation of Sacs and Foxes to parley over the murder of a white man which occurred when he attempted to force his attentions on an Indian maiden. See Perry A. Armstrong, *The Sacs and the Black Hawk War*, 59–60.

hauk is uplifted, waiting only for a leader to direct the blow."[3]

Visiting the Sacs, Foxes, and Iowas, Boilvin noted that they had been tampered with. After smoking with them, he was confident he had repaired the damage. He was unduly optimistic; that winter the Sacs were again visiting the Prophet. The Americans regarded the Shawnee's activities with increasing alarm. Indian agents included the Sacs and Foxes among the tribes the Prophet planned to launch against the frontier settlements. The Americans suspected that behind the Indian hostility lay the machinations of British agents.

Believing war inevitable at the moment, officials in Canada had taken steps to insure Indian support. The Lieutenant Governor dispatched an agent to Amherstburg to learn the role the Indians of the Northwest could be expected to play if hostilities began. After negotiating with the Prophet and other chiefs, the British arrived at the conclusion that the Indians were generally hostile to the Americans but required support before they would break openly. Meanwhile, the course of events on the Mississippi aggravated the discontent of the Sacs and Foxes.

Late in September, 1808, a detachment of American troops moved up the Mississippi to a point about fifteen miles above the mouth of the Des Moines. Although the personnel and equipment for the long-promised factory accompanied the troops, the tribesmen were quite perturbed when the soldiers began to erect Fort Madison. Black Hawk led a party of warriors down the river to protest. A parley with the commanding officer served to allay their fears somewhat, but relations remained strained. Early in the spring, reports of an impending attack hastened work on the fort. Until April, when the work had been sufficiently completed to permit occupation, the soldiers slept on their arms.

The caution of the garrison was justified, as Black Hawk

[3] Charles Jouett to the Secretary of War, August 22, 1807, in Carter, *Territorial Papers*, VII, 472–73.

and a party of Sacs made an attempt to take the fort by a ruse. After several days of trading and negotiating at the fort, during which time they repeatedly professed friendship, the Indians tried to rush the gate under cover of a war dance. Confronted with a loaded cannon and lighted matches in the hands of an alert garrison, the Sacs abandoned their pose and withdrew precipitately.[4] Had the Indians obtained an entrance, they would have massacred the whites, Black Hawk states. Prompt reinforcement of the garrison discouraged any further attacks for the moment.

Throughout the next three years tension continued to mount as the British, the Shawnee Prophet, and his brother Tecumseh labored to turn the Indians of the Northwest against the Long Knives. At an interview with Harrison in the summer of 1809, the Prophet denied recent attempts to ally Indians against the United States. He did admit receiving British invitations to go to war the previous autumn and participating in war talks with the Sacs and Iowas. However, he insisted that the hostile sentiments were confined to the tribes on the Mississippi. Sincere or not at the time of the interview, the Prophet did not long refrain from incendiary activities. The next spring he lashed with impassioned oratory an estimated eleven hundred visiting Sacs, Foxes, and Winnebagos. Harrison believed that the Sacs and Foxes, who later met in council with the British, were ready whenever the Prophet gave the signal.

In the summer of 1810 the Sacs slew four settlers on the frontier above the Missouri, dramatically highlighting the horrifying possibilities of an Indian war. From St. Louis a few months later, William Clark warned Governor Harrison at Vincennes that the Sacs were completely committed to the projected confederacy.[5] The Prophet and the traders operating out of Canada had done their work well.

---

4 Kate L. Gregg, "The War of 1812 on the Missouri Frontier," *The Missouri Historical Review*, Vol. XXXIII, No. 8 (1939).

In the law against the importation of British goods, which inconvenienced them considerably, the British traders had a real grievance. In addition, enterprising American traders were beginning to invade what had long been private British preserves on the upper reaches of the Mississippi. Nicholas Boilvin, whose agency had been moved from the Lower Rapids to Prairie du Chien on Campbell's death in 1808, found the British traders particularly trying. He attributed much of the unrest of the tribes frequenting Prairie du Chien to the traders' misrepresentation of American motives and ability. Not content with telling the Indians that their American father was so poor that he could not furnish them with a single blanket, they added that the Americans themselves had to apply to the British for necessities! The Americans, the traders insisted, had prevented the British from bringing the Indians what they needed. However, the warriors should be patient as, "Soon their English father will declare war against the Americans, and will again take under his protection his beloved red children."[6] Liberal gifts accompanied this misinformation, and the traders, to confirm their statements, could always point to the treatment the British accorded the Sacs and Foxes.

As long as the British supplied their wants, the Indians, enjoying at best a marginal existence, could not be blamed for visiting Malden and Amherstburg in droves. The Sac receiving at the latter post an "elegant" rifle, fifty pounds of lead for bullets, twenty-five pounds of powder to propel them, and three blankets, ten shirts, and other cloth to cover his nakedness might well be expected to love his British father. And the British generosity was particularly impressive when contrasted with American largess. Sacs calling at Amherstburg

5 Harrison to the Secretary of War, July 5, 1809, Secretary of War, Letters Received, NA; Harrison to the Secretary of War, June 14, 1810, in *Messages and Papers*, I, 422–30; Harrison to the Secretary of War, August 7, 1810, in *ibid.*, I, 455–56; Harrison to the Secretary of War, June 6, 1811, in *ibid.*, I, 512–17.

6 Boilvin to Secretary of War, February 11, 1811, in Nicholas Boilvin Letters, 1811–23 (ed. by Marian Scanlan), State Historical Society of Wisconsin.

in the summer of 1810 and visiting Governor William Hull of Michigan Territory on their return had an object lesson in this. From their British father they received gunpowder and lead. Of Hull they asked clothes and food, but received only the latter, along with plenty of free advice against visiting Canada and associating with the Shawnee Prophet. The Americans did not profit from the Indians' comparison of the generosity of their two fathers.

In treating the Indians so liberally the British were not deliberately "sending firebrands into the Mississippi Country," as one agent charged. Even Harrison, no man to underestimate the villainy of British and Indians, admitted that the Sacs visiting Canada in the summer of 1810 had not been urged to war against the Americans. Although the Sacs told the British that they had taken up the tomahawk at the request of the Prophet and had come for arms and ammunition, the king's agent admonished them not to go on the warpath. He agreed to supply their wants but strongly advised the tribe to remain at peace. Nevertheless, knowledge of the agent's advice did not shake the suspicious Governor's basic belief in British iniquity.

To cope with the rising tide of hostility the American officials tightened their defenses and attempted to placate the Indians. In any plan of defense devised by the frontiersmen, Prairie du Chien, at the mouth of the Wisconsin River, played an important role. Visited by over six thousand Indians a year, the straggling little village of thirty to forty houses, occupied principally by French Canadians and their Indian wives, assumed an importance out of all proportion to its size. As the headquarters of the British traders for the upper Mississippi it was the logical site for an American fort. Finally, in the spring of 1812, the Secretary of War announced that the United States would establish a post at Prairie du Chien whenever troops were available. There the matter rested when news reached the frontier of the declaration of war.

Fortunately for their constituents, the governors of Indiana and Illinois territories and the District of Louisiana were aware of the danger and doing all in their power to place the frontier in a state of preparedness. Governor Ninian Edwards of Illinois Territory was particularly alarmed at the concentration taking place under Tecumseh and the Prophet. A Marylander by birth, Edwards had been reared in Kentucky. In 1809, President Madison appointed him governor of Illinois Territory. As governor he acted quickly and energetically, although not always wisely.

Edwards despaired of peace until troops dispersed the Prophet's party and chastised the hostile bands along the Illinois River. He might have added—and until a more intelligent direction were given to Indian affairs. Events currently transpiring at Dubuque's lead mines on the Mississippi graphically illustrated this need.

When Boilvin returned to Prairie du Chien from Washington in July, 1811, sixty white men accompanied him. They were employees of two enterprising Americans, purchasers of the claims of the deceased Julien Dubuque. Disturbed at the prospect of so numerous a body of whites settling among them, the Sacs and Foxes protested vehemently against the party taking possession. They were even opposed to the Americans leaving their boats.[7]

A most perplexing problem confronted Boilvin. The Indians claimed that in 1788, as a mark of the respect and affection with which they regarded him, they had made the grant to Julien Dubuque for the duration of his life. However, Dubuque had had the Spanish government approve his claim and grant him the area in fee simple. Then when he died in debt, his creditors took over the grant as a legitimate part of his assets. Such legal technicalities made no impression on the infuriated Sacs and Foxes, and they refused to permit the whites to occupy the mines.

[7] Boilvin to the Secretary of War, July 7, 1811, in Carter, *Territorial Papers,* XVI, 168–69.

Only by reminding the Indians that Dubuque had incurred the debts in clothing them and persuading them that to "induce the great Spirit to receive him with charity his debts must be paid" was the tactful Boilvin enabled to prevent bloodshed. The Indians consented reluctantly to allow the administrators of Dubuque's estate to sell his property at the mines. As soon as the whites had left the area, the tribesmen burned the buildings and "swore never to give up their land untill they were all dead." Although they had taken no scalps, the Sacs and Foxes were in an ugly mood.[8] Boilvin's invitation to the chiefs to visit Washington that winter did not entirely mollify them.

The invitation which he extended to the chiefs of other tribes on the frontier also was part of the effort to conciliate the Indians. Such measures, especially the more liberal policy on presents, might have succeeded had they come earlier. Unfortunately, early in November, 1811, the Prophet led his warriors against the army of Harrison, encamped on Tippecanoe Creek near the Prophet's village. The indecisive clash which resulted in Tecumseh's absence did much to counteract the new policy.

No Sacs and Foxes were among the warriors straggling back to the Mississippi after the bloody encounter that cold, rainy morning in November. They had failed to fulfill their promise to be ready the previous spring, nor had they rallied to the Prophet's side in the fall. Prior to the Battle of Tippecanoe the Shawnee sent a message and wampum to the tribes, chiding them for their delinquency and requesting them to be ready by the spring of 1812.[9] Clark believed that the reinforcement of the Fort Madison garrison had been largely responsible for the cooling of Sac and Fox ardor for the confederacy. However, the British agent at Amherstburg estimated that

[8] Boilvin to the Secretary of War, August 31, 1812, Secretary of War, Letters Received, NA.

[9] Forsyth to Clark, November 1, 1811, Forsyth Papers, Missouri Historical Society (hereafter cited as Forsyth Papers).

should war erupt two thousand warriors would be available from those tribes to supplement His Majesty's forces.[10]

The news of the engagement at Tippecanoe, which assumed greater proportions as a victory with each retelling, did not lull the Americans. The governors continued to fortify their frontiers and maintain their meager military forces ready for action. None realized the necessity for vigilance better than Nicholas Boilvin, wintering at Prairie du Chien. Throughout the cold winter months he conferred with a number of bands of Sacs, Foxes, Sioux, Menominees, and Winnebagos. He found the Indians wavering. British agents were active among them, and Boilvin was busy turning back parties of Indians on their way to Canada. The Indians explained that they were going to see their English father and procure clothes for their women and children, as the King had promised them help whenever they were in need.[11]

The need was certainly there. Following a dry summer, the winter had been particularly trying for the Indians. In circumventing the American nonimportation law the British traders had arrived on the Mississippi too late in the fall to outfit many of the Indians for their winter hunt. Four thousand Indians received American rations for a month at one big council Boilvin held at Prairie du Chien. Over the pipes in the discussions, which lasted for twenty days, Boilvin learned that the Indians were actually in receipt of British invitations to join them in the impending war. The chiefs frankly admitted that they were restrained principally by a fear of American retaliation. With no orders to enlist the Indians as active allies the best the agent could do was to urge neutrality.

The Foxes appeared to be relatively friendly. Repeatedly professing friendship, they interceded on behalf of miners whom the Winnebagos attacked. As he was convinced Fort

10 Clark to the Secretary of War, November 23, 1811, Secretary of War, Letters Received, NA; Matthew Elliot to William Claus, December 9, 1811, in *Messages and Papers*, I, 660–62.

11 Boilvin to the Secretary of War, December 13, 1811, in Boilvin Letters.

Madison would soon resound to the war whoop, the anxious factor there needed any reassurance he might obtain. "Every hour I look for a war party, and God only knows when it will end," he moaned.[12]

Benjamin Howard, a Kentuckian appointed by Madison to the governorship of the District of Louisiana, and William Clark both argued for action. Howard recommended a campaign against the Indians in the spring, and Clark urged cutting the communications between the lakes and the Mississippi by seizing the mouth of Fox River. Although they did not approve either of these plans, authorities in Washington were not totally inactive. Early in January, 1812, Congress authorized the recruiting of six companies of rangers to protect the frontier. However, the project moved slowly, and Governors Edwards and Howard each decided in March to call out a company of rangers. The governors warned Secretary Eustis that the Prophet was regaining his influence and that Tecumseh was successfully visiting the frontier tribes, among them the Sacs and Foxes.[13]

Although Americans generally regarded the Foxes as trustworthy, opinion differed on the Sacs. For example, in February and March of 1812, Clark first reported that the Sacs had declined to go on the warpath with the Winnebagos and then cited Tecumseh's success among the Sacs.[14] Old Indian fighter Harrison had a solution for the conflicting reports. When informed that his colleague Ninian Edwards was negotiating with representatives of the Northwestern tribes, including the

12 John Johnson to Governor Benjamin Howard, January 7, 1812, in *American State Papers: Indian Affairs*, I, 805.

13 Ninian Edwards to the Secretary of War, March 3, 1812, in Carter, *Territorial Papers*, XVI, 193–94; Clark to the Secretary of War, March 22, 1812, Secretary of War, Letters Received, NA. See also, Acting Governor Attwater of Indiana Territory to the Secretary of War, January 21, 1812, in Carter, *Territorial Papers*, X, 376–78.

14 Clark to the Secretary of War, February 13, 1812, Secretary of War, Letters Received, NA; Clark to the Secretary of War, March 22, 1812, Secretary of War, Letters Received, NA.

Sacs, Harrison recommended, instead of talking, "A war of extirpation." Advocates of an appeasement policy were in the saddle, and they ignored Harrison. The projected Washington trip for the chiefs of the Sacs and Foxes, and other tribes was on the program for that summer, and Boilvin was already preparing to escort chiefs to St. Louis on the first leg of the long journey. For the second time in seven years Sacs and Foxes were to visit Washington.

Floods on the Ohio slowed the progress of the party of twenty-seven, principally Osage, Sac, and Fox chiefs, which Clark led from St. Louis in June. Several days behind them came Boilvin with a small contingent of Sioux, Winnebago, and Iowa chiefs. Somewhere in their journey up the turbulent Ohio to the carriages that awaited them at Pittsburgh for the trip overland to Washington, the parties encountered the news which spread like wildfire—the United States and Great Britain were at war! The chiefs could be assured of a warm reception in Washington. In announcing the long-expected news to Clark and the territorial governors, the Secretary of War laid down the policy to be followed toward the Indians by the agents of the government: "No exertion or reasonable Expenses will be spared to keep the Indians quiet and friendly."

In the years immediately preceding the war, the British and Americans had contended for Indian favor. With the aid of Tecumseh, the Prophet, and smooth-talking Canadian traders, and a policy of liberality, the king had enjoyed considerable success, but the position of the majority of the Sacs and Foxes remained in doubt. It was to be seen whether they would maintain the neutrality desired by their American father or join the redcoats and drive him from their land.

5. Initial Disappointments and Successes

UNTIL THE FALL of 1813 the Sacs and Foxes and their British and Indian allies had cause for elation. Incompetent commanders and ill-trained, insubordinate, and poorly equipped troops botched four American invasions of Canada. Horrifying reports of massacres at Fort Dearborn, Fort Mims, and on the River Raisin quickly extinguished settler expectations of an early end to the British-Indian menace.

The outbreak of hostilities had not altered the American determination to keep the Indians of the Northwest neutral. While the chiefs of the western tribes were in Washington, anxious officials made every effort to impress upon them the necessity of remaining at peace during the war precipitated by a British attack on the "eighteen fires." For the chiefs, the President gave a summary of British-American relations from the time of the Revolution, which he attributed to efforts of the British king "to make them [the United States] dig and plant for his people beyond the great water." "And I say to you, my children," proclaimed President Madison, "your father does not ask you to join his warriors. Sit still on your seats and be witnesses that they are able to beat their enemies, and protect their red friends."[1] As he spoke, friends of his red friends were making their way toward Detroit in expectation of sharing in the assault on that American post. The American plans might involve keeping the Indians neutral, but those of the British called for active Indian participation.

The key to the British activities in the Northwest was Robert Dickson, the redheaded Scotch-Irish trader whose home adjoined Boilvin's agency in Prairie du Chien. No white man on the upper Mississippi enjoyed more prestige among the Indians than did Dickson, or the Red Head, as they called him. Leading a unit of Indian auxiliaries, he distinguished himself in the operations concluded by the surrender of Mackinac to the British in July, 1812. Although no Sacs and Foxes were in his force at this time, a failure by officials in Washington to appreciate the dependence of the Indians on the credit system soon sent warriors from those tribes to swell the ranks of Dickson's auxiliary forces.

When President Madison had addressed the chiefs in Washington, he had mentioned that the United States had established factories among them to supply their wants. However, no effort was made to alter the customary cash policy of the factories to accommodate the Sacs and Foxes. To make matters worse, the chiefs, either as a result of wishful thinking or faulty interpreting, returned to their villages from Washington with the news that the factor at Fort Madison would supply them on credit. Black Hawk and the other chiefs and warriors who had not made the trip to Washington had already learned that the factor had no authority to do so.

The tribesmen were in a quandary; without supplies from the traders they might starve before completing another winter's hunt. Long hostile to the Long Knives, a fear of retaliation restrained most of them from taking the warpath. A few

[1] *Niles Register,* May 14, 1825.

warriors would have chosen the side of their British father regardless, but the granting of credit to the two tribes would have ensured the neutrality of the great majority of Sacs and Foxes. This failure to appreciate fundamental facts of the Indian way of life proved extremely expensive in terms of American lives and property, because the Sacs and Foxes, debating what course to pursue, received rumors of British traders with goods at Rock River. The news ran through the camp "like *fire in the prairie.*" Hurriedly assembling their meager belongings the Indians set out for Rock River. Black Hawk rationalized that they had been *"forced into* WAR *by being* DECEIVED!"[2]

On their arrival at Saukenuk they found a British trader with two boatloads of goods and a message from Dickson. The trader, Edward Lagoterie, gave them a warm welcome and presented them with a large silk British flag, a keg of rum, and other presents. After agreeing to supply the king's red friends with goods on credit, the trader broached to Black Hawk the subject of service with His Majesty's forces. Lagoterie had little trouble in convincing the Sac war chief that his interests lay with the British. The news that Dickson was at Green Bay with twelve boats loaded with the spoils of Mackinac was sufficient for the Indian, who had never befriended the Long Knives. At the suggestion of the trader, who informed him that the Potawatomis were also on the way to join Dickson, Black Hawk quickly assembled a party of two hundred warriors and departed for Green Bay. At this strategically important terminus of the Fox-Wisconsin waterway, Dickson was waiting to welcome the Sacs.[3]

Dickson chose Black Hawk to lead the Indians assembling at Green Bay. The war chief fancied to raid the American settlements on the Mississippi, but the king's agents persuaded

2 *Life of Black Hawk,* 52.

3 Ernest Alexander Cruikshank, "Robert Dickson, The Indian Trader," in *Collections of the State Historical Society of Wisconsin,* XII, 141. (These will hereafter be cited as *Wisc. Colls.*)

him that they must first defeat the Americans concentrating along the lake frontier. Placing a British medal around Black Hawk's neck and the Union Jack in his hand, Dickson hurried him and five hundred painted warriors to the aid of the British forces operating against Detroit. The Indians arrived too late to participate in that British victory. Without having bloodied their spears, Black Hawk and his fellow tribesmen returned to the Mississippi to prepare for the winter hunt.

Although unaware that a party of Sac warriors had already responded to Dickson's recruiting, American officials had serious doubts about this tribe. In July, Thomas Forsyth, the newly appointed Indian subagent for the Potawatomis and former spy for William Clark, learned that during the previous month one hundred Sacs had visited Malden. Two months later he warned Governor Howard of Missouri Territory that although they had not yet committed themselves, "The Sackies, Foxes & Sieux are all waiting to see how their brethren come on. When an opportunity offers it will be like a Clap of thunder. Take good care of the Sackies! They are deceitful People."[4] The St. Louis officials disregarded these warnings. They continued to pay annuities to the tribes and failed to separate the hostile element from those who wished to remain neutral.

A council the Prophet held with chiefs and warriors of the Sacs, Sioux, Iowas, and Winnebagos at Saukenuk sustained Forsyth's serious view of the Sac menace. Aware of it, Governor Edwards, in a move to relieve the continued pressure on the frontiers of Illinois, led a small force of three hundred men against the Miamis and Kickapoos at the head of Peoria Lake. The expedition only increased the Governor's headaches, as the fugitive Kickapoos and Miamis sought shelter with the Sacs on Rock River.[5]

[4] Forsyth to Governor Edwards, September 7, 1812, in Carter, *Territorial Papers*, XVI, 261–65.
[5] Governor Edwards to the Secretary of War, July 21, 1812, in *ibid.*, XVI, 244–47.

The year 1813 was but a few days old when Edwards suggested to President Madison that the United States take action against the Sacs. He voiced sentiments reminiscent of Harrison's remarks on Edwards' own efforts to negotiate with the Indians in April, 1812. Convinced that a majority of the Sacs were hostile and that their proximity and numbers rendered them formidable, the Governor cautioned the President: "Too long have we confided in Indian professions, the most melancholy consequences have resulted from it."[6] Fearing that any mistake in the course pursued in regard to the tribe would be disastrous, Edwards proposed a wise solution. Either the Americans should hold the Sacs responsible as a tribe for the action of individuals or bring the friendly members within the white settlements where their actions would be above suspicion. If the tribe refused to co-operate, the doughty governor advised an attack in preference to waiting passively for "their meditated blow." Edwards called for armed boats on the Wisconsin and Illinois rivers and an expedition to build forts at Peoria and on the Rock and Wisconsin rivers.

In St. Louis also, the use of armed boats and the advisability of an expedition into the Indian country were being considered. Late in November, 1812, William Clark, a brigadier general in the militia as well as an Indian agent, returned from Washington. Apprised of the situation on the frontier he directed that several gunboats be built to patrol the waters in the vicinity. Governor Howard had a more ambitious project. He proposed that he raise a force of four thousand mounted troops to "scour" the country between St. Louis and Prairie du Chien and build forts on Rock River. In Washington, the new secretary of war, John Armstrong, would sanction only the building of four gunboats to patrol the Illinois, Mississippi, and Missouri rivers. With their hopes of a spring offensive against the British and Indians blasted, the Americans re-

[6] Governor Edwards to President James Madison, January 16, 1813, in *ibid.*, XVI, 285–89.

doubled their efforts to isolate the Sacs and Foxes and prepare the settlements for the expected attack.

Ninian Edwards had not given up his plan to bring the friendly Sacs within the white settlements. If the Secretary of War did not accept his proposal, he predicted, the tribe would "to a man unite against us."[7] This convinced Armstrong, and he relented and delegated to Clark the responsibility for implementing Edwards' cherished scheme. A shift of personnel brought Clark added powers to apply to the task at hand; he was chosen to replace Howard as governor of Missouri Territory. Clark continued to function as Indian agent, although the office itself was abolished, its duties being merged with those of the governor.

Although the responsibility for isolating the Sacs and Foxes rested with Clark, Nicholas Boilvin and Maurice Blondeau, a Fox half-blood, negotiated directly with the Indians. Blondeau and another half-blood had been among the tribesmen most of the winter of 1812–13, trying to repair the damage done by a party of rangers. While on a patrol along the Mississippi, the rangers had met a lone Indian and, on general principles, killed and scalped him. To the distress of Clark and his subordinates it was discovered that the warrior was a brother of Quashquame, a signer of the Treaty of 1804 and one of the principal Sac chiefs. They were even more chagrined to learn that the regulation-bound commanding officer of Fort Madison had refused the request of the relatives of the slain warrior for a present "to put out the blood." In an effort to conciliate the Indians, Blondeau took $125 worth of presents to the Sacs.[8]

Help for the Americans in their contest with the British for the favor of the Sacs and Foxes came from an unexpected quarter, the Winnebagos. Occupying roughly the area between the Rock and the Wisconsin and eastward toward Lake Michi-

[7] Edwards to the Secretary of War, March 14, 1813, in *ibid.*, XVI, 305–306.

[8] Copy of Maurice Blondeau to Nicholas Boilvin, January 23, 1813. Enclosed in General Howard to the Secretary of War, March 6, 1813, Secretary of War, Letters Received, NA; Blondeau to Boilvin, February 17, 1813, in Boilvin Letters.

gan, the Winnebagos were strongly pro-British and had suffered heavily at the hands of Harrison at Tippecanoe. When they came to blows with the Foxes, the warriors of that tribe looked to the United States for assistance and drew the Sacs along with them.

This placed the Sacs in an even more awkward position than they had hitherto occupied. Eight or ten lodges had already separated from the main part of the tribe and had taken up a position farther up Rock River. To the pleas for assistance which the embattled Foxes directed at another band of Sacs, the latter replied that they could not aid their old comrades as it would bring down upon their heads the wrath of the British and their Indian allies. Boilvin agreed that the fears of the neutral Sacs were justified. In March he forwarded to Washington their plea for garrisons to save them from the necessity of throwing themselves into the arms of the British.[9]

Secretary Armstrong's decision to adopt Edwards' scheme to quarantine the friendly Sacs and Foxes on the Missouri had come none too soon. Even the Kickapoos, Potawatomis, and Sioux were sending delegations to press Black Hawk's people. The British promised them ample supplies if they would go to the British posts and threatened them with extermination if they refused.[10]

In April, to save them from their predicament and insure their neutrality, Boilvin sent word to fifteen Sac and Fox chiefs to bring their followers south and place them under the protection of the Americans.[11] By the end of the month the tribesmen were beginning to congregate on the Des Moines. The unceasing efforts of Blondeau and Boilvin had been rewarded. A large segment of the two tribes, perhaps a majority, spurned

[9] Council held by Maurice Blondeau with the Sacs, January 22, 1813; Boilvin to Secretary Armstrong, March 20, 1813; both in Boilvin Letters; Barony Vasques to Boilvin, February 27, 1813, in Carter, *Territorial Papers*, XVI, 306–308.

[10] Council held by Maurice Blondeau with the Sacs and Foxes, April 29, 1813, in Boilvin Letters.

[11] Boilvin to Secretary Armstrong, April 17, 1813, in *ibid.*

the British offers and defied the British threats. Even a few bands of Sioux were willing to abandon their usual haunts for the protection of the Long Knives. The Americans had cause to feel that Clark and his agents had proved a match for the redhead from Canada.

However, Dickson was not idle in the spring of 1813. Armed with a bountiful supply of goods and a commission as agent for King George III among the Indians west of the Mississippi, the former trader busied himself recruiting warriors, with the promise of a return to the boundaries of Wayne's Treaty of Greenville. On his way to Prairie du Chien from Chicago he negotiated with the hostile Sacs on Rock River and assured them that they had nothing to fear in the way of an American attack up the Mississippi, as the Long Knives were employing all available forces to take Detroit and "deprive you of your wants." It was, therefore, to the interest of the Sacs and Foxes that they supply one hundred warriors for the campaign on the lakes. As evidence that the two tribes might look to Prairie du Chien and himself for their future wants, Dickson sent them, from the king's stores at the Prairie, kegs of powder, casks of liquor, and bales of cloth. Most of this good-will offering Black Hawk's band retained, and their leader once again led Sacs and Foxes to the aid of their British father.[12]

At Detroit the Indians under Black Hawk joined the growing throng of warriors and their dependents who were consuming British rations at an alarming rate. Forced to employ his restless and expensive auxiliaries before they became discouraged and slipped off for home, the British commander, General Henry A. Proctor, laid siege to Fort Meigs on the Maumee River in Ohio. Temperamentally ill-equipped for siege operations, the Indians rapidly lost interest and departed by bands. Finding Fort Meigs' defenses too much for his diminishing force, Proctor moved on to Fort Stephenson. Early in August, 1813, in an effort to accomplish something

[12] Cruikshank, "Robert Dickson," 143–47.

before his army dwindled away completely, the General ordered an attack. Undertaking to assault one face of the fort, the Indians failed to hold up their end of the attack, and the Americans easily repulsed the British and their red-skinned allies.

The Sacs and Foxes had had enough of the white man's style of fighting "in the open daylight . . . regardless of the number of warriors they may lose!" Black Hawk and his followers were "tired" of the campaign, their "success being bad, and having got no plunder," and so the valiant Sac led his warriors back to Rock River.[13] In his absence from Saukenuk that fall a rival for his leadership of the hostile faction had arisen. An operation General Howard planned while Black Hawk and his warriors were serving with the British had been responsible.

In St. Louis, generals Clark and Howard were following opposite courses in dealing with the Indian problem. Clark was occupied with his negotiations to draw the neutral element of the Sacs and Foxes beyond the reach of British agents, and Howard was reviving his plans for an expedition into the Indian country to intimidate the savages. Although the previous spring Secretary of War Armstrong had failed to approve his proposed expedition, early in July, 1813, Howard repeated his request to lead a force up the Mississippi and erect a fort at Prairie du Chien. Before he could receive an answer from Armstrong, a band of Potawatomis besieged Fort Madison. The troops set fire to their fort and escaped in the confusion.

Howard made no attempt to rebuild Fort Madison but led his mixed force of thirteen hundred rangers, mounted Missouri and Illinois militiamen, and regulars across country to Peoria. Here, late in September, they destroyed the Indian villages and began the erection of Fort Clark. One hundred men, under Major Nathan Boone, son of the famed Daniel, escaped the

13 *Life of Black Hawk*, 58, 62.

labor detail when the General chose them to reconnoiter in the direction of Rock River. Although they failed to move within forty-five miles of their objective, reports of their approach terrorized the inhabitants of Saukenuk, who had visions of Howard's entire force descending upon them.

Expecting any moment to see Americans charge into the village, the chiefs and warriors gathered in council to decide whether to fight or flee across the Mississippi. In the absence of Black Hawk and the more daring spirits, the counsels of despair prevailed. As they streamed from the council lodge, a young Sac, unable to enter as he had as yet killed no enemy, learned the decision and begged permission to address his tribal leaders. Although shocked at the audacity of the youth, something in his manner caused them to re-enter the lodge and permit him to speak. As the tumult subsided, Keokuk, or the Watchful Fox, as the brash young Sac was known, rose to address the council.

The chiefs and warriors saw a handsome young man of medium build whose features, though of Indian coloring, betrayed the presence of French blood in his veins.[14] Known in the village as an intelligent youth with some ability as an actor and speaker, Keokuk launched into an ardent oration. Scourging the cowards who would abandon their lodges to the Long Knives, he fired his audience with a determination to fight for their village. Offering to assume full responsibility for the defense, he swept all opposition aside and emerged from the council as the nominal leader of the Sac forces.

When the attack failed to materialize, the grateful tribesmen hailed Keokuk as a hero. Black Hawk returned to find the Sacs recognizing as the war chief of his nation a youth who at the time of his departure had not even held the right to speak in council. In the handsome and intelligent young

---

[14] Thomas Forsyth to Thomas L. McKenney, August 5, 1830, Draper MSS., 6T140–47; Maximilian, *Travels in the Interior of North America, 1832–1834,* 225.

brave, the veteran Black Hawk had real competition for the chief position of leadership among the two tribes. Over the years their rivalry became an important factor in determining the course of relations between the Americans and the tribesmen. Keokuk, a shrewd politician, eventually became the friend of General William Clark, who in October of 1813 was laboring to detach as many Sacs and Foxes as possible from the ranks of the young war chief's supporters.

Throughout the spring and summer of 1813 small parties of Sacs and Foxes and occasional Winnebagos, Iowas, and Sioux came to parley with Clark and seek shelter among the Americans. Aware that the Indians were in dire circumstances and that if the United States did not care for them they would be forced to resort to Dickson at Prairie du Chien, Clark planned a general removal of friendly Sacs and Foxes to winter quarters on the Missouri. By September the operation was in progress. Clark delegated Blondeau to conduct the warriors and youths overland to their new home and Boilvin to escort the old men, women, and children by water.[15]

In September, 155 canoes of Sacs and Foxes gathered at the little village of Portage des Sioux to smoke with William Clark. Once again they agreed to live in peace with the Osages, with whom they would be in close contact in their new location. They immediately prepared to move up the Missouri with the factor, who was to keep them supplied with goods. In all, more than fifteen hundred members of the two tribes chose to resist the blandishments of Dickson and the other British agents and trust in the good faith of their American father. The settlers on the frontier applauded the separation of the friendly Sacs and Foxes from the hostile fellow tribesmen on Rock River. "Our army will now meet an enemy in every savage band, and ... that vengeance they have so long merited will fall on them

15 Clark to Secretary Armstrong, September 12, 1813, Secretary of War, Letters Received, NA.

with redoubled fury," wrote a citizen of St. Louis of Howard's force operating east of the Mississippi.

St. Louisans were certain in the fall of 1813 that the end of the war was in sight. Coupled with the welcome news from Portage des Sioux came reports that Perry had stopped the British on the lakes, General Howard had built a fort in the heart of the Indian country, and William Henry Harrison had slain Tecumseh and defeated a force of British and their Indian allies at the Battle of the Thames. Moreover, Harrison had concluded a treaty with several of the most important tribes of the Northwest, by which they agreed to give up their prisoners, surrender hostages, and attack any Indians at war with the United States. The occasion called for a celebration, and the happy townspeople, who only a few months before were building a stockade in anticipation of a British-Indian onslaught, responded with a general illumination highlighted by a blazing canoe which they pulled through the streets.

By the end of 1813 the Sacs and Foxes had no cause for elation. The tribesmen were divided over the role they should play in the war, and many of them had abandoned long familiar haunts to take up residence, under American guardianship, on the Missouri. Even more important for the future of relations between the Americans and the Sacs and Foxes had been the emergence of Keokuk as a Sac war chief.

6. Redcoats and Redskins Defeat the Long Knives

T HE YEAR 1814 was to be a good one for the Indians and their allies. In the East, rampaging redcoats put the torch to the Capitol and the White House. Only Captain Thomas Macdonough's brilliant victory on Lake Champlain averted a disastrous invasion from Canada. Generals Andrew Jackson and Jacob Brown were the only American army commanders able to win victories of consequence.

With the arrival of the new year the complacency of the frontiersmen had evaporated. On the Missouri the friendly Sacs and Foxes found their pledge given at Portage des Sioux the previous fall incompatible with close contact with their old enemies the Osages. In January, 1814, the citizens of St. Louis began hearing that the two tribes planned to attack the Osages and retreat to the Mississippi. Moreover, the stubborn and unaccommodating British refused to concede, and with spring came rumors of preparations for a descent upon St. Louis by the redcoats and redskins.

In the absence of the regular district commander the responsibility for the defense of the Missouri frontier fell upon

General Clark's broad shoulders. Learning that Dickson had arrived on the Mississippi with five large boatloads of goods for the Indians and was recruiting a sizable force to invade Missouri Territory, the Governor checked his feeble defenses. To reassure the alarmed local citizenry, Clark proposed to the Secretary of War that he recruit volunteers to man the large keelboats built the previous year. By patrolling the Mississippi as high as Prairie du Chien these craft could disperse any small boats encountered and destroy supplies which the British might try to accumulate for the threatened invasion. The small size of Clark's proposed force made an actual occupation of Prairie du Chien impractical.

Confronted with the problem of relieving General Wilkinson, an old acquaintance of the Sacs and Foxes, and getting results in more important theaters of war, Secretary Armstrong referred Clark's proposal to General Howard, about to resume his duties at St. Louis. Clark did not wait for Howard's approval. Confident that the General would agree, as they had frequently conversed on the subject, Clark acted. The arrival of a small detachment of sixty-one regulars under Major Zachary Taylor offered him the opportunity to revise his plans to include a fort at Prairie du Chien. With this strategic point occupied, the American position in the Northwest would be considerably strengthened and Dickson would be forced to establish a new base of operations from which to inflame the savages with tales of the perfidy of the Long Knives.

The Governor did not dally. On the first of May he embarked his two hundred men under Lieutenant Joseph Perkins, with orders to build and garrison a fort at Prairie du Chien. To support the regulars, Clark intended to leave an armed boat with a complement of militia until he could send reinforcements. The success of the project rested on the possibility of reinforcing the garrison before the enlistments of the militia expired, as they could not be expected to remain one day longer than their enlistment.

Good winds on a river full to its banks carried the fighting governor and his men toward their objective. Until they reached the mouth of Rock River, nothing of consequence occurred, hostile Indians being conspicuous by their absence. As the expedition approached Saukenuk, small bands appeared, but they failed to deliver a concerted attack. Some approached too close to the boats, and the Americans fired on them and, in several cases, took canoes and arms from Indians falling into their hands.

Overawed by the display of armed might, the Sacs and Foxes asked for peace. Clark granted it, on condition that they attack the Winnebagos, who had not appeared to ask for terms. The Foxes at Dubuque's mines likewise saw the wisdom of accepting Clark's proposal. The road to Prairie du Chien was open.[1] On June 2 the Americans landed unopposed at the village and took possession. Failing to get assurance of support from the local militia and neighboring Foxes and Sioux, the small British garrison had fled to fight another day. However, by the morning of July 20 the British, under Colonel McKay, were once again in control at Prairie du Chien and the only Americans to elude capture were aboard the gunboat *Governor Clarke,* somewhere between Rock Island and Prairie du Chien. Partially completed Fort Shelby promptly became Fort McKay.

Back in St. Louis, General Howard had taken over and, aware of the potential danger, was scheming to reinforce Fort Shelby before the militia left. He wished to employ regulars, as he considered the service period of the militia too short for garrison duty. Repeatedly, he implored Secretary Armstrong to send him troops, but in vain.

Realizing that he could not delay, the General moved without instructions. By an act of providence he got sixty regulars from Fort Knox. To these he added sixty-four rangers and, placing them all under Major John Campbell, started them up

---

[1] Clark to the Secretary of War, June 5, 1814, Secretary of War, Letters Received, NA.

the river. He hoped that they might hold the fort until he was able to send more reinforcements or withdraw the entire garrison.

Major Campbell's route led him through the Rock River Sacs and Foxes, who had been restless throughout the spring and summer. The Americans charged them with many of the minor raids which had harassed the poorly defended frontier. On the Missouri the supposedly friendly element of the two tribes, after a visit from their friends and relatives from Rock River, displayed alarming pro-British symptoms. They even raised the British flag in council! Although they had not attacked the Osages as he had expected earlier in the year, the factor who had accompanied the two tribes up the Missouri became sufficiently alarmed to retreat to St. Louis with his stock of goods.[2]

The abject capitulation of the Rock River Indians to Clark's imposing force in May had evidenced their respect for the strength of the expedition rather than a change of heart. They still preferred American scalps to Winnebago or British. But Major Campbell and his men did not anticipate any serious effort to hinder their progress upstream. Indeed, Campbell permitted women and children to accompany the expedition. In addition he was burdened with the responsibility for boats carrying the goods of the fort's sutler and contractor.[3]

On July 13, while still about eighty miles below Rock River, the party of approximately 133 men, women, and children met Indians bearing dispatches to Clark. The redskins reported all quiet on the Mississippi. Five days later, as McKay's force was

[2] Gregg, "The War of 1812," 330.

[3] *Missouri Gazette,* July 30, 1814. The account of Campbell's skirmish is based on the following: Report of Lieutenant John Campbell, July 24, 1814; Report of Jonathan Riggs, July 26, 1814, in the U. S. Miscellaneous Archives in The State Historical Society of Wisconsin; "Papers from Canadian Archives," in *Wis. Colls.,* XII, 115; *Life of Black Hawk,* 72–74; Lieutenant Colonel William McKay to Lieutenant Colonel R. McDouall, July 27, 1814, in *Collections and Researches Made by the Michigan Pioneer and Historical Society,* XV, 623–27; and Boilvin to the Secretary of War, September 9, 1814, in Boilvin Letters.

attacking Fort Shelby, nine Indians with a white flag met Campbell and offered to conduct him to the friendly Sacs and Foxes, who wished to parley.

The next day the American relief force arrived at the mouth of the Rock. Five more warriors met them and repeated the Indian request for a council. Campbell consented, and 150 warriors assembled to talk with the American war chief. To the usual query concerning presents, the Major replied that he had some for them if they proposed to attack the Winnebagos as they had promised in the spring. The spokesman for the Sacs said that he had made no such promise but that the Sacs would comply with the request if the United States provided arms and ammunition. Campbell, ill and not at his best, did not consider the conversation of much significance and, after treating the Indians to some firewater, he terminated the council.

As the Indians appeared to him to be "friendly and well disposed," the Major elected to remain overnight in the vicinity. The next morning he dispatched letters by the Sacs to Perkins at Prairie du Chien and to Howard at St. Louis. Written as the garrison of Fort Shelby was opening its gates to the British, Campbell's letters never reached their destination.

After proceeding as far as the rapids of the Mississippi, a few miles above the mouth of Rock River, the Americans anchored for the night. Early on the morning of July 21, 1814, they headed upstream. With only a sergeant's guard aboard, the contractor's and sutler's boats passed through the rapids and were some distance ahead of the next two craft, manned by rangers. Two miles behind them, as the wind rose to near gale velocity, Campbell was having difficulty finding the main channel. Unable to made headway, his boat drifted into shoal water a few yards from an island's high bank covered with tall grass and dense undergrowth.

Despairing of further progress until the wind abated, Campbell decided to post sentries and prepare breakfast on the island. Preparations for the meal were forgotten in the war whoops of the attacking Sacs. The first volley disposed of the sentries, and before the troops could regain the boat, nearly half of the thirty-three regulars were killed or wounded. Indian-loaded canoes appeared from all directions. It appeared to the embattled Long Knives that hundreds of shrieking, howling savages were concentrating for their destruction.

Under cover of the high grass, bushes, and willows clothing the island the Indians approached to within a few yards of the boat and opened a galling fire. The men on the boat replied as best they could with a swivel and small arms, but their situation was desperate. Black Hawk personally launched fire arrows which set the sail ablaze, and the warriors swarmed about the craft. Some fired through the port holes; others attempted to cut holes in the boat's bottom or set fire to her. Even the Indian women took a hand, jumping aboard and flailing about with their hoes like amazons, breaking heads and casks alike. Fortunately for the Americans, the rangers up the river caught sight of the smoke and turned back to investigate. The commander of one boat, Lieutenant Rector, anchored above Campbell and raked the Sacs, now reinforced by parties of Kickapoos and Foxes. The other boat, under Lieutenant Riggs, drifted about one hundred yards below Campbell's and stranded.

The original target for the Indians, Campbell's craft, was burning, and immediate action was necessary or the scalps of the badly wounded Campbell and his men would be danced through the streets of Saukenuk. Riggs was unable to move upstream to his commander's assistance, and it remained for Rector and his rangers to stage a dramatic rescue. Ignoring the hail of lead which descended upon him and his men and closing his ears to the murderous cries of the Indians, outraged that their victims were being snatched from their grasp, the unruffled Rector cut his anchor cable and drifted down river until he came abreast of the beleaguered boat. Throwing out nearly all of the provisions to lighten his craft, Rector calmly took the survivors off the burning vessel and then fell downstream. Riggs remained to defend himself as best he could.

Exhausted by the several-hour-long battle, the Indians inflicted several casualties but failed to prevent Riggs from freeing his boat and slipping down the river to join the others. Meanwhile, the *Governor Clarke* had encountered the boats of the sutler and the contractor above the rapids. When the firing had subsided, the gunboat managed to shepherd them through the danger zone to the open water below the mouth of the Rock.

After sharp fighting the Indians had won. Campbell had fourteen men killed and seventeen wounded, two of them fatally. In addition, the Indians killed one woman and a child and severely wounded another woman. The attackers lost only one woman and two warriors. At Prairie du Chien, McKay exultingly proclaimed it one of the most brilliant Indian performances since the commencement of the war.

A move made by McKay to intercept the *Governor Clarke* in its flight from Prairie du Chien had proved to be the unsuspecting Campbell's undoing. Believing that the boat might run aground at the rapids, McKay had sent to Rock River four kegs of gunpowder and a request that the Sacs harass the gunboat should it do so. Reaching the Indians on the evening Campbell camped at the rapids, the message and the gunpowder had their desired effect.

The delighted British loaded the victorious Indians with presents. To the proud warriors who brought the news of the victory and a request for ammunition, the elated McKay gave ten kegs of gunpowder and some presents to take back to Saukenuk. He later distributed among the Sacs and their jubilant Kickapoo and Fox allies more powder and fourteen bales of goods. The powder was particularly welcome to the Indians, as a few weeks after the battle reports began to reach Saukenuk that the Long Knives were planning another attack.[4]

The harrowing tales the survivors of the battle of July 21 bore down the Mississippi stung Howard to prompt counteraction. Assembling the 430 troops then available, mostly rangers and militiamen, with a sprinkling of regulars, the enraged General placed them under twenty-nine-year-old Major Zachary Taylor and dispatched them up the river in eight boats, with orders to destroy the Rock River villages. Following the success or failure of this mission the muscular, stocky Virginian was to drop down to the mouth of the Des Moines to erect and garrison a fort. To deceive the Indians on Rock River, Howard and Taylor allowed the rumor to circulate that the objective was Prairie du Chien. "We set out with hearts elated and sails filled," one of Taylor's rangers confided to his diary on August 22, 1814.

At no time prior to the arrival of the expedition at Rock River did the Americans sight hostile Indians. However, they found indications that Indians had detected the expedition. As he approached their stronghold, the Major exercised extreme caution, in order that they might surprise the Indians rather than be surprised by them.

On the night of September 3 the boats, under cover of darkness, moved up to a point about fifteen miles below the mouth of Rock River. A good night's rest would have been more beneficial, as the Indians were well aware of the expedition's approach and a real shock was in store for the Americans.

Shortly after his recapture of Prairie du Chien, Colonel McKay returned to Mackinac, leaving Captain Thomas G. Anderson in charge of Fort McKay. A veteran of many years trading on the upper Mississippi, Anderson knew the territory and the people. Learning that a boat abandoned by Clark in the spring was still lying on the banks of the Mississippi, about two miles above the charred ruins of Fort Madison, he decided to seize it or burn it. To carry out the project, Anderson chose

4 Lieutenant Colonel McKay to Lieutenant Colonel McDouall, August 1, 1814, "Papers from the Canadian Archives," in *Wis. Colls.*, XII, 115–17.

Duncan Graham, a trader before the war and currently a lieutenant in the British Indian Department.

On August 15, a week before Taylor started up the Mississippi, Graham departed from Prairie du Chien with a small party. The Lieutenant carried a supply of tobacco to enlist the Rock River Indians for his mission, but he found them agitated and unwilling to co-operate. They had learned that a large force of Americans was on its way to attack them. Three Foxes were even then on their way to Prairie du Chien for arms, ammunition, and reinforcements to repel the Long Knives.[5]

At Fort McKay, Anderson gave the suppliants a cool welcome. He found their warning quite indefinite concerning the location and size of the American force and concluded it was a stratagem to obtain more supplies. Since McKay had already informed Black Hawk that he need not expect any more munitions until new supplies reached Prairie du Chien, Anderson did not hesitate to deny their requests. Meanwhile, Graham despaired of aid from the Indians and prepared to descend the Mississippi alone. The arrival of two Missouri Sacs caused him to abandon the proposed trip and sent him scurrying to Anderson with the news that the Americans were really on their way up the river.

Convinced of the authenticity of the report, Captain Anderson decided to try to stop the Americans at the Mississippi rapids above the mouth of Rock River.[6] From his small garrison, Anderson drew thirty men and armed them with a three-pounder and two swivels. The detachment, under the command of Graham, left Fort McKay the morning of August 27. The following day more than one hundred Sioux, Foxes, and Winnebagos, chanting their war songs, left Prairie du Chien and followed Graham down the river to assist their allies

[5] Anderson to Graham, August 26, 1814; Anderson to Lieutenant Colonel McDouall, August 29, 1814; both in "Captain Thomas G. Anderson's Journal," in *Wis. Colls.*, IX, 219–21.

[6] "Anderson's Journal," in *ibid.*, IX, 213.

against the invaders, then about midway between St. Louis and Saukenuk.[7]

Duncan Graham reached the village on August 29 and found the Indians "much animated to meet the enemy." The Sacs were more pleased with the arrival of the British "than if all the goods in the King's store in Mackinaw had been sent them," as they were now firmly convinced that their English father was determined to support them against "the ambition and unjust conduct of their enemies." As scouts returned with reports that the Americans were approaching, Graham evolved a plan of defense.

Judging, incorrectly, that Prairie du Chien was the invaders' target, the Lieutenant decided to concentrate his defenses along the rapids above Saukenuk. On September 5 the British emplaced their guns to command the narrowest part of the channel and awaited Taylor's approach. They did not have long to wait, as the American craft hove into view late in the afternoon of that same day.

As they came in sight of the mouth of the Rock, Taylor and his men discovered that the prairies along the Mississippi were covered with grazing horses—"doubtless to lure us ashore," surmised the wary Major. In order to select a site from which his artillery might command the village and perhaps ambush the Indians, no shots having yet been fired, Taylor altered Howard's plan. The General had proposed that the expedition pass the Sacs and Foxes as if they intended to proceed on to Prairie du Chien and then return stealthily in the night and surprise the Indians in their lodges. Instead, Taylor resolved to hoist a white flag to lure the Indians into parleying with him. Thus, he might ascertain the situation at Prairie du Chien and perhaps the strength of the Indians themselves. Moreover, if the Indians would consent to meet in council, the implacable

7 The account of the ensuing skirmish is based on "Anderson's Journal," in *ibid.*, IX, 220–32; Edgar B. Wesley, "James Callaway in the War of 1812," in *Missouri Historical Society Collections*, V, 69–75; and Taylor to Howard, September 6, 1814, in *Niles Weekly Register*, Supplement to Vol. VII, 137–38.

Major expected to retaliate "on them for their repeated acts of treachery" by attacking them in council. If the Indians did not respond to his flag of truce, Taylor planned to draw them out of their defenses by continuing toward the rapids and then, by a quick countermarch, destroy the Indians before they could regain their defenses. Unknown to Taylor, his opponents now numbered about one thousand warriors. Reinforcements of Missouri Sacs and Foxes, Winnebagos, and Sioux had reached Rock River.

The American commander first resorted to the deceptive flag of truce. But the Indians, who appeared by the hundreds along the shores and darted back and forth in their canoes, well out of range, did not fall for the ruse. As the boats approached the head of Credit Island, which lay athwart the mouth of the Rock, the elements came to the assistance of the Indians. The favorable wind which had carried the squadron to the mouth of the Rock began to shift and, by the time the boats reached the head of Credit Island, had turned into a small gale which blew downstream.

Deluged by the rain which accompanied the high wind, Taylor found himself unable to proceed up the river and decided to put his alternate plan into operation. With difficulty, and still flying their white flag, the Americans managed to land at a small willow-covered island in the middle of the river. Posting sentries, the Major allowed his men to eat and bed down on the boats for the night. Until shortly before dawn only the glow of a large fire on the Illinois shore reminded the sentries of the presence of the enemy. However, warriors were even then infiltrating the sentry posts.

In violation of the orders of Lieutenant Graham, who wished the Indians to attack at his command, a few impetuous warriors had crossed under cover of darkness to the island off which the boats were anchored. Employing the tactics so effective against Lieutenant Campbell's detachment earlier in the summer they approached to within point-blank range of the sentries without being detected. The first indication the Americans had of their presence was a volley and a chorus of blood-chilling war whoops. Following a preconceived battle plan the troops remained on the boats and returned the fire as best they could.

When the sun had risen sufficiently to illuminate the scene, Taylor cleared the island of the enemy with a charge through the willows. After wounding two Americans, the Indians escaped by wading to a near-by island. To dislodge them the Major ordered Captain Rector, the veteran of Campbell's defeat, to rake it with his guns. Rector complied, but no Indians appeared to be shot. After about thirty minutes he landed and destroyed several canoes beached below him. Having accomplished this, Rector began to re-embark his men. At this moment, to the amazement of the astounded Americans, solid shot appeared out of nowhere, splintering the hulls, masts, and steering oars and shredding the sails. The Indians also opened a rapid fire punctuated by scalp-tingling war whoops. Howard and Taylor had not anticipated the three pieces of artillery revealed so disconcertingly to the stunned Major.

Following the predawn attack which opened the engagement, Graham had abandoned his position at the rapids and moved his guns to a site covering Taylor's boats. Working rapidly, Graham soon had the guns emplaced behind a knoll and ready to fire. Taylor's initial reaction to the hail of lead was to order a piece of artillery landed to return the fire. After a moment he realized that this would prove ineffectual, as the British were defiladed and would sink his boats before he could bring effective fire upon them. The fire from behind the knoll becoming more accurate as Graham's men became "base enough to knock the Splinters into the men's faces," as a ranger wryly described it, Taylor gave the order to fall down the river. His boat led off, to be followed by the others.

As the boats ran rapidly before the wind, Graham kept them in range as long as he could by rolling his guns down the beach.

On the prairies, which the previous day had been lined with grazing horses, screaming warriors brandished their weapons and kept up a heavy if inaccurate fire on the descending boats. After running this gauntlet for two miles the Americans outdistanced their pursuers, and, a mile farther down the river, Taylor gave the order to land so that they might treat the wounded and repair the boats. Indians in canoes arrived on the scene shortly, but when the Americans drew up in battle array, the warriors beat a hasty retreat. The next move was in Taylor's hands.

Gathering his officers together the Major asked their advice. Outnumbered at least three to one and running short of provisions, the disheartened officers advised retreat. This was enough to convince the equally discouraged Taylor, and in conformity with the second part of his orders he descended the river to the mouth of the Des Moines and began the construction of Fort Johnston. Although they had inflicted only eleven casualties on the invaders, the Indians, with the aid of the British detachment and its artillery, had clearly defeated the Americans.

By the end of 1814 the Sacs and Foxes were more unified in their opposition to the Long Knives than at any previous time. Although a few bands remained under Clark's protection on the Missouri, the twice victorious tribesmen on the Rock considered themselves a match for the Americans. Wholesome respect for the strength of the United States no longer tempered the hatred engendered by the Treaty of 1804 and a decade of friction.

Black Hawk

From a painting by George Catlin in 1832. *Smithsonian Institution.*

Appanoose, a contemporary of Keokuk.

From a daguerreotype made in the 1840's. *Smithsonian Institution.*

Keokuk in 1847.

From a daguerreotype. *Smithsonian Institution.*

Treaty of 1867 being read to delegation in Washington.
Left to right: Ukquahoko, Manahtowah, Muttattah, Cheko-
skuk, Keokuk, Commissioner of Indian Affairs Lewis V. Bogy,
Chief Clerk of the Indian Bureau Charles E. Mix, and
three Kaws.

7. Peace Comes to the Upper Mississippi

THE NEXT TWO YEARS were to see bewildering changes and grievous disappointments for the Sacs and Foxes. In the fall of 1814 they were flushed with victory. A year later, though still undefeated, they were at the mercy of the Americans.

The defeat of Taylor's command had renewed the confidence of the exultant British and Indians on the upper Mississippi. The grateful redcoats singled out for particular attention the Indians who had deserted the American reservations on the Missouri and showered the Sacs and Foxes and their allies with presents. The British commander at Prairie du Chien recognized the value of the victory in heartening his fickle allies, "For had the enemy put their design in execution, and had murdered the Sauks in that inhuman and American-like manner, as was their intention . . . the Indian tribes on the Mississippi would not have been easily brought to understand or believe that our Government's intention to support them is real."[1]

1 Anderson to McDouall, October 18, 1814, in "Prairie du Chien Documents, 1814–1815," in *Wis. Colls.*, IX, 269–72.

Spurred on by the British, a party of Sacs reconnoitered down the Mississippi and discovered Taylor's men constructing Fort Johnston at the mouth of the Des Moines. Until they evacuated the fort and burned it, the soldiers knew no peace. Small bands of Indians from Rock River hovered around the fortification and attacked any working parties straying too far from the defenses. Other parties raided along the Missouri frontier, and Sacs brought ten American scalps to Prairie du Chien, with assurances that they would "continue to bring them in as they do ducks from the swamps." Only a shortage of provisions prevented the British and Indians from attacking Fort Johnston and driving the garrison back to St. Louis. But supply deficiencies also hampered the Americans, and late in October they evacuated the fort.

As snow began to fall along the upper Mississippi, hostilities ceased. On the Iowa River the Sacs and Foxes joined the Kickapoos for their winter hunt. The Indians asked Captain Anderson at Fort McKay for a trader whom he couldn't furnish, but his successor, Captain A. N. Bulger, sent them twenty-five sleigh-loads of presents. Colonel McDouall had ordered Bulger to support the Sacs "in consequence of their bravery, and good conduct, & of their being your advance guard."[2] Reports of plans afoot in St. Louis for a spring expedition by land and water against Prairie du Chien encouraged Bulger to cultivate the Indians.

Bulger decided to concentrate the defense at Prairie du Chien and send raiding parties to the vicinity of St. Louis to distract the Americans and force them to employ their troops in defense. To hearten the Sacs and Foxes, he hoped to "impress on their minds that it is *solely on their account* that the war is now carried on. That the King their Great Father always true to his promises is resolved not to lay down the Casse-tete

2 "Anderson's Journal," in *Wis. Colls.*, IX, 250; Bulger to McDouall, January 15, 1815, in "The Bulger Papers," *ibid.*, XIII, 54–60; McDouall to Bulger, October 17, 1814, in "The Bulger Papers," *ibid.*, XIII, 14–19.

[tomahawk] until the Indians are restored to their rights, and their future independence secured."[3]

Colonel McDouall confirmed Bulger in his pronouncement that the British were continuing the war only to aid the Indians. McDouall informed him by letter that the British demand that the Americans withdraw behind the boundary Wayne established in 1795 had stalemated negotiations. In compliance with orders of Governor Sir George Prevost, McDouall forwarded a speech to be read to the Indians.

In accordance with McDouall's instructions to "leave no means untried to excite their enthusiasm and perseverance," Bulger sent runners to the surrounding tribes. To the nearly twelve hundred Menominees, Winnebagos, Ottawas, Chippewas, Sacs, Foxes, and the Sioux who assembled to hear the Colonel's message, it constituted a powerful appeal to continue the war. According to McDouall, the deceitful Americans realized defeat was inevitable and had "sent commissioners across the Big Lake to treat for peace." However, the king, faithful to his red children, refused to treat unless the Americans agreed to restore the lands stolen from the Indians since the Treaty of Greenville. Their lands freed of the Americans, "The Indian nations, whose rights were in future to be held sacred," would be completely independent.

Nor was the king content merely to refuse the American proposals. The British spoke of "great" reinforcements arriving at Quebec and large fleets and armies even then attacking the Americans "on the side of the Great Lake [Atlantic]" and at the mouth of the Mississippi. The delighted Sacs and Foxes and their allies enthusiastically received McDouall's speech and Bulger's appeal to carry the war to the enemy.[4] After this council they placed little faith in the peace reports emanating from St. Louis. Only a few days after Bulger addressed the

[3] Bulger to Guillory, April 8, 1815, in "The Bulger Papers," *ibid.*, XIII, 127–29.

[4] Alfred Edward Bulger, "Last Days of the British at Prairie du Chien," *ibid.*, XIII, 156.

eager council at Prairie du Chien and sent an agent to Rock River to spark Sac and Fox raids on the American frontier, an old friend of the Sacs and Foxes, the gunboat *Governor Clarke,* anchored off the mouth of the rock. It carried word of the Treaty of Ghent and a warning that if the Indians did not cease hostilities they would lose the benefits the British had secured for them.

Duncan Graham, the capable commander of the artillery which had stopped Taylor the previous September, was present at Rock River when the *Clarke* arrived. He agreed to carry the news to Prairie du Chien and arrived at Fort McKay just in time to halt the departure for the Missouri frontier of the main Indian force. Unfortunately, he arrived after several war parties had already left to carry the war to the Long Knives.

Bulger immediately began recalling all war parties he was able to contact. By May 10 more than eight hundred highly excited and indignant Indians were at Fort McKay. To the principal chiefs, astounded and angry after being assured that the British would fight until the Americans were driven behind the frontiers of 1795, the British commander reluctantly announced the terms of the treaty.

In a council with the king's men, Black Hawk displayed the war belt he had received at Quebec and declared vehemently, "I have fought the Big Knives, and will continue to fight them till they are off our lands. Till then my father, your Red Children can not be happy." With that he stalked angrily from the chamber to lead a war party down the Mississippi. So bitter did the Indians appear that Bulger feared that they intended to attack Fort McKay and, for a fortnight, kept the garrison under arms.[5] Meanwhile, oblivious of the fact that the war was over, raiding parties which Bulger had been unable to recall were wreaking havoc on the frontier. Clark be-

5 Bulger, "Last Days," *ibid.,* XIII, 157–58; "An Indian Council," in "The Bulger Papers," *ibid.,* XIII, 131–32.

lieved that it would be "necessary to cut off the Rocky River Tribes before we shall be at peace."[6] As one of the commissioners appointed by President Madison to reach a peace settlement with the western Indians, the vexed Governor became even more convinced of that fact before the year was over.

Early in May, Clark and his two colleagues, Governor Ninian Edwards of Illinois Territory and Auguste Chouteau, gathered in St. Louis to send out announcements of the council to be held at Portage des Sioux in July. The commissioners directed several of the talks to the Indians of Rock River. Earlier attempts to communicate with those tribes had met with only partial success. One of the messengers lost his scalp, and even the British warned the commissioners to beware of the Rock River Indians. Clark, Edwards, and Chouteau complained to the Secretary of War that a show of force would be necessary and asked directions on how to proceed with them.[7] Before the letter was more than a few miles from St. Louis, a Sac attack near Fort Howard at the mouth of Cuivre River resulted in the Battle of the Sinkhole.

About noon, May 24, Black Hawk and his war party ambushed five men of the garrison of Fort Howard, killing four. A detachment from the fort immediately began a pursuit of the Sacs. They soon overtook the Indians, who took refuge in a sinkhole. Improvising a breastwork on two wheels, the whites approached the hole near enough to fire on its occupants. Before any decision could be reached the approach of darkness halted the firing. The next morning the soldiers found that Black Hawk, leaving five corpses behind, had led the Sacs to safety. From the blood found on the scene the Americans concluded that they had wounded several other In-

[6] Clark to the Secretary of War, April 17, 1815, Secretary of War, Letters Received, NA.

[7] Thomas Forsyth to the Secretary of War, April 30, 1815, in Draper MSS., 7T29; Clark, Edwards, and Chouteau to the Secretary of War, May 22, 1815, in *American State Papers: Indian Affairs*, II, 7.

dians. The redskins had done well themselves; white losses totaled eleven killed and three wounded.[8]

While Black Hawk and his party were lurking around Fort Howard, Captain Bulger, preparatory to the evacuation of Fort McKay, held his last Indian council. He had received confirmation of the peace from Colonel McDouall only two days before and moved rapidly to perform his disagreeable duty. May 22, in the very council house in which not two months before he had delivered McDouall's inflammatory speech, Bulger officially discharged the Indians from their obligation to war on the Long Knives. Displaying the great belt of wampum, dyed red when used to summon the Mississippi tribes to war and now dyed blue to signify peace, he passed a beautifully decorated peace pipe among the Indians. Aware of the reception his speech would receive, Bulger made preparations to handle any sudden outburst of resentment. In the fort, alert gunners stood by their cannon with lighted matches. Happily, the chiefs and braves did not give vent to their emotions. In stunned silence they heard Bulger announce that the treaty of peace contained no references to the Treaty of Greenville and that the Indian prewar status was unchanged. Although bitterly disappointed at the unexpected news, a Sac chief declared that he would attempt to restrain his people, although he could not vouch for their actions should the Americans further trouble them.

Two days later the uneasy British withdrew from Prairie du Chien, leaving Fort McKay a pile of glowing embers. Prior to their departure, Captain Bulger endeavored by a lavish distribution of presents to offset the shock of the treaty. He assured McDouall that he had left the Indians on the Mississippi "above want."

The *Missouri Gazette* regarded such activities in a different light. In reporting British generosity toward the Sacs, the St.

[8] Extract of Lieutenant Drakeford to Colonel William Russell, May 25, 1815, in *Niles Weekly Register*, July 1, 1815; *Life of Black Hawk*, 65–66.

Louis paper spoke of the departure of "captain Duncan Graham, deputy-scalping-master-general, from Rock River after bestowing on his worthy comrades, the Sacks, ten barrels of gun powder and twenty fusees, as a reward for their services in butchering the helpless women and children on the frontier." At the same time the *Gazette* reported that the Sacs and Foxes had finally evidenced a willingness to negotiate.[9]

Early in June a strong delegation of Foxes from the other villages and a few Sacs and Foxes from Rock River met the commissioners at Portage des Sioux. Clark concluded the opening address to the Indian delegations with an expression of surprise at the absence of the principal Sac chiefs. He directed that those Rock River Indians present send for the absent chiefs at once, as their failure to appear in thirty days would mean war.

When the interpreters translated this strongly worded warning to the other Indians, the Shawnees, Delawares, Sioux, and Omahas sprang up and expressed their approval by vehement yelps which appalled the Sacs. That night the commissioners posted a strong guard to protect them. Nevertheless, the Sacs, whom observers had noted on arrival to "frown and strut around with the most insufferable impudence," slipped down to their canoes and hurried back to their villages.

The one Sac chief who had come to Portage des Sioux had stated that even if a treaty should be concluded with all the chiefs, the tribes would never consent to relinquish the lands previously ceded.[10] Less than two weeks later, the commissioners, hearing of additional Indian depredations on the frontier, feared that a war with the Rock River Indians was unavoidable.

Not every American considered the Indians solely at fault for the postwar unpleasantness. The embittered Boilvin laid

9 *Niles Weekly Register,* July 22, 1815.

10 Clark, Edwards, and Chouteau to the Secretary of War, July 11, July 16, 1815, in *American State Papers: Indian Affairs,* II, 8–9; Gregg, "The War of 1812," 347.

the blame at the door of the "administration at St. Louis" and denounced Clark as a warmonger. The actions of the tribesmen he attributed to the failure of the British to inform them of the treaty and to the fact that the Indians mistrusted the individuals sent to make peace. Boilvin declared, with no pretense of modesty, that all would have gone smoothly had he been sent to announce the treaty to the chiefs.[11]

Even though Sac chiefs did not appear within the thirty days allotted them by the commissioners, the threat to use force was not carried out. Instead, Boilvin and an interpreter were sent after them. Given an opportunity to exercise his influence, the agent enjoyed a measure of success, although he arrived at Rock River at a most inauspicious time. The Indians were "dancing" American and French scalps! After negotiating with the Sacs for three days and hearing their frequently reiterated fears of an American ruse, Boilvin granted the Indians a pardon, on their promise to remain at peace and send a proper delegation to the treaty council. True to their word, a party of chiefs straggled into Portage des Sioux two weeks after the commissioners had adjourned. The Americans told them to return the next spring.[12]

Although the Rock River Sacs caused the commissioners considerable anxiety, the Foxes and that small portion of the Sacs remaining on the Missouri under the tutelage of the United States proved entirely amenable and confirmed the Treaty of 1804. In addition, the Foxes agreed to surrender their prisoners and the Missouri Sacs promised "to remain distinct and separate from the Sacs of Rock River, giving them no aid or assistance whatever until peace shall also be concluded between the United States and the said Sacs of Rock River." Thus effected, the breach between the two parties of

[11] Boilvin to the Secretary of State, July 24, 1815, in Boilvin Letters.
[12] Boilvin to the Secretary of War, January 11, 1816, Secretary of War, Letters Received, NA; "Councils of Different Tribes Held at Prairie du Chien and Rock River by Nicholas Boilvin, Agent," in Boilvin Letters; Gregg, "The War of 1812," 347.

Sacs gradually widened in the succeeding years. The Indians from Rock River never completely forgave the Missouri contingent for their desertion.

The commissioners continued to complain to Secretary of War William H. Crawford of the conduct of the Sacs. Nevertheless, late in November the affable Georgia giant decided that, although their conduct merited "the severest chastisement," the United States would be liberal with them. He authorized Clark, Edwards, and Chouteau to treat with the Rock River Indians after they had surrendered stolen property in their possession.[13] To insure that the Indians appreciated the liberal American policy, a detachment of infantry troops left St. Louis to erect a fort near the mouth of Rock River.

While the troops moved up the Mississippi, Boilvin, "Surrounded by hostile savages who are in the daily habit of intercourse with the British traders urging them to hold themselves in instant readiness for another war," passed an uncomfortable winter at Prairie du Chien. Handicapped by a lack of presents, Boilvin was hard pressed to counteract the traders' insinuations. That the Indians appeared at all in St. Louis in May, 1816, to treat with the commissioners was evidence that the agent actually had considerable influence among the tribes on the upper Mississippi.

Despite Boilvin's presence the negotiations between the Sacs and the commissioners did not run smoothly. The Indians assumed that the Americans would permit British traders to remain among them. When Clark announced that this would not be allowed, a chief, to the applause of the other Sacs, scathingly charged that the Americans spoke with two tongues. Stung by the implied insult, the normally lenient Governor summarily broke off negotiations, and the apparently unrelenting Sacs retired to their camp.

The timely maneuvers of a detachment of artillery in the

13 Secretary of War Crawford to Clark, Edwards, and Chouteau, November 24, 1815, in *American State Papers: Indian Affairs*, II, 12.

vicinity of the Sac camp led the Indians to reconsider. The next day, humble and contrite, the chiefs asked Clark to resume their conversations. He graciously consented, and at the ensuing meeting the offending chief offered the ingenious explanation that Clark had misunderstood him; he had meant simply that the Long Knives spoke with two tongues, French and English! On May 13 the chiefs and braves attested to their change of heart by placing their X's on the treaty the Americans presented to them.[14]

Similar to the one signed by the Foxes and the Missouri Sacs the previous year, the treaty provided that the Rock River Indians should "unconditionally assent to, recognize, re-establish, and confirm" the Treaty of 1804. Among the braves who "touched the goose quill to the treaty" was Black Hawk, the implacable enemy of the Americans. Years later he pleaded ignorance to the significance of the confirmation of the Treaty of 1804. Had he known that the site of Saukenuk was surrendered by the treaty, Black Hawk said he would never have signed.[15] Undefeated in battle, the war chief remained a proud and defiant enemy of the Long Knives. Nor did the desertion of the British shake his allegiance to them. Although Keokuk and most of the other influential Sacs and Foxes recognized that in the future they would be unable to depend on British aid, Black Hawk continued to look to Canada.

For the moment, at least, peace reigned on the frontier. So long as the Indians were not disturbed in their actual possession of the land, they could afford to ignore or remain in ignorance of the Treaty of 1804, which their chiefs and braves had recently reaffirmed in St. Louis. Not for several years would they be again confronted with the necessity of fighting for their villages and corn fields at the mouth of the Rock.

[14] Timothy Flint, *Recollections of the Past Ten Years*, 153–54.
[15] *Life of Black Hawk*, 86.

8. Postwar Problems

ALTHOUGH the Rock River Indians had signified by their X's that they recognized the supremacy of the Long Knives, the Americans were taking no chances. Early in May, 1816, as Keokuk, Black Hawk, and the other Sac chiefs and braves negotiated with the commissioners at St. Louis, a regiment of the United States infantry appeared off the mouth of Rock River. In the following months Fort Armstrong rose on the lower end of Rock Island, where perpendicular cliffs of limestone dropped thirty feet into the rushing waters of the Mississippi.

Before leaving Rock Island for Prairie du Chien to construct Fort Crawford, the commanding officer of the regiment invited the sullen tribesmen to parley with him, but they refused. The Sacs and Foxes, who had twice sent these Long Knives scuttling back to St. Louis in defeat, strongly resented the garrison, obviously established to overawe them. The island, with its profusion of berries, fruits, and nuts, had been a favorite haunt of the Indian youth. No longer did the Sacs and Foxes see the guardian of the island, the good white spirit with swan's wings. The Indians had been careful to refrain from unnecessary noise near the cave abode of the good spirit, but the ignorant Long Knives were so noisy that they drove him away. Black Hawk had no doubt that a bad spirit replaced the good one.[1]

To strengthen their guard over the obstreperous Sacs and Foxes, the Secretary of War transferred Thomas Forsyth to Rock Island. In 1812 the veteran frontiersman and trader had entered the Indian service as a subagent at Peoria under Governor Ninian Edwards. Only a subagent in 1816, Forsyth was promoted to full agent two years later. Intelligent and benevolent, he was a competent speaker and commanded the respect of his charges. When available for service he was a very capable agent.

To discharge his first duty to the Rock River Sacs and Foxes, Forsyth left St. Louis in May, 1817, with their annuities. When he arrived at Rock River, the Foxes refused their share. They declared that "they would do without food and live on roots rather than part with their lands." Declining to argue, Forsyth bluntly told the scowling Indians that they could take the annuity or leave it, as they desired. Take it they did, after he had left their village to visit Saukenuk.[2]

Surprisingly, the Sacs received the agent hospitably and accepted the annuity without quibbling. In compliance with Clark's directions the agent queried them concerning the possibility of their removing to land west of the Mississippi. The Indian reply was evasive; they said perhaps they might but as yet they did not know. Lord Selkirk, the proprietor of a large settlement in the Red River region of Canada, was currently encouraging the Sacs and other tribes to migrate to that area. Although only a part of the Sacs were considering the proposal, Forsyth believed that if any of the Indians went the rest of the nation would follow.[3] The War of 1812 had not terminated

1 *Life of Black Hawk*, 87.

2 Forsyth to Clark, June 3, 1817, in Draper MSS., 7T40–43.

3 Extract of Benjamin O'Fallon to Governor Ninian Edwards, February 19, 1818, in *Niles Weekly Register*, August 1, 1818; Forsyth to Clark, June 3, 1817, in Draper MSS., 7T40–43.

the close connection between the Indians of the Northwest and the British. Although the Sacs did not accept Lord Selkirk's invitation, their annual visits to the British posts clearly manifested their attachment to the English. In 1819, for example, the British agent at Malden distributed among 340 grateful Sacs an estimated $3,400 worth of trade goods, including ammunition.

At Detroit, Lewis Cass, the sober, dark-complexioned governor of Michigan Territory, suspected the Canadian visits of the red men. Not only did the visitors keep the frontier in a state of alarm by their pilfering and destruction en route, but Cass believed that the discontented Indians were hoping for the appearance of another Tecumseh. In 1817 the uneasy governor heard that Sacs and Foxes calling at Drummond's Island had boasted of destroying surveyors' markers and had declared that they would not only keep the surveyors from returning, but would kill any Americans who attempted to settle on Indian lands.

By the spring of 1821, Forsyth incorrectly assumed that he had "weaned" the tribes from their habit of visiting the British posts. Black Hawk and Keokuk both told him that since he treated them so well they would cease visiting Malden. That summer Black Hawk did not go to Malden, but he did call at the British post on Drummond's Island. To the British he declared defiantly that, although the Americans surrounded the Sacs, "We are ever ready to meet them," and he requested "a double proportion of my Great Father's bounty." However, the Sacs went away displeased and empty-handed. The British, who had told the Indians three years earlier that presents might be obtained only at Amherstburg, refused to give them any presents at Drummond's Island.[4]

Sheer economic necessity was an important factor behind the Indian pilgrimages to the British posts. Game had so de-

4 Forsyth to Clark, May 2, 1821, in Draper MSS., 4T87; "Papers of Thomas G. Anderson, British Indian Agent, 1814–1821," in *Wis. Colls.*, X, 45.

creased that hunting was no longer a pleasure for the Indian but had become real labor. Even the Anglophobe Cass admitted this,[5] and Henry R. Schoolcraft, later an Indian agent known for his scientific interests, agreed. "The causes of this increasing intercourse are to be found," Schoolcraft averred, "not so much in any increased efforts of the British agents to alienate these bands from our government, as in the necessitous and impoverished state of the Indians."[6] More fortunately situated on fertile lands than the northern Indians, the Sacs and Foxes came to depend less on British largess. But they had troubles of their own.

As settlers' cabins encroached on their hunting grounds along the Missouri and forced them north and away from their old rivals, the Osages, the Sacs and Foxes collided with a powerful confederacy roaming the northern plains, the Sioux. As the prewar years were marked by clashes with the Osages, so the postwar years were marked by clashes with the Sioux. Most of the skirmishes occurred where the hunting grounds of the Indians overlapped, and the honors were about even. Although the Sioux were more numerous, they were scattered, and the Sacs and Foxes, concentrated in a few villages, could usually muster as many or more warriors at any given time.

The initial difficulty occurred as a result of a number of Sioux attacks on Fox intruders. When, in the summer of 1818, the Foxes finally retaliated, they handled the Sioux roughly and took five prisoners. After much procrastination on the part of the Foxes, Forsyth, Boilvin, and the commandant of Fort Crawford at Prairie du Chien co-operated in getting the prisoners returned to their people. Thus begun, some fighting between the tribes occurred practically every summer for years, although the Indian agents arranged frequent peace councils.

In August, 1820, Governor Cass ordered Boilvin to take immediate steps to end the current hostilities. The agent re-

---

[5] Cass to Calhoun, October 24, 1821, Stock Transcripts.
[6] Schoolcraft to Cass, July 18, 1822, Cass, Letters Received, Photostat WHS.

doubled his efforts and succeeded in holding a council of the Sioux, Sacs, Foxes, and Winnebagos. The Sacs and Foxes blamed the continuation of the war upon their "foolish young men" and expressed a willingness to "bury our Hatchets underground." Fearing that if the fighting continued their traders would be afraid to visit them, the Sioux hastened to agree. The council closed with the difficulty presumably resolved. However, the Sioux delegation represented only that portion of the tribe residing along the Mississippi, whereas the plains Sioux had been most belligerent.[7]

An outbreak in the summer of 1821 led to another peace conference the next spring between the Foxes and the Mississippi Sioux bands, but large war parties continued to leave Rock River in search of Sioux. One party which went out in April, 1822, returned about the middle of June after suffering seven or eight casualties, but the proud warriors brought in twenty scalps and fourteen child prisoners. Heartened by the success of this party, a force of five hundred Sac, Fox, and Iowa warriors rode from their villages in search of Sioux scalps. They acquired some, but they lost about as many in the process. Undismayed, two months later two hundred more painted warriors set out to display their manhood. Meanwhile, at Prairie du Chien fresh negotiations were in progress between the chiefs of the Foxes and Sioux. Conducted by Boilvin, these talks resulted in a truce between the two tribes. War between the Sacs and the Sioux continued unabated.

Although they were constantly at odds with the Sioux during these years, the bellicose Sacs and Foxes also found time to exchange scalps with the Otos and Osages on the Missouri. For a short time, at least, they even fought their old allies, the Iowas. Because of the extension of white settlements along the Missouri such activities brought friction with the Americans. In June, 1820, William Clark accused the tribesmen of feign-

7 Cass to Boilvin, August 9, 1820; Council Held Between Sioux, Sacs, Foxes, and Winnebagos, September 5, 1820; both in Boilvin Letters.

ing a war against the Sioux, "When in reality their object is to destroy our Traders and attack the small tribes immediately in the neighborhood of our troops."[8] Clark threatened the Sacs and Foxes with war, but Secretary of War Calhoun only authorized him to withhold presents and annuities if the outrages continued.

The next June, when Forsyth went to Rock Island to distribute the Sac and Fox annuities, he also demanded the warriors implicated in the murder of a Frenchman the previous year. This time the Foxes took their annuities without dispute. However, the sewing silk and short pieces of linen which made up a part of their annuity provoked the Sacs to derisive laughter. They declared there were too few goods for so many Indians and refused to accept them. However, within a few days they changed their minds. In Forsyth's opinion, the Sacs delayed in accepting the annuity not because of the quality of goods but because they believed that the Foxes were getting more than their share. Having accepted the annuity, the Sacs also agreed to surrender the murderers if they personally could deliver them to St. Louis.[9]

As they had promised, the tribe sent a deputation of their leaders, including Keokuk, to St. Louis with the two murderers and four Oto prisoners taken the previous summer on the Missouri. Before the actual surrender of the prisoners and the two Sac warriors, Keokuk, who was responsible for the delegation's presence in St. Louis, informed Clark privately of what was to occur. In order that the incident might "enhance the worth and popularity of Keokuk," Clark, on receiving the Sacs and Foxes, did not demand the murderers but waited until the Indians volunteered them.[10] Fortunately for Keokuk's status in the tribe the United States lacked sufficient evidence to convict the two warriors and released them.

[8] Clark to Forsyth, June 4, 1820, in Draper MSS., 2T52.
[9] Forsyth to Clark, June 13, June 14, and June 18, 1821, in Forsyth Papers.
[10] Clark to Forsyth, June 30, 1821, in Draper MSS., 1T55.

Clark recognized the value of cultivating Keokuk, whom he regarded as the future head of the Sac nation. He thoroughly appreciated the war chief's efforts to harmonize relations "between the Whites and reds." To keep such an influential brave friendly, Clark was attentive to the wants of Keokuk and his friends when they visited St. Louis. On the occasion of the surrender of the two murderers, Keokuk and his party received about $300 worth of goods, ranging from butcher knives and blankets to plumes and black silk handkerchiefs. One coat for Keokuk cost $21.50 alone. This particular act of generosity may explain Keokuk's willingness to co-operate. The Americans had learned to appeal to his weak points, his cupidity and love of display.

While Keokuk was arranging for the surrender of his fellow tribesmen, his American-hating rival, Black Hawk, was visiting the British at Drummond's Island. Keokuk, who was by now the confidant of both Clark and Forsyth, could dispense with British presents. Not only did Clark receive him hospitably at St. Louis but Forsyth remembered Keokuk's two wives with handsome gifts. The agent was certain that "if things are well managed in two or three years more his word among the Sauks and foxes will be their law."[11] As Keokuk rose in influence in the councils of his people, Black Hawk declined. In 1823, Forsyth did not consider Black Hawk, only a few years earlier the toast of the British, sufficiently important to be included in a list of the five leading Sacs and Foxes.

When the lead region occupied by the tribes began to attract whites up the Mississippi, the Americans profited by having such a worthy advocate as Keokuk among the Indians. Despite the reception accorded the creditors of the estate of Julien Dubuque in 1811, United States authorities, out of reach of scalping knives, granted mining leases to some Kentuckians. The recipients of the leases could locate their claims anywhere in Illinois or on land the Ottawas, Chippewas, and Potawato-

11 Forsyth to Clark, August 5, 1821, in Forsyth Papers.

mis ceded the government in 1816. However, the Sacs and Foxes claimed the land, and the Americans were forced to deal with them before they could sink the first pick in the ground.

The Secretary of War instructed Forsyth and Boilvin to negotiate with the tribes and prepare them for an influx of miners. The assignment was a difficult one. Forsyth admitted, "I cannot see how the major part of the Foxes, and some of the Sauk could exist without those mines."[12] Nevertheless, accompanied by the lessors, Forsyth took the annuities to the tribesmen in June, 1822, and announced to them in council at Fort Armstrong that the whites had come to mine lead on Fever River. The agent told the Indians, who themselves had been mining mostly in the Fever River area, that the generous whites had no objection to their working mines the whites did not occupy. However, to avoid friction it would be wise for the Indians to transfer their activities to the west side of the Mississippi. The indignant Fox chiefs denied in vain having sold any land above the mouth of Rock River. To the discomfiture of the Foxes, the Sac chiefs displayed a shocking lack of racial solidarity by declining to support the Fox cause. Forsyth closed the council and moved up to Fever River, where Boilvin and Colonel Willoughby Morgan of the United States Army joined him for another conference with the Foxes.

Once again the Indians denied the right of the United States to lease the land to anyone, but in the face of American insistence the Foxes offered to lease the land for four years. The whites refused this proposition and cautioned the Indians that resistance to the United States occupation "would only draw upon them the displeasure of their Great Father & perhaps his chastisement." At this thinly veiled warning the opposition evaporated. The agents differed regarding the sincerity of the Fox protest. Ever sanguine, Boilvin believed it was merely a maneuver to get presents, but Forsyth thought that only the

[12] Forsyth to the Secretary of War, August 18, 1822, in Draper MSS., 7T96–97.

size of the military escort kept the Indians from destroying boats and tools and generally interfering with the working of the mines.[13]

The postwar years had certainly not brought any marked improvement in Sac and Fox relations with the Americans. The tribesmen maintained their British contacts, and the frontiersmen remembered the death and destruction visiting the settlements in the past as a result of such associations. And the hostilities between the Sioux and the Sacs and Foxes increased the opportunities for trouble along the fringe of white settlement. Nor were the confederated tribes satisfied with the course of events. Throughout the six years they had manifested a great uneasiness in regard to the land they occupied and on several occasions had denied the validity of the Treaty of 1804. Only the increasing popularity and influence of Keokuk and the corresponding decline of Black Hawk's prestige was an encouraging sign to the American officials. The future held no great promise of peace and amity between the Sacs and Foxes and their white brothers.

13 Forsyth to the Secretary of War, June 24, 1822, in Draper MSS., 7T89–93; Boilvin to Secretary Calhoun, June 19, 1822, in Boilvin Letters.

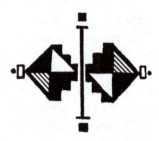

9. The Sac and Fox Position Worsens

IN THE YEARS FROM 1822 to 1828 the advance of white settlement further aggravated the relations between the Sacs and Foxes and the Americans. Although halted temporarily in 1825 by a great council of the Northwest Indians, trouble between the two tribes and the Sioux continued. As earlier, the Sacs and Foxes repeatedly manifested suspicion of American interest in Indian lands. Such sentiments led a delegation of the tribes to visit Washington in 1824.

In the summer of 1821 Sac and Fox civil chiefs had complained to agent Thomas Forsyth about the status of their land west of the Mississippi. They admitted selling in 1804 the land as high up the Mississippi as the mouth of the Two Rivers, erroneously described in the treaty as the River Jeffreon. But whites were beginning to settle above the mouth of the Two Rivers, on land which the Indians insisted they had not sold. In reply the agent described the 1821 Sac and Fox boundaries as the mouth of the Des Moines on the south and a line opposite Prairie du Chien on the north. Forsyth could not tell the tribes from whom the United States purchased the section between the Des Moines and the Two Rivers. Disgruntled, the chiefs left, only to return a few days later accompanied by a number of braves—Keokuk and Black Hawk among them. They now requested that Forsyth write the President a letter, which they dictated and signed.

"We wish to do what is right, yet it is hard for us to see our property taken away by the white people without complaining," the Indians told the President. They asked their Great White Father to "take away everything from before our eyes, so that we may see clear and know what we own."[1] Forsyth forwarded the letter to the Secretary of War, but Calhoun had no answer for the chiefs.

In September, 1823, the chiefs, still dissatisfied on the issue, asked permission to send a delegation to Washington in the spring. Secretary Calhoun reluctantly consented, if Clark and Forsyth could not otherwise satisfy the Sacs and Foxes. Clark, now occupying the recently created office of Superintendent of Indian Affairs at St. Louis, believed that if he could make them some presents and give an influential half-blood a section of land he could satisfy the tribesmen. Renewed hostilities between the Sacs and Foxes and the Sioux caused him to abandon the plan to dissuade the Rock River Indians from visiting the President.

In the winter of 1822–23, Nicholas Boilvin had tried to bring the tribes to an understanding but failed. The next June, when Forsyth returned to Rock Island, he found the Indians in a state of alarm, with scouting parties out to intercept a reported Sioux invasion. The attack did not materialize, and later in the summer a party of Sac and Fox buffalo hunters attacked a war party of Sioux and killed six. But seven Sac and Fox warriors were killed and eighteen were wounded.[2]

---

1 Sacs and Foxes to the President, September 14, 1821, in Draper MSS., 7T75–76.

2 Boilvin to Calhoun, November 3, 1822, and January 14, 1823, in Boilvin Letters; Forsyth to Calhoun, June 3, 1823, in Draper MSS., 4T165–66; Forsyth to Calhoun, August 15, 1823, in Draper MSS, 4T175–77.

In the hope that the presence of their Great White Father would cause the warring tribes to bury the hatchet, Clark decided to permit the Sioux agent, Lawerence Taliaferro, to escort a party of Sioux and Chippewa chiefs to Washington in June, 1824. The Indian Superintendent proposed to accompany the Sac and Fox chiefs himself. In May, when the home-loving Forsyth left St. Louis for Rock Island, he carried Clark's orders to select for the Washington trip not more than ten sober, influential, well-informed Sacs and Foxes. On arrival the agent found that two hundred of his charges were even then combing the plains for the Sioux. He sent runners to recall them, but they refused to return. Although many young men continued to slip away to join the war party, the chiefs accepted Clark's invitation to visit Washington and quickly selected ten of their number, including Keokuk but not Black Hawk. Because of their prominence, Clark permitted Tiamah, a Fox chief, to take his wife and daughter and Keokuk to take one of his wives.

Late in June the Sacs and Foxes and representatives from five other tribes left St. Louis. As the delegation awaited a boat to carry them to Louisville on the first leg of the long journey, the large war party of Sacs and Foxes which Forsyth had attempted to turn back captured four Sioux on the St. Peters River. Unable to decide which warriors should have the prisoners, the members of the war party calmly settled the argument by killing them.[3]

At Washington, the Sacs and Foxes displayed more interest in the land problem than in reaching agreement with the Sioux. Keokuk spoke ardently and well for the Sac and Fox title to the land in dispute, between the mouth of the Des Moines and the mouth of the Two Rivers. To Secretary Calhoun he disavowed any claim to land his tribe had sold to the United States, but he protested strongly against the Americans purchasing the disputed area from the Osages. The adroit

[3] Forsyth to Calhoun, July 8, 1824, in Draper MSS., 4T190–92.

94

Keokuk declared that the Sacs and Foxes claimed that land by the same right by which the United States claimed its land, by right of conquest. They had driven the Osages from the land, and therefore those Indians had no right to sell it.[4] In the face of this logic—some observers noted that the Indian employed a style of oratory similar to that of the august Secretary of War—the South Carolinian capitulated and drew up a treaty, which the tribesmen signed August 4.

In return for $1,000 in cash or merchandise, the addition of $500 to each of the tribes' annuities for ten years, the service of a blacksmith as long as the president deemed proper, a store of farming utensils and cattle, the services of instructors in agriculture for a period to be set by the president, and a few concessions to half-bloods of their tribes, the Sacs and Foxes gave up all claim to the area in dispute. In addition, Secretary Calhoun promised the Foxes, who voiced a fear that the Americans would take over the lead mines on the west bank of the Mississippi, that he would direct Forsyth to keep off any intruders.[5]

To impress the chiefs with the wealth and population of the United States, Clark escorted them on a tour of some of the eastern cities. Traveling by coach to Baltimore, where they resided, appropriately, at the Indian Queen Hostel, the party proceeded to Philadelphia by steamboat and then on to New York. At the latter city they visited Scudder's Museum, Castle Gardens, and a circus. The other spectators at the circus were disappointed to see that the wild Indians had discarded their colorful native dress and wore the uniform of army officers, complete with caps and swords. The war whoops with which the braves and chiefs first voiced their approval of the performers, particularly the clown and the equestrians, delighted the crowd.

Pleased with the courteous treatment accorded them and

4 Keokuk to the Secretary of War, July, 1824, Stock Transcripts.
5 Secretary Calhoun to Pee-Mash-Kee, August 7, 1824, Photostat WHS.

convinced of the strength of their Great White Father—it is significant that Black Hawk did not take this trip—the chiefs made the long journey back to their homes on the Mississippi and its tributaries. However, as a pacifier the expedition was a failure.

Of the delegation which Taliaferro led from St. Louis to join the other Indians in burying the hatchet in the presence of the president, one Sioux chief, Little Crow, did not reach Washington. Overcome with nostalgia he made the tragic error of leaving the party before it reached Pittsburgh. While the other Sioux continued up the Ohio in the steamboat, he struck across country for home. Reaching the Mississippi, Little Crow encountered a family of Foxes. Having lost relatives at the hands of the Sioux, the Fox woman persuaded her husband to bury his hatchet in Little Crow's head.[6]

Nor was this the only incident heightening tension on the frontier. Even while the chiefs negotiated in Washington, the prairies resounded to war whoops. Under cover of darkness one night in August, forty-five Sac warriors surrounded a Sioux camp of one hundred lodges and before daylight launched a whirlwind attack upon the unsuspecting occupants. Before the bewildered Sioux could arouse themselves, the attackers, with fifteen scalps and one prisoner, were in full retreat. Rallying rapidly, the Sioux sent in pursuit a large party which killed eight Sacs and freed the prisoner.[7] It would take much smoking to remedy the damage done by clashes like these.

While in Washington, the chiefs and braves had requested that the government hold a grand peace council of the Northwest Indians. Congress approved one for the purpose of establishing boundaries and promoting peace among the tribes. To share Clark's task of reconciling the Indians, James Barbour, Calhoun's successor as secretary of war, chose Governor Lewis Cass of Michigan Territory. For three years, Cass had been

[6] Forsyth to Calhoun, August 24, 1824, in Draper MSS., 4T192–95.
[7] Forsyth to Calhoun, September 9, 1824, in Draper MSS., 4T204–207.

compiling a report for the War Department on the Indians of the Northwest, having requested the appointment in order to further his knowledge of the tribes to meet at Prairie du Chien.

By August 3, 1825, all the Indians except the Sacs and Foxes and their allies, the Iowas, had arrived at the rendezvous. For miles above and below the little settlement, Indian lodges lined the banks of the Mississippi, even extending into Prairie du Chien itself. The Sioux chiefs, with the skins of skunks attached to their heads as symbols that they never ran, the tall and warlike Chippewas, the Winnebagos, fierce neighbors of the Sacs, the Ottawas, the Menominees, and the Potawatomis beheld the dramatic approach of more than one hundred of Forsyth's charges August 4. Chanting their war songs, the Sacs, Foxes, and Iowas stood erect in their canoes and passed and repassed the council ground. Beaching their canoes, they drew up as if for battle and, armed with spears, clubs, guns, and knives, glared defiantly at the Sioux.

The Sac, Fox, and Iowa warriors were a formidable, frightening array. They had shaved and painted their heads, except for the scalp lock, which was tied with red horsehair like the crest on a Roman helmet. Other tufts of red horsehair dangled from their elbows, and necklaces of bear's claws encircled the throats of the warriors, who were nude except for breechclouts, moccasins, and leggings. Bearing flags of feathers, beating drums, and whooping murderous cries, they paraded menacingly toward the council area. Henry R. Schoolcraft, the scholarly agent from Sault Ste Marie, had never seen so fully depicted, "The wild, native pride of man, in the savage state, flushed by success in war, and confident in the strength of his arm." Their conduct in council in the succeeding days bore out Schoolcraft's first impression of them. "Their martial bearing, their high tone, and whole behavior . . . was impressive and demonstrated, in an eminent degree, to what a high pitch of physical and moral courage, bravery and success in war may lead a savage people."[8]

The day after the Sacs and Foxes made their entrance, Clark opened the council in a pavilion of green boughs near the fort. In his initial address he tactfully claimed that peace was the only American objective. He suggested to the Indians that fixed boundaries between their hunting grounds were the most feasible means of ensuring peace and, after passing a pipe among the chiefs and braves, adjourned for the day.

Twelve more days of parley, oratory, and smoking of the peace pipe were necessary before the Indians came to an agreement. As the commissioners had expected, the boundaries between the Sioux and their rivals to the north, the Chippewas, and those between the Sioux and the Sacs and Foxes were the most difficult to fix. Black Hawk's rival, Keokuk, spoke often and well for his people, shaking his lance at the Sioux as if "he wanted but an opportunity to make their blood flow like water."

The Sacs and Foxes and the Sioux finally concurred on terms August 17. Two days later the relieved commissioners reassembled the tribesmen, read the treaties, and all present signed them—in triplicate. Clark then circulated a great belt of wampum depicting the "Great village" and a number of smaller villages representing the tribes party to the treaty. On the following day the commissioners distributed copies of the peace treaty. Articles I and XIII contained the heart of the treaty. The first provided that "There shall be a firm and perpetual peace between the Sioux and the Chippewas; between the Sioux and the confederated tribes of Sauk and Foxes; and between the Ioways and the Sioux." Article XIII stated: "It is understood by all of the tribes, parties hereto, that no tribe shall hunt within the acknowledged limits of any other, with-

[8] Henry R. Schoolcraft, *Personal Memoirs of a Residence of Thirty Years with the Indian Tribes on the American Frontier,* 216–17; *The Michigan Herald* (Detroit), September 20, 1825.

out their assent." The influence of Cass, ever suspicious of British tampering with the Indians, was apparent in Article X, which read: "All the tribes aforesaid acknowledge the general controlling power of the United States and disclaim all dependence upon, and connection with, any other power."

After the chiefs and braves received their copies of the treaty, all joined in smoking the peace pipe. Many of the Indians delivered short speeches indicating satisfaction with the proceedings and expressing good will toward all. Clark then adjourned the council, and the redskins sat down to a feast provided by the commissioners. As Clark and Cass, the latter a strong temperance man, did not furnish them any straight whiskey, the disappointed Indians grumbled about the penny-pinching commissioners. To disprove the charges of stinginess the Americans lined up a number of tin camp kettles, filled them with whiskey, and, after some pertinent remarks, emptied them on the ground. The demonstration astounded the Indians. "They loved the whiskey better than the joke," noted Schoolcraft. This concluded the council, and the bands began to drift away from Prairie du Chien. Clark and Cass, versed in Indian ways, did not exude optimism. They were too well aware of the role of war in Indian society and the difficulty of restraining ardent young warriors.

Two years after the Treaty of Prairie du Chien, Black Hawk demonstrated that the young warriors were not the only unstable element in the tribes. The summer of 1826 had passed uneventfully, and the Rock River Indians had even sent a delegation with a peace pipe in a futile search for Sioux bands. In May, 1827, Forsyth was surprised to learn from his friend Keokuk that the sexagenarian Black Hawk was organizing a war party to lead against the Sioux. The old warrior, who had not been present at Prairie du Chien in 1825, refused a bribe of three horses and other property to drop the scheme. The agent asked Keokuk to warn Black Hawk that if he went to war Forsyth would put him and his war party in irons and send them down to St. Louis to spend the remainder of their days in prison. And if the tribe refused to surrender the culprits, the agent threatened to call upon Clark and his two thousand troops for assistance.

For more than two weeks the issue of war and peace hung in the balance.[9] Black Hawk stubbornly turned down a new offer of seven horses and scorned Forsyth's warning with the declaration that only death would stop him. Morgan, a half-blood Fox at Dubuque's mines and likewise a non-signer of the 1825 treaty, also prepared to lead a war party. Despairing of preventing their departure, Forsyth warned the Sioux. Just as the renewal of tribal hostilities appeared inevitable, Black Hawk and Morgan inexplicably abandoned their plans. Such were the trials and tribulations of an Indian agent.

Although for the moment the Rock River Indians maintained an uneasy peace with the Sioux, they took lightly the obligation, explicit in the Treaty of Prairie du Chien, to sever their connections with the British. Cass had good grounds for including the article. During the two years preceding the treaty bands of Sacs and Foxes had journeyed to Canada. In 1823 the agent at Malden told the Indians that Britain and the United States were at peace and that the red men should refrain from depredations. Less appreciated by the Americans was the assurance of the Englishman that the Sacs and Foxes were entirely justified in assaulting the Sioux. He added, patronizingly, that the Indians shouldn't blame the American agents for not being generous with them, as the king, not the president, was the real father of the Sacs and Foxes.[10]

In the autumn of 1824 the British indirectly invited the tribesmen to repeat their visit in the summer of 1825. They showed a Potawatomi, whom they knew would pass the word

[9] Forsyth to Clark, May 24, 1827, in Draper MSS., 4T265; Forsyth to Clark, May 24, 1827, in Draper MSS., 4T269–70; Forsyth to Lawerence Taliaferro, May 28, 1826, in Draper MSS., 8T54; Forsyth to Clark, June 15, 1827, in Draper MSS., 4T271–72.

[10] Forsyth to Calhoun, September 23, 1823, in Draper MSS., 4T177–78.

on to the Rock River Indians, a quantity of trade goods reserved for them. The anticipated generosity of the British meant more to the Sacs and Foxes than Article X of the treaty which their representatives had signed at Prairie du Chien, and each summer bands of the Rock River Indians visited British posts. *Niles Weekly Register* reported that in 1826 not less than five thousand Indians from the United States visited Malden, "England's scalp-market" in the late war. The Sacs and Foxes who made the trip were disappointed at the presents they received and at the British agent's statement that the king was at peace with all the world and particularly the United States.[11]

In the spring of 1827 the Indians had other worries besides the abortive expeditions Black Hawk and Morgan were planning against the Sioux. That spring a rumor was abroad in the Northwest that the United States and England were about to go to war. Should such a war eventuate, Lawerence Taliaferro, the able Sioux agent at St. Peters, predicted that the Sacs and Foxes and the other tribes on the frontier would side with the British.[12] The Winnebagos demonstrated their hostility to the Americans in a series of incidents which the settlers dignified by calling the Winnebago War of 1827.

Although the Winnebagos sought aid from the Foxes in case of a war with the whites, neither the Foxes nor the Sacs came to their assistance. Instead, those tribes aided General Henry Atkinson, the tall, slender North Carolinian commanding the American troops. The General had wisely followed Clark's advice to approach the Sacs and Foxes through Keokuk. As a mark of his appreciation of the war chief's services the White Beaver, as the Indians called Atkinson, gave Keokuk a saddle and bridle.[13]

11 Forsyth to Clark, August 25, 1826, in Draper MSS., 8T49; Forsyth to Clark, June 27, 1826, in Draper MSS., 8T42–43.

12 Forsyth to Clark, May 24, 1827, in Draper MSS., 4T265; Taliaferro to Clark, October 7, 1827, Photostat WHS.

13 Clark to Forsyth, July 14, 1827, in Draper MSS., 2T32; Atkinson to Clark, July 24, 1827, Stock Transcripts.

The White Beaver did not employ the confederated tribes against the Winnebagos, but Forsyth did use Sacs as spies to report on the movements of the hostile tribe. They were particularly suited for this duty, as many of them had relatives living a few miles up Rock River at the village of the Winnebago Prophet. This unsavory character presided over a band of half-blood Sacs and Winnebagos and renegades from both tribes. Following the surrender of the Winnebagos he visited Rock Island and assured the agent that Atkinson had taught the hostiles a lesson they would never forget. The Prophet blamed the Indians from Prairie La Crosse for the mischief and declared that they should all have been killed. His attitude and that of the Sacs demonstrated the lack of unity among the Indians. Certainly the Rock River tribesmen were in a position to have sympathized with the Winnebagos, as the influx of whites into the area imperiled them as much as the Winnebagos.

The proximity of the settlements had intensified the friction between whites and Indians. Unscrupulous settlers took advantage of the Indians' weakness for liquor and plied them with it, collecting in return many times its value in horses, blankets, or peltries due the warriors' trader for credit advanced. The agents tried to break up the liquor traffic, but to no avail. Forsyth even encouraged the Indians to retake forcibly property the whites purchased for liquor. Often the alcohol-enflamed Indians committed acts which injured innocent white men. Nor were the whites entirely guiltless of violence. Forsyth reported a number of Missourians for badly beating two warriors with the Indians' own ramrods and swords.

Each year, as the settlements crept closer to Rock River, the game upon which the Sacs and Foxes subsisted diminished. By 1824, Black Hawk and his fellow hunters had to go two hundred to three hundred miles from their homes to reach good hunting. This necessitated more horses, and horses had to be purchased with peltries needed to buy traps, ammunition, knives, and kettles. The annuities the United States paid the tribes were never sufficiently large to be of much assistance. The Sacs rarely saw any of their $1,100, nor did the Foxes usually handle any of their $900. Traders' bills and settlers' claims for property damage took most of the annuities. As late as 1826 the Indians were still paying claims on property destroyed by them in 1815.

The firm of Farnham and Davenport always obtained its share of tribal annuities. In 1827, for example, the traders received $1,491 of the $2,000 paid the Indians. This is not to infer that George Davenport and Russell Farnham were selfish, grasping individuals; the tribesmen placed great faith in their traders. Now affiliated with the American Fur Company, they enjoyed a good reputation on the upper Mississippi. Even Forsyth grudgingly admitted that they were "a moral and good people . . . not wanting in good advice (occasionally!) to the Indians." As he seldom wintered at Rock Island, Forsyth depended to a considerable extent on the traders to exert a proper influence on the Indians. The agent never gave up his residence in St. Louis, although Governor Edwards' protests on this score had led to his transfer to Rock Island and Clark repeatedly rebuked him for his extended absences from his post.

Thomas Forsyth was a competent official and performed his duties efficiently—when he was at Rock Island. But as the relations between the Sacs and Foxes and their Indian and white neighbors constantly brought on disputes, the long suffering Clark was entirely correct in attempting to keep him at his post. Indeed, the Secretary of War had found it necessary to employ a subagent and interpreter for the Foxes at Fever River. Fear of the loss of their villages and cornfields made the Indians nervous and complicated dealings with them. The apprehension was manifested in many ways in the years from 1822 to 1827.

In 1822 they were extremely reluctant to sign a paper agreeing to the removal of the government factory from Rock Island, for fear that they would also be signing away land. In 1824 they had insisted upon visiting the President to discuss their lands west of the Mississippi. Government regulation required that the Indians sign receipts for their annuities, but the tribes usually balked at this, and Forsyth would instead have to take certificates from witnesses. On one occasion the Indians explained their refusal to sign for annuities by saying that "not a man, woman or child of their nation would ever sign any paper as they had little enough land for their own use."[14] In 1826 any remaining Sac and Fox faith in the good intentions of the Americans was shaken when they learned that the United States had bought land claimed by them from the Kansas Indians. Forsyth had never seen Indians "so thunder struck about any thing" as the chiefs and braves were when he mentioned the transaction to them.[15]

Greater shocks were in store for the Sacs and Foxes. In the midst of the disturbances the Winnebagos created in 1827, Governor Ninian Edwards of Illinois appealed to the Secretary of war for the removal of all Indians from ceded land in Illinois. Edwards, Illinois' first senator following his nine years as territorial governor, occupied the state governorship from 1826 to 1830. No friend of the redskins and anxious to clear them from Illinois' land, Edwards objected not only to Indians occupying ceded territory but also to their hunting and traversing any part of it. Such conduct "has been borne by the people for a few years past with great impatience, and cannot be submitted to much longer," warned the old Indian fighter.[16]

Forced to match scalping knives with the Sioux as the ad-

---

[14] Forsyth to the Secretary of War, July 7, 1823, in Draper MSS., 7T113–14.

[15] Forsyth to Clark, June 27, 1826, in Draper MSS., 8T42–43.

[16] Edwards to the Secretary of War, September 4, 1827, in Ninian W. Edwards, *History of Illinois from 1778 to 1883 and Life and Times of Ninian Edwards,* 351–53.

vancing line of settlement drove them from their own hunting grounds, the Sacs and Foxes were about to be confronted with the spectre of the Treaty of 1804. Black Hawk's days in the Rock River Valley were numbered.

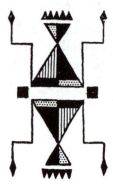

10. The Indians Leave Saukenuk

L IKE A SPOT of raccoon grease on a blanket, to use the frontier simile, the Long Knives were spreading in all directions. Among the Americans flocking to the lead mine region in 1827 was one Colonel Henry Dodge. Nearly six-feet tall, courageous and aggressive, Dodge was a natural leader of men. People remembered that when a grand jury indicted him as a henchman of Aaron Burr, the pugnacious Dodge thrashed several of the jurors and the remainder reconsidered their verdict. A few months before the Winnebagos went on the warpath in 1827, Dodge arrived in the mining district, and the miners promptly chose him to lead their volunteer contingent under Atkinson.

Although the Sacs and Foxes were not directly concerned in this affair, Dodge typified the quality of the opposition the Indians were encountering. The whites moving into the area were a rough, belligerent lot, not greatly concerned with Indian rights or with statutory law. On one occasion when Joseph Street threatened to use troops to evict Dodge from Indian land, he answered with the ringing challenge, "Let them march, Sir, with my Miners, I can whip all the old Sore Shined Regulars that are stationed at Prairie du Chien."

The Indians Leave Saukenuk

In Governor Edwards of Illinois the miners had a sympathetic observer. In the spring of 1828 the Governor was dissatisfied with the results of his complaints of the previous fall. A dispute between Potawatomis and settlers goaded Edwards into notifying Clark that Illinois was tired of applying to Washington for relief from the Indian problem. Unless the government acted promptly, he wrote, "Those Indians will be removed, and that very promptly."[1] The harassed Superintendent replied that he and his agents had tried for several years to induce the Indians to move from the ceded lands. To insure results the Governor carried his complaint of this "annoyance [to] which no free and independent State of this Union is bound to submit," to Clark's superior, the Secretary of War.[2] Secretary Peter B. Porter, James Barbour's successor, also advocated removing Indians beyond the Mississippi to lands unsuitable for white settlement. He promised that, except for some Kickapoos, Indians in Illinois would remove beyond the Mississippi by May 25, 1829.[3]

At a meeting with Forsyth late in May, 1828, the Sac and Fox chiefs stoutly protested against the agent's injunction to move the next spring. The Indians vehemently denied having sold any land north of the mouth of the Rock. Proclaiming that they would not move from the land in which lay the bones of their ancestors, the chiefs vowed that they would defend themselves against any power sent to remove them. Despite this uncompromising—even insolent—stand, a few weeks later Forsyth assured Clark that although the Indians could not remove in 1828, as they had already planted their corn around

1 Edwards to Clark, May 25, 1828, Photostat WHS.

2 Edwards to Clark, May 29, 1828, in E. B. Washburne (ed.), *The Edwards Papers,* 339–40.

3 Edwards to the Secretary of War, June 17, 1828, in *ibid.,* 343; Secretary of War Porter to Edwards, July 7, 1828, photostat in possession of Illinois State Historical Society; Secretary of War to Edwards, July 22, 1828, in Evarts Boutell Green and Clarence Walworth Alvord (eds.), *The Governors' Letter Books,* 139.

Saukenuk, they were planning to move the next spring to new villages west of the Mississippi.[4]

In the summer of 1828 the confederated tribes had other worries besides removal. The winter hunt had not been a success, and the warriors fared little better in the summer. Even the British failed them; a party of one hundred Sacs and Foxes received few goods and scant courtesy on a visit to Malden. However, a Canadian veteran of the late war told them that British troops would aid them in holding their land and villages.[5]

To protest the Treaty of 1804, Morgan led a party of Foxes to St. Louis early in the summer of 1828. In an interview with Clark the Indians pleaded ignorance of the reason for the Fox annuities. The Superintendent explained their treaties to them and then demonstrated his skill with the red men by extracting a promise from Morgan that in the near future the tribe would sell Dubuque's mines.[6] When Morgan returned to his village and informed the other chiefs of his action, they, as he might have expected, would not even consider the idea of a sale. The headstrong Morgan indignantly responded that he was the one who had fought to keep those lands in the past but now the other chiefs would have to fight. With that he led a war party from the village and deliberately invited war by killing one Sioux woman and taking prisoner another woman and a child. Fellow tribesmen of Morgan's victims pursued the Foxes to the Mississippi. The outraged warriors lost the trail of the Foxes but happened on a Sac encampment and killed a chief and his wife and stole a number of horses. Al-

---

[4] Forsyth to Clark, May 24, 1828, in Draper MSS., 6T81; Forsyth to Clark, June 2, 1828, in Draper MSS., 6T83; Forsyth to Clark, July 6, 1828, in Draper MSS., 8T83.

[5] C. D. St. Vrain to P. Chouteau, Jr., April 30, 1828, and George Davenport to Russell Farnham, August 19, 1828, both in P. Chouteau-Maffitt Collection, Missouri Historical Society; Forsyth to Clark, June 22, 1828, in Draper MSS., 8T78; Forsyth to Clark, June 10, 1828, in Draper MSS., 6T84–86.

[6] Forsyth to Clark, June 20, 1828, extract in Clark Papers, Kansas Historical Society.

though General Joseph Street, an officer in the Illinois militia who had replaced the deceased Boilvin as agent at Prairie du Chien, obtained the release of the Sioux prisoners, the uneasy truce was over.

While out on the hunting grounds the Sacs were planning war parties against the Sioux, whites were moving into the lodges of Saukenuk. When the Indians had left for their winter hunt, the rumor had circulated widely that they would not return. During the winter and spring of 1828–29 about twenty families squatted on tribal lands in the vicinity of Rock Island.

In his winter lodge, Black Hawk heard of the invasion and walked all the way back to investigate. Although the old brave found a squatter occupying his lodge, he contented himself with a verbal rebuke and returned to his winter camp. But when the Sacs rendezvoused to go to their new village on the Iowa River, Black Hawk defied his tribal chieftains and led a number of followers back to Saukenuk. The old warrior did not fear the Long Knives. Had he not twice seen them flee before his young men? Black Hawk scoffed at the reports of those who had visited Washington, New York, and Philadelphia. Even if the Long Knives were as numerous as the leaves of the forest, if they attempted to keep him from the land of his fathers their scalps would festoon his lodge poles. In the hope of preventing trouble, the chiefs deputized Keokuk to accompany the old firebrand.

On return to Saukenuk the Indians found some of their lodges destroyed, others damaged, and squatters' fences enclosing their best cornfields. Although violence was avoided for the moment, the situation was potentially dangerous. Each day that the Sacs and the whites remained shoulder to shoulder increased the possibilities of trouble. The fences the Indians erected around their cornfields would not turn the settlers' stock, and when Keokuk called on the whites and requested that they put up their cattle at night, one foolish settler refused to co-operate. The Indians retaliated by turning the man's cattle into his own cornfield.

Twice Sac deputations called on Forsyth to complain about the presence of the squatters. At the first visit, Quashquame, a signer of the Treaty of 1804, denied, as he had the previous May, having sold any land above Rock River. Black Hawk also denied the sale and declared that the whites habitually said one thing to the Indians and put another on paper. Reminded that at the treaty negotiations in 1816 the American commissioners refused to smoke with him until he reaffirmed the agreement of 1804, the old Sac retorted that the subject of land had not been mentioned to him in 1816. If it was in the treaty, Black Hawk accused the commissioners of including it secretly. Forsyth blocked any further discussion and even refused his friend Keokuk's private request to remain with a few friends to raise some corn they had planted.

A few days later another Sac deputation visited their agent. This time Keokuk was not present to restrain his fellows and the braves spoke "very fiercely" of defending their village in the late war and continuing to do so as long as they lived. Defiantly they asserted that they had formed an alliance with the Chippewas, Ottowas, Potawatomis, Kickapoos, and Menominees, and that those tribes were prepared to assist them at any time.[7]

Forsyth saw nothing but trouble for the ensuing summer, especially if the Indians obtained whiskey. Keokuk, whom the chiefs had hoped would be a moderating influence, was dejected. The Sacs at the village preferred Black Hawk's counsel, and the whites aggravated the situation by assaults on the Indians. One of the principal braves protested against the plowing up of his cornfield, and the offending white man beat the Indian with a bean pole for objecting.

The settlers likewise protested to Forsyth, to the commandant of Fort Armstrong, and to Governor Edwards. They repre-

[7] Forsyth to Clark, May 17, May 22, 1829, in Draper MSS., 6T97–101.

sented themselves as peaceful settlers who had come to Rock River expecting that the Indians, who had been ordered to remove, would not return. However, the red men had returned and were throwing down their fences, stealing their horses, and threatening to kill them if they did not leave Saukenuk. The commandant told the whites that he lacked the authority to remove the Indians, and Forsyth responded to their appeals by saying that he could only request the Sacs to depart. Only the Governor remained, but the settlers were confident that Edwards would aid them.

Clark correctly blamed the white squatters for the strained situation. Had they not intruded at Rock River, the Sacs would probably have removed peacefully within a few months. The Superintendent said he had no power to keep the settlers off ceded land and little influence with the Sacs involved, as they had always looked to Canada for advice.

After the Sacs departed for their summer hunt in 1829, the tension eased, although the few Indians remaining at the village quarreled almost daily with the squatters. One white man threatened to shoot a young Sac who objected to the settler striking his mother. Forsyth sympathized with his charges. "It appears hard to me," he wrote Clark, "that the Indian property should be stolen, their huts torn and burned down, and their persons insulted by Strangers . . . who are now quarreling and fighting with each other about the corn fields." The agent hoped that "our Government will render some justice to those Indians, and not encourage those intruders."[8]

The government's answer was to demand that the Sacs remove and to place their land around Saukenuk on sale. The Secretary of War had decided that the Sacs would have to cross the Mississippi.[9] Early in July the General Land Office advertised that the land around Saukenuk would go on sale at

---

[8] Clark to Forsyth, June 4, 1829; Forsyth to Clark, June 17, 1829; both in Draper MSS., 6T104-105.
[9] T. L. McKenney to Clark, June 17, 1829, Photostat WHS.

Springfield, Illinois, on the third Monday in October, 1829. For better or worse, the decision had been made. Article VII of the Treaty of 1804, which had provided that the confederated tribes might use the land until the government sold it to actual settlers, no longer protected the Indians.

The summer of 1829 had been a discouraging one for Black Hawk. A visit to Canada had been fruitless, and he appealed in vain to former Governor Edward Cole and Judge James Hall when they stopped at Rock Island. From Forsyth he learned that the land occupied by Saukenuk and the Indian cornfields would be sold and that the Sacs must remove beyond the Mississippi. The whites were selling whiskey to the Indians, and his arch rival, Keokuk, "A coward, and no brave," was at Prairie du Chien negotiating with the white men.

In the spring of 1828, President John Quincy Adams had authorized negotiations with the Indian tribes claiming mineral lands between the Illinois River and the mines on Fever River. The commissioners were unable to assemble the representatives of the tribes in time to hold a general treaty in 1828, and it was postponed to the summer of 1829. Clark suggested that the time might be favorable to extinguish the Sac and Fox claim to mineral lands west of the Mississippi. One factor the Superintendent offered for consideration was "their belief that they have been defrauded of an immensely valuable country by the Treaty of 1804 held with a few of their tribe . . . and their apprehension . . . produces unfriendly feelings, particularly among those who are under British influence."[10] Thomas L. McKenney, head of the Indian Bureau of the War Department, declined to include the Sacs and Foxes in the coming treaty, because to include them in a discussion of Indian claims to land east of the Mississippi might imply that they had such claims.

Nevertheless, Keokuk, Quashquame, and Tiamah led a dele-

[10] Clark to McKenney, August 2, 1828, Photostat WHS; Clark to the Secretary of War, May 20, 1829, Photostat WHS.

gation to Prairie du Chien. Here, late in July, 1829, the commissioners, General John McNeil of the army, Colonel Pierre Menard, a fur trader turned politician, and Caleb Atwater, the intellectual pioneer, opened the negotiations. The bargaining for the valuable mineral tract drew a large group of spectators and speculators from Paris, London, and Liverpool as well as from every large city in the Union. After concluding treaties with the other tribes present, the commissioners negotiated with the Sacs and Foxes.[11]

As in 1825, the Sacs and Foxes made a dramatic entrance. This time Keokuk brought with him two deserters from the garrison of Fort Crawford, whom he had captured as they attempted to escape down the river. The confederated tribes performed several other services at the direction of the commissioners, among them a war dance which Keokuk led to intimidate the fractious Winnebagos. Keokuk's language in council certainly did not indicate the subservience to the whites that his other conduct implied. When queried on the Sac and Fox mineral lands west of the Mississippi, Keokuk spoke for the tribes in a manner which left little doubt of the Indian reluctance to become involved in any more land deals with the United States. The Sac brave declared that General Harrison had cheated the Sacs and Foxes in 1804 and that Quashquame had deceived them also, but that he, Keokuk, did not propose to be cheated. The other Indians joined their plain-spoken war chief in refusing to sell their mineral sites and railed against trespassers on their lands. To explain their problems to the President, they asked to go to Washington. Unable to agree to this, the embarrassed commissioners attempted to placate the tribesmen with $850 worth of presents.

One of the issues the commissioners and the Sacs and Foxes

11 Caleb Atwater to the Secretary of War, October 28, 1829, Stock Transcripts; Atwater, *The Writings of Caleb Atwater*, 243; Journal of Prairie du Chien Treaty of 1829, Stock Transcripts; Forsyth to Clark, August 8, 1829, in Draper MSS., 6T108–109; McNeill, Menard, and Atwater to the Secretary of War, September 11, 1829, Photostat WHS.

touched upon was the renewal of hostilities with the Sioux. Keokuk correctly attributed it to Morgan, also present at the council. In the summer of 1828, following the attack on the Sac encampment by the Sioux in pursuit of Morgan, the Rock River Indians had conferred and decided to leave their women and children in camp and make a muskrat hunt. They proposed to fight only if attacked. To insure that they would not succumb to the first opportunity to lift a few Sioux scalps, a trader in the employ of Farnham and Davenport accompanied them. But twenty vengeful warriors eluded the vigilance of the trader and attacked a Sioux camp, capturing a woman. Then the warriors rejoined the main band, which retreated to the Mississippi "without making one Skin," to the extreme annoyance of the trader.[12]

During the winter of 1828–29, Farnham and Davenport were quite concerned at the trade prospects. The Sacs and Foxes had brought them relatively few pelts the preceding year, and since Morgan's attack the hunters feared a Sioux ambush and refused to venture far from the Mississippi. And, so long as the hunters remained in close proximity to the river, unscrupulous settlers with whiskey to barter made serious inroads on Farnham and Davenport's trade. The partners at Rock Island saw little prospect of any spring hunt if the Sacs and Foxes remained at odds with the Sioux.

Russell Farnham and George Davenport were not the only traders losing money because of the hunters' belligerency. The Sioux on the Mississippi dealt less with Joseph Rolette, a veteran of the king's forces and trader at Prairie du Chien for the American Fur Company. In June, 1829, the voluble General Street managed to arrange a truce between the Foxes and the Sioux, and Rolette advised the American Fur Company at St. Louis to "prevail" on Clark to capitalize on Street's ten-

---

12 George Davenport to P. Chouteau, December 23, 1828; Farnham and Davenport to P. Chouteau, February 16, 1829; both in P. Chouteau-Maffitt Collection.

tative agreement. As the Sioux were preparing for their winter hunt and hostilities continued to imperil the Indian trade, the agent visited Robert Stuart, the harsh Scot presiding over the American Fur Company fortunes on the upper lakes.

On hearing Rolette's tale of woe, Stuart wrote McKenney of the Indian Bureau that unless the government took immediate steps to reconcile those tribes the war would become general and "cost the United States, at least, the trouble & expenditures of a Treaty, and a great loss in the Fur Trade, beside the effusion of human blood &c." McKenney was able to reassure John Jacob Astor himself, when the founder of the American Fur Company wrote the War Department that Clark was prepared to act. Astor's son, William B., directed his company's manager in St. Louis to give Clark "no peace night or day."

In August, 1829, when Forsyth delivered the Sac and Fox annuities totaling $2,000, the Indians turned over $1,900 to Farnham and Davenport to apply on their debt. The Indian agent retained the remaining $100 to satisfy settlers' claims for depredations. While the chiefs were receiving and disbursing the tribal annuities, a Sac and Fox war party high up the Missouri swam the river to wipe out a band of sixteen Sioux on the opposite bank. Although, with the exception of Morgan, the responsible chiefs of all three tribes desired peace, their inability to control their warriors made a peaceful settlement extremely difficult. And the fundamental trouble remained; the more extensive the settlers' encroachments upon the Sac and Fox hunting grounds, the more necessary it became for those tribes to invade the Sioux territory. Refusing to recognize the roots of the conflict, Clark hoped by distributing four thousand or five thousand presents to prevent further trouble.

While the whites debated the course of action to pursue with the warring tribes, scalping parties continued to leave the Indian villages. Forsyth feared that they would not attempt to take prisoners, since the Indians had learned to their irritation that the Americans demanded the return of any that they took. As the winter of 1829–30 approached, traders prophesied a general Indian war. The Foxes had ceased to discriminate closely in their scalping and had included a Winnebago and a Menominee among their victims. Davenport and Robert Stuart expected the tribes of the slain to join with the Sioux in a concerted attack on the Sacs and Foxes.

In the hope of averting the threatened calamity, Clark received a delegation of the confederated tribes in St. Louis in March, 1830. Meeting in his St. Louis council room and museum, a large chamber decorated with weapons, canoes, gaily colored blankets, and other souvenirs of his travels, the Indians presented their grievances. Speaking for his people, as usual, Keokuk complained that the line the Treaty of Prairie du Chien established in 1825 was not keeping the Sioux out and that the Sacs claimed land the United States had bought from the Kansas nation. Clark commented that he understood that they were also dissatisfied with the Treaty of 1804, contracted by chiefs who "imposed themselves on the Commissioners as the principal chiefs of the nations, and were stated as such by the Traders." However, he reminded them that after having the treaty explained to them at Portage des Sioux in 1815 and again in 1816, they had confirmed it. In reference to the rift within the tribes, the Superintendent said that he had appreciated the fact that the tribes wished to reunite with "the British party" (Black Hawk's band). To prepare the way for the Sac and Fox removal from Rock River and the sale of their mineral lands on the west side of the Mississippi, Clark attributed their difficulties to the river, pointing out that it offered an avenue by which intruders might separate those tribesmen at Saukenuk from those west of the Mississippi.[13] The Indians did not accept this theory, however, and reiterated an earlier request

[13] Clark to the Secretary of War, April 6, 1830; "Minutes of a Council Held by William Clark with the Sacs and Foxes," March 26, 1830; both Photostat WHS.

that Clark permit them to visit the President. The Secretary of War did not approve, as he had previously decided to summon the warring tribes to Prairie du Chien for a peace council in July. The stupidity of Captain Wynkoop Warner, the newly appointed subagent to the Foxes at Dubuque's mines, endangered the whole project.

When a Fox delegation, because of overindulgence, failed to present themselves for a scheduled council at Prairie du Chien, Warner neglected to inform them that the meeting had been cancelled. Recovering from their drinking bout the principal Fox chiefs and braves, with the exception of Morgan, left the village at the mines for Prairie du Chien. En route, the unarmed party of sixteen men and one woman was surprised by a war party of more than one hundred Sioux and Menominees. All the Foxes but one were slaughtered. He was allowed to escape because he was half Winnebago.

Not content with the scalps they had taken, the Sioux hovered around the Fox village and kept its inhabitants in a state of panic. Afraid that the Sioux intended to attack them in their lodges, the Foxes appealed to the Indians at the mouth of Rock River to send reinforcements and canoes to evacuate them. The Indians of Saukenuk rushed two hundred warriors to aid their allies and shifted the Foxes to a point on the west side of the Mississippi, opposite Fort Armstrong. Although the tribesmen were clamoring for war, Forsyth managed to restrain them and gladly granted their wish to visit Clark at St. Louis.[14]

Late in May, for the second time in three months, the Superintendent received a party of Sacs and Foxes. They demanded that the Americans, whom they blamed for the massacre, "cover the Dead" by liberal gifts. Confident of their ability to beat their enemies, the confederated tribes practically refused to go to Prairie du Chien for the peace conference. They intimated that they now might consider selling their mineral lands west of the Mississippi.

[14] Street to Clark, May 27, 1830, Photostat WHS; Forsyth to Clark, May 6, May 17, 1830, in Draper MSS., 6T125–31.

On their return to Saukenuk, Forsyth held a feast. He reasoned that on a full stomach the Sacs and Foxes might consent to go to Prairie du Chien, but the well-fed Indians said that this would be walking over their dead relatives to shake hands with their enemies. The tribesmen declared that if their enemies wanted to council, they could come to Rock Island. Once again they asked to visit Clark, and once again Forsyth agreed.

In St. Louis for their third interview in succession with the Superintendent the Indians simply repeated their refusal to council with their enemies anywhere except at Rock Island. Concluding that a "firm and decisive course" was necessary to deal with the Sacs and Foxes, who "have more national character than any tribes we have within this Superintendency," the exasperated Clark ignored their refusal and proceeded with his plans for the conference at Prairie du Chien.[15]

Authorized by the War Department to expend $5,000 to "cover the Dead" of the Sacs and Foxes, Clark was able to conciliate them for the moment for only $1,000. Stopping at each village on his way to Prairie du Chien, the Superintendent harangued the Indians and persuaded about seventy of them to accompany him. When they reached the council grounds they found a number of Winnebagos and Menominees waiting for them.

Over a period of nine days the representatives of the hostile tribes reached an agreement with each other and one with the United States. By the terms of the first, the Sacs, Foxes, Sioux, Winnebagos, Menominees, Omahas, Iowas, and Otos agreed to bury the hatchet. On July 16, 1830, the Indians surrendered to the United States a considerable area between the Missouri and the Mississippi, which was divided into hunting grounds for the tribes concerned. For their share of the purchase price the Sacs and Foxes received annuities of $6,500 for ten years.

The commissioners wanted to broach the subject of a pur-

15 Clark to McKenney, June 16, June 19, 1830, Photostat WHS.

chase of the Sac and Fox mineral lands, but the tribes' price was too high. Becoming aware of the value of their land the Indians were prepared to ask for an annuity of $32,000 for fifty or sixty years, plus salt, tobacco, and the payment of $60,-000 owed Farnham and Davenport. Russell Farnham offered to settle the debt for $40,000 if the government would agree to the Indian proposal. The commissioners disappointed Farnham by taking no action. Although Clark was optimistic about the negotiations, as far as the trader was concerned they were a failure.

When the Indians departed from Saukenuk in September, 1829, Keokuk had assured Forsyth that neither he nor any of his followers would return in the spring. The Watchful Fox was quite despondent. At the direction of the Sac chiefs he had given up his summer hunt and remained at Saukenuk in a futile effort to keep peace. Unable to please either those who wished to remain at Rock Island or those who wished to remove, Keokuk was ready to wash his hands of the whole business.[16]

Black Hawk also had troubles. Forsyth had made it clear that the government was going to sell the land around Saukenuk and that the Indians could not return there in the spring of 1830. Then the elderly brave learned that his old friends George Davenport and Russell Farnham had bought more than two thousand acres around the mouth of Rock River. Black Hawk and his outraged followers held several councils to determine what to do. They not only decided to return but even laid plans to murder those whom they held responsible for their predicament. The angry Indians condemned Davenport, Forsyth, Clark, the interpreter LeClaire, the commandant of Fort Armstrong, and Keokuk.[17] They might well have included the hero of New Orleans, President Andrew Jackson.

---

[16] Forsyth to Clark, October 1, 1829, in Draper MSS., 6T113-15.
[17] *Life of Black Hawk*, 111-13.

A notorious hater of Indians and British alike, Jackson was a strong supporter of the removal policy. In his annual message in December, 1829, Old Hickory denounced as a violation of states' rights the presence of Indians within state boundaries. Late in May Congress fell in line with an appropriation of $500,000 to move tribes to land west of the Mississippi which was not a part of any state or territory. The bill related to the Sacs and Foxes only as an indication of the government's policy, as the bill explicitly excluded from its provisions those tribes covered by previous treaties.

In the spring of 1830, despite the Treaty of 1804, its affirmation in 1816, numerous lectures on the subject by Clark and Forsyth, and the desires of the principal chiefs, Black Hawk led his followers back to Saukenuk following their winter hunt. The Indians discovered even more whites in the vicinity than the previous year, and the women had to locate their corn patches in the small areas the squatters had not enclosed. When Forsyth arrived at his post, he called before him Black Hawk's band and Keokuk and the other tribesmen present at Rock Island for their spring trade.

Forsyth told the Indians that Clark had directed him to tell them for the last time to move. Keokuk replied soothingly that his faction had been trying to get "those Mutinous Indians" to remove to the new village on Iowa River. The Watchful Fox was only awaiting their final answer, to be given when their leaders returned from a visit with the Winnebagos of Rock River. The friendly chiefs advised the agent to coerce the recalcitrants by withholding their blacksmith services. Having already threatened to turn the matter over to the White Beaver, General Atkinson, and having suspected Black Hawk's band of procrastinating, the incensed Forsyth favored a show of force. The right moment, he believed, would be at the change of garrisons, which was to take place shortly. At that time an unusually large number of troops would be available for duty at Fort Armstrong. If these were not sufficient, he advised Clark to ask the governor of Illinois to call out three hundred to four hundred militiamen.

The garrison was relieved, but the troops applied no pressure to remove the Sacs from their village. When some of Black Hawk's band visited Forsyth and asked that the blacksmith do some work for them, the agent took Keokuk's advice and refused. When the Indians began to declaim resentfully about their land east of the Mississippi, he declined to argue. Having threatened them with force, Forsyth thought it foolish to discuss the matter further, "For to use threats to Indians and not put them into execution is worse than nothing."

Incidents bringing the whites and Indians to the verge of bloodshed continued to occur. A teetotaler, Black Hawk objected strenuously to the squatters selling liquor to the Indians. He feared that a drunken redskin might kill a white. After repeated warnings to one man who persisted in vending firewater, the old Sac led a party of his young warriors to the settler's cabin and rolled out his barrels and stove them in.

As the plans progressed for the Prairie du Chien council of the Sioux and the Sacs and Foxes, Black Hawk left Saukenuk in search of advice. Revisiting the British post at Malden he was assured that if the tribes had not sold their village site, and certainly the lone surviving signer, Quashquame, denied it, their American father would not dispossess them. When he returned to Saukenuk, Black Hawk told his agent that his band was determined to occupy their village again in the spring of 1831 and that he planned to visit Clark at that time to settle the issue.[18] The agent to whom he addressed these sentiments was not Thomas Forsyth.

Always desirous of wintering near St. Louis, Forsyth no longer had to disobey Clark to do so. In April, 1830, the irritated superintendent deplored Forsyth's refusal to conform to orders and depart for Fort Armstrong, and the Secretary of War took the opportunity to discharge Forsyth. To replace

[18] Felix St. Vrain to Clark, October 8, 1830, Photostat WHS.

the veteran he chose Felix St. Vrain, an inexperienced resident of Peoria.

In August, St. Vrain arrived at Fort Armstrong to take up his duties. Both whites and Indians protested to him in the usual vein, and St. Vrain was at a loss about how to proceed. He believed it useless for him to say anything, as his predecessor had threatened the Indians on several occasions to no avail. St. Vrain was correct. Black Hawk, still dreaming of his victories in 1813 and 1814, had demonstrated that he would not leave peacefully the village and lands of his ancestors. The Illinois frontiersmen, lusting for the rich acres around Saukenuk, were willing to remove him by force.

Keokuk and most of the other Sacs and Foxes recognized the hopelessness of their situation. Although Keokuk might haggle over the terms of land sold to the United States, he confined his objections to the council chamber. The tribesmen might risk battle with the Sioux and Menominees, but war with the Long Knives was suicide.

Black Hawk and his son, Whirling Thunder.

From a painting by John W. Jarvis. *The Thomas Gilcrease Institute of American History and Art.*

Sac and Fox chiefs of the 1880's.
Oklahoma Historical Society.

Moses Keokuk and son Charles, 1868.

From a photograph by A. Z. Shindler. *Smithsonian Institution.*

Sac and Fox chiefs and headmen, 1885. Pawshepawho standing in front of wickiup.

From a photograph by W. S. Prettyman. *Oklahoma Historical Society.*

11. The Corn Treaty of 1831

B Y 1831 the white population of Illinois had passed the 150,000 mark. A few cabins, sometimes many miles apart, were scattered along the Mississippi River as far north as Galena and eastward along the Illinois to Chicago. But the northern third of the state, with the exception of the lead-mining region, the vicinity of the mouth of the Rock, and the settlement at the mouth of the Chicago River, was virtually an uninhabited wilderness. As yet, few of the settlers had ventured onto the prairies, and their rude cabins generally huddled near one of the numerous wooded creeks and rivers that threaded the area.

The Sacs and Foxes, whose land settlers were beginning to occupy, had a difficult time in the winter of 1830–31. The band which had followed Black Hawk back to Saukenuk the previous spring was short of guns, traps, and other equipment, its warriors having traded too freely with the whites for whiskey. Another band, which had visited St. Louis in the fall, returned to the hunting grounds late and did little that winter except loiter around their trader's establishment, drinking and begging. Heavy snows handicapped the industrious Indians attempting to hunt, and in January, Russell Farnham feared that all his horses as well as some of the Indians would starve. Only one band of forty lodges made a good hunt. These were not the only Sac and Fox troubles. "We were a divided people," relates Black Hawk. The aged recalcitrant headed one faction within the two tribes and his rival Keokuk, who had traveled as far east as New York and realized the futility of resistance, headed the other. Possessed of a "smooth tongue," Keokuk employed all his persuasive powers to dissuade the deluded Sacs from following Black Hawk's lead. And the latter's few white friends joined Keokuk in advising the old warrior to give up his plan to return to Rock River in the spring of 1831. Rationalizing that he and his band had had no part in selling the land and that the treaty provided that the Indians might occupy the land until the United States disposed of it to settlers—he chose to ignore the sale that had already taken place—Black Hawk determined to return to the spot for which he felt a "sacred reverence." His one consolation was that the women, tillers of the fertile acres around Saukenuk, were solidly behind him. Some of their attachment to the aged warrior can be explained in terms of alarm at the incredible rumor circulating among the tribesmen that the Americans intended to castrate all males and import negro men to breed a fresh stock of slaves.[1]

Black Hawk hoped for outside aid. He was in constant communication with the Winnebago Prophet at his village on Rock River, and in the fall of 1830 a small party of warriors, including Black Hawk's son, left to visit the Creeks, Cherokees, Osages, and other tribes as far southwest as Texas. Carrying quantities of black wampum, Black Hawk's emissaries inveighed against the avaricious, defrauding Americans and summoned the tribes to join the Sacs and Foxes in a general onslaught on the white settlements.[2] But Black Hawk and the Winnebago Prophet were not Tecumseh and his brother.

[1] Tiamah and Apanos-okimant to Clark, July 22, 1832, Photostat WHS.
[2] *Life of Black Hawk*, 115; P. L. Chouteau to Clark, June 27, 1831, extract

While the deputation from Rock River was seeking support among the southwestern tribes, a new governor of Illinois was moving to forestall the return of Black Hawk's band to Rock River. After a career which included service in the War of 1812 and terms on the Illinois Supreme Court and in the Illinois General Assembly, John Reynolds had been elected in 1830 to succeed Ninian Edwards. Within a short time he received complaints from settlers about Sac and Fox conduct. The Old Ranger, as he was known for his exploits in a ranger company in the War of 1812, was no Indian lover. A lifelong resident of the frontier, he considered the Indians incapable of civilization and intruders in states whose claims transcended those of any Indian.

Reynolds transmitted the settlers' charges of theft, trespass, damage, and assault with intent to rape to the General Assembly. The irate governor recommended, unsuccessfully, that it vest in him the power to call out the militia to protect the citizens from Indians and to remove the latter from ceded land. However, the General Assembly did agree on resolutions stating that the actions of the Sacs and Foxes "justify a resort to immediate force," unless the President took prompt steps to remedy the situation. The legislators united in instructing Illinois' representatives in Congress to request the President to remove the Indians from ceded land in Illinois and prevent Black Hawk's return.[3]

Federal government officials were likewise concerned at Black Hawk's probable return to Saukenuk. While the Illinois General Assembly debated the issue, Clark asked the Secretary of War for instructions. He estimated that about one-

in Clark Papers; Clark to Eaton, June 29, 1830, Clark Papers; General Edmund P. Gaines to Lewis Cass, August 10, 1831, in Black Hawk War Papers, Illinois Historical Library; St. Vrain to the Secretary of War, September 6, 1831, Photostat WHS. (The Black Hawk War Papers will hereafter be cited as BHWP.)

[3] Josephine Louise Harper, "John Reynolds, 'The Old Ranger' of Illinois, 1788–1865," unpublished Ph.D. dissertation, University of Illinois, 1949, 105–106; "Preamble and Resolutions by the General Assembly of Illinois re Indians on the Northwest frontier," January 19, 1831, Photostat WHS.

sixth of the Sacs were members of Black Hawk's band and attached to the British interest. Expecting the band to recross the Mississippi following their winter hunt, the Superintendent predicted that if an increase in annuities did not change their minds, force would be the only alternative. If the Secretary of War agreed and the tribes consented, the purchase of their mineral lands would furnish the increase in the annuity.

Before the government took any action, the British Band followed Black Hawk back to Saukenuk. St. Vrain being absent, their leader called on the interpreter and George Davenport. To no avail, both advised the Indians to remove. The women began to plant their corn, and three hundred warriors, although as yet manifesting no hostility, appeared determined to remain. Trouble was not long in coming. The settlers accused Black Hawk's band of burning fences, destroying crops, and vowing to exterminate any settlers foolhardy enough to remain. Receiving no satisfaction from the agent or the commandant of Fort Armstrong, the indignant whites, whose charges were discounted by some, petitioned the Old Ranger for assistance. They recounted their difficulties and implored speedy relief, stating that otherwise "we must leave our habitations to these savages."

After his return to Rock Island, St. Vrain had been at a loss concerning the proper procedure to adopt. Until late in May none of the Indians called on him, and when they did they presented Quashquame to testify against the Treaty of 1804. Not content with words, the warriors did oust one settler who had the temerity to plow up a few of the Indians' patches of corn. Before this news could reach the ears of John Reynolds, the impatient Governor decided to call out seven hundred members of the militia to remove the Indians "dead or alive." In the hope of making "this disagreeable business" unnecessary the Old Ranger informed Clark of his plans so that the Superintendent would have the opportunity to try to remove them peaceably before the militia acted.[4]

Fortunately, when the Superintendent received Reynolds' communication, General Edmund P. Gaines, commander of the Western Department of the army, was in St. Louis. Clark promptly referred it to the General. Although personally opposed to the removal policy, the irascible Gaines lost no time in dispatching troops to Rock River. He informed the Governor that unless the size of the disaffected band increased, the regular army could handle the situation without the assistance of the militia.

The day after General Gaines' arrival at Rock Island, he summoned Black Hawk and his principal braves to counsel with him and also asked Keokuk and others of the peaceful faction to be present. To the alarmed army officers, traders, and friendly Indians assembled at the council house, Black Hawk and his men resembled a war party more than a peace delegation. Profusely painted and well armed, they bounded to the council house whooping and brandishing their lances. So hostile did the Indians appear that Gaines increased the guard and kept the entire command under arms.[5]

The General opened the council by reminding the Sacs of their treaties of 1804, 1816, and 1825 and of the fact that they had been permitted to remain as long as the land was not needed. Now, Gaines announced, the growing population of whites necessitated their removal. Quashquame then recited his familiar version of the Treaty of 1804, and the General quickly countered by reading a part of the treaty and the names of the signers, including Quashquame's.

At this, Black Hawk, his expression stern and unrelenting, rose and, throwing back his blanket to free his right arm for

[4] Reynolds to Clark, May 26, 1831, Photostat WHS.

[5] For an account of the council I have depended almost entirely on an unsigned article, "Voyage on the Upper Mississippi," in *The Military and Naval Magazine of the United States*, Vol. III (July, 1834), 245–52, 349–57. From similarities between this article and George A. McCall's *Letters from the Frontiers*, I have concluded that McCall was author of the article as well. Black Hawk also speaks of the council, in *Life of Black Hawk*, 122, and Gaines reports on it in Gaines to Reynolds, June 5, 1831, BHWP.

gestures, declared that the Great Spirit had placed the Sacs at Rock River and that his braves were unanimous in their determination to remain. Leaping to his feet the choleric General challenged Black Hawk's right, when chiefs were present, to speak for his tribe. Gaines cautioned the Indians against following Black Hawk and asserted imperiously that he did not propose to argue the validity of the Treaty of 1804. He was there to see how long it would take them to comply with its provisions.

Wrapping his blanket tightly around him, the chastened Black Hawk sullenly resumed his seat. Other braves, however, rose in succession and violently and ferociously reiterated their decision to remain at Saukenuk and "lay their bones with those of their ancestors." Gaines replied to this outburst with the blunt statement that they could either go peacefully or before bayonets and advised them to wait until the next day before rendering a final decision. As Gaines prepared to close the council, Black Hawk rose again and, taking a position in the center of the chamber, offered Gaines his hand, saying with all the dignity he could muster, "You have asked, who is Black Hawk?—know, that he is a Sac, and that his father was a great warchief." After referring to the popularity he had enjoyed as a leader of war parties, the old brave concluded, "Black Hawk is satisfied with the lands the Great Spirit has given him. Why then should he leave them?" Gaines replied scathingly that white men as well as red were strongly attached to their places of birth, but that when the whites sold their inheritance, they left it without quibbling. With that, he summarily dismissed the Indians, who left glowering.

That night, Keokuk, who with his party was camping under the protection of an enormous white flag, circulated among Black Hawk's band, pleading with his misguided friends and relatives. Nearly fifty families succumbed to his eloquent persuasion and moved their camp to the white flag.

Accompanied by a few of his party, Keokuk called on Gaines

early the next morning. Strikingly attired to best display his fine physique, the light-skinned Sac entreated the Americans to refrain from violence until he could withdraw as many of the British Band as could be reasoned with. Nor was he harsh with the ones who persisted in remaining. Keokuk sympathized with those who had planted crops at Saukenuk and would suffer greatly if forced to abandon them. Highly commending the war chief's course of action, Gaines generously offered him time to continue his proselytizing. The General strengthened Keokuk's hand by authorizing him to promise his friends, if they would remove, supplies equivalent to their harvest.

Despite his faith in Keokuk's ability and good intentions, Gaines was pessimistic about the chances of a peaceful removal. He had heard that Black Hawk's British Band had invited the Winnebago Prophet's followers and some Kickapoos and Potawatomis to join them. Therefore, he decided to call on Reynolds for the militia and to summon troops from Prairie du Chien in order to punish the Sacs should the report be true. George Davenport was equally pessimistic about peace, but the unlettered but practical trader consoled himself with the knowledge that "We expect to get the annuetys in our hands today."

To investigate the rumor regarding the Winnebagos, General Gaines called on Colonel Henry Gratiot, agent for that tribe and lead-mining son of a prominent St. Louis trader. The agent found the Prophet and some of his men at Saukenuk and succeeded in persuading them to return to their own village. However, the tricky Prophet did not remain in his lodge but continued up the Rock to the Winnebago villages high up that river, in an unsuccessful effort to recruit aid for Black Hawk against the Long Knives.

In his early forties, the Winnebago—some said he was half Sac—was nearly six feet tall and, although inclined to obesity, strongly built. The Prophet's long matted hair, low forehead, large, deeply sunken eyes, fleshy nose, thick lips, and generally unkempt appearance gave him a savage expression. Normally wearing a deep frown, he managed to convey an impression of brutality and cunning. And his appearance accurately reflected his character. On her death bed one of his wives accused him of murdering her. The Prophet was a dangerously vicious individual, and it was to such a man as this that the simple Black Hawk turned for advice. The unprincipled Winnebago assured the Sac that the Americans were bluffing in an attempt to frighten him away.

After the council with Gaines, Black Hawk indignantly consulted his evil genius again. The Prophet told him that in a dream the Great Spirit had directed that the daughter of a deceased chief long friendly to the whites should request Gaines to permit the Indians to remain long enough to harvest their crops. The gullible Black Hawk swallowed the story, and three days after the council he reappeared before the General with a party of his braves and "an extremely ill-looking hag." Before introducing the chief's daughter, Black Hawk launched into a lecture, the main burden of which was that although he and his warriors wished peace and would not strike the first blow, their bones would whiten the prairies before they would remove!

He then introduced the chief's daughter, but before the "smoke-dried dame" could get well underway in her tirade, the provoked General cut her short. It was unnecessary to say more on the subject; action was needed now, and the Indians had exactly three days to evacuate or be evicted. In deep silence the Indians began to leave. On his way out, Black Hawk made a gesture of conciliation. However, when the appointed time came the Sacs did not recross the Mississippi. Gaines wisely chose to await the arrival of Reynolds and the militia before attempting to coerce the Indians.[6]

6 *Life of Black Hawk,* 121–23; "Voyage on the Upper Mississippi." According to Black Hawk he did not accompany the woman.

The fourteen hundred militiamen were ready to move June 20. Reynolds later described them rather ambiguously as drilled and trained "with as much accuracy as if they were regulars, so far as raw troops were capable." Indeed, the brigade possessed "all the qualities except discipline, that were necessary in any army." The absence of this essential quality made it difficult to control the troops, who "entertained rather an excess of the *Indian ill-will,* so that it required much gentle persuasion to restrain them from killing, indiscriminately, all the Indians they met."

Back at Rock Island, Gaines waited impatiently for the arrival of the militia. To reconnoiter the Sac positions he armed the steamboat *Winnebago* and sent her up the Rock to a point above Saukenuk. Although the Americans saw many women, children, and old men, few warriors were in evidence. The Indians appeared alarmed at first, but none attempted to flee. The General, no Indian hater, refrained from loosing his artillery at the tantalizingly vulnerable lodges. He wished to avoid bloodshed if at all possible.

Not until the afternoon of June 25 did the militia contingent, weary from a march protracted by flooded streams, reach the rendezvous several miles below the mouth of the Rock. While the men drew fresh supplies of ammunition, cleaned their equipment, and recuperated from the difficult march, the generals and their staffs planned the coming operation. The tacticians evolved a plan calling for the militia to attack Saukenuk the next morning from the south side of the Rock River while the regular troops advanced from Fort Armstrong. Caught between these two forces and prevented by the Winnebagos from escaping in canoes, the British Band could either surrender or be exterminated.

At sunrise June 26, Gaines set the troops and steamboat in motion. After a preliminary bombardment the troops swept into the village without meeting any opposition. The whites, who had not heard a war whoop all morning, were not surprised to find an old, mangy dog the lone occupant of Sauke-nuk. A driving rain began soon after they occupied the village and further discomfited the troops, embarrassed at the escape of their prey from the elaborately contrived trap. Unable to vent their wrath on the owners of the lodges, the mortified volunteers set fire to the huts, although it meant the loss of their only shelter against the torrential rain. In several instances the frontiersmen amused themselves by opening the graves of former inhabitants of Saukenuk and scattering their grisly contents. One corpse was thrown on a fire built to warm the chilled bones of some of the drenched militiamen.[7]

Although the volunteers had not distinguished themselves by their discipline or training, they had accomplished their mission. The mere report of the approach of the "multitude of *pale faces* . . . under no restraint of their chiefs," had sufficed to send the Indians stealthily out of their village the night before the attack. Although a few of the Sacs moved up Rock River to the Prophet's village, the majority followed Black Hawk across the Mississippi and camped under the protection of a white flag.

The day following the attack, General Gaines ordered the Indians to Rock Island for a council. Several of the leaders responded, but not Black Hawk. The General impatiently repeated his command and threatened to move on Black Hawk's new camp if he did not comply. Keokuk exerted his influence in Gaines' behalf, and Black Hawk finally agreed to appear and sign an agreement never to return to Saukenuk. On June 30 the old warrior and members of his band landed on Rock Island and proceeded to the council house. There was no whooping and brandishing of weapons as there had been a few weeks earlier. After the Indians were seated, Gaines' aide, Lieutenant McCall, read slowly the "Articles of Agreement

7 J. W. Spencer and J. M. D. Burrows, *The Early Day of Rock Island and Davenport* (ed. by Milo Milton Quaife), 47–48; Thomas Ford, *A History of Illinois from Its Commencement as a State in 1818 to 1847*, 112–15; "Voyage on the Upper Mississippi"; St. Vrain to Clark, July 23, 1831, BHWP.

and Capitulation" which the General and the Governor had drawn up, and the interpreter carefully translated them.

By the terms of the document, Black Hawk and his followers agreed to submit to Keokuk's authority, remove to the west side of the Mississippi and never return without permission, abandon all communication with the British, and grant the United States rights for military and post roads. For its part, the United States agreed to guarantee them their lands west of the river. An article also provided that if Keokuk's band could not enforce the treaty stipulations they were to inform the nearest military post.[8]

Following the reading of the articles the Indians advanced one by one to the table bearing the document and affixed their *X*'s. After Quashquame had signed, Black Hawk was summoned. Silence fell over the room as the old warrior, his face marked by grief and humiliation, "strode majestically forward." When he reached the table, the aide handed him the pen and indicated where the *X* should go. While the spectators waited with bated breath, Black Hawk took the pen and deliberately drew "a large bold cross with a force which rendered *that* pen forever unfit for further use." Then, politely returning it, he resumed his seat with the same measured stride.[9] "I touched the goose quill to this treaty, and was determined to live in peace," related Black Hawk.

Although it was not included in the articles, Gaines charitably agreed to supply the Indians with corn equivalent to that left in their fields. To estimate the amount due the Indians he appointed two Rock River settlers, one the white whom the Sacs had evicted. The volunteers, camping in the vicinity since the attack on Saukenuk, were not pleased with the treaty. Around their campfires of fence rails—one settler estimated they did him ten times the damage the Indians had done—the frontiersmen ridiculed the "corn treaty." The volunteers, who

8 "Terms for British Band Surrender in 1831," June 30, 1831, Photostat WHS.
9 McCall, *Letters from the Frontiers*, 240–41.

had not heard a shot fired in anger during the farcical campaign, prescribed a diet of lead for the dirty, thieving redskins who kept white men out in such miserable weather.

As the volunteers began to disperse to their homes, the Indians prepared to make a winter hunt. Presumably, the issue was closed, although in St. Louis, Clark advised keeping the British Band under observation for some time. Crusty Governor Reynolds announced that if he found it again necessary to call on the militia he would muster "such force, as will exterminate all Indians, who will not let us alone."[10]

Indian complaints to St. Vrain indicated that all was still not quiet on Rock River. When the Sacs attempted to return to their old village to rebury the corpses exhumed by the volunteers, the calloused settlers hindered them. Other whites fired on Indians as they descended the river and took their canoes or destroyed them if the red men landed. As the supply of corn Gaines had delivered to the Indians proved inadequate, as might have been expected considering the identity of the men appointed to set the amount, the women and children lamented the loss of their roasting ears, beans, and melons in the fields around Saukenuk. Unable to withstand their cries any longer, a party of venturesome warriors slipped back to Saukenuk to harvest their fields. Pitiless whites fired on them and drove the Indians empty-handed back across the river. Other Sacs formed war parties and sought compensation at the expense of the Sioux. On the Mississippi the Sacs and Foxes were about to launch an attack on the Menominees, ending the truce between the tribes on the frontier and swelling the ranks of the disaffected band of Black Hawk.

Before the sun rose on the morning of July 31, about one hundred Sac and Fox warriors surprised a Menominee encampment about two miles from Fort Crawford. Working quietly and swiftly with lance, knife, and tomahawk they slew twenty-five and wounded several more of the camp's thirty to

10 Reynolds to the Secretary of War, July 7, 1831, Photostat WHS.

forty occupants. The attackers escaped with few casualties. Not only had they had the advantage of numbers and surprise, but the Menominees were unarmed. The previous evening they had been engaged in a drinking bout, and their women had hidden their weapons as a safety measure. Thus, the Sacs and Foxes gained bloody vengeance for the Sioux and Menominee massacre of the Fox chiefs the previous year.[11]

An outraged chorus greeted the audacity of the war party and their disregard of treaties and agreements. General Street warned the Secretary of War that unless they were "signally chastised and deeply humbled . . . White men will next be missing near the Sacs and Foxes." At St. Peters, the Sioux agent, Lawerence Taliaferro, who had offered to lead five hundred Sioux and Chippewas against the Rock River Indians in the late campaign, fairly seethed. Sacs and Foxes had recently killed two Sioux on their own hunting grounds, confirming the agent's low opinion of them. The principal chief of the band of Sioux involved assured the agent that his people would not seek revenge before the first of October. But if at that time the United States had not punished the guilty warriors, he would carry the war to the Sacs and Foxes. General Henry Atkinson could foresee nothing but further conflicts among the tribes, "For they hold no faith under Treaties, compacts, or obligations of any sort." The new Secretary of War realized the gravity of the situation.

In Washington the reaction to Peggy O'Neill Eaton's lurid past had cost her husband John his post as Secretary of War. To succeed his friend, President Jackson chose Lewis Cass, the temperance-minded Governor of Michigan Territory. Described by Thomas L. McKenney, himself an Indian expert, as "the best informed man in the United States on Indian affairs," Cass knew the character of the red men well enough to appre-

11 General Street to Clark, August 1, 1831, Photostat WHS; Loomis to Street, August 1, 1831, Photostat WHS; Atkinson to Gaines, Office of Adjutant General Document File, Box No. 194, National Archives (hereafter referred to as OAGDF, NA).

ciate the effect on the Menominees if the government did not move swiftly to punish the guilty Sacs and Foxes. Jackson concurred in this opinion and ordered the surrender of the principal Indians involved in the massacre.

Shortly after learning of the incident, Secretary Cass directed General Atkinson and William Clark to parley with the confederated tribes at Rock Island and demand the murderers and perhaps a few hostages. General Atkinson had already ordered Major John Bliss, commanding Fort Armstrong, to interrogate the Sacs and Foxes on the subject of the Menominee massacre. The morning of September 5, 1831, the Major met the principal tribesmen in council at Fort Armstrong.

Major Bliss opened with a recapitulation of the Treaty of 1830, by which the Indians had agreed to refrain from attacks on their neighbors. Then, after referring to the massacre of the Menominees, the officer demanded that the Sacs and Foxes surrender the offenders. Keokuk was the principal speaker for the Indians; Black Hawk commented sullenly that since his band had not attended the negotiations in 1830 he had nothing to say. The burden of the Indian defense was the old familiar plaint that the chiefs were unable to control their young men. As usual, Keokuk spoke ably and forcefully for his people. He maintained that the recent incident only balanced the Sioux and Menominee massacre of the Fox chiefs in 1830. Referring to an Iowa's murder of an Omaha, which act the United States had ignored, Keokuk declared that he suspected a government bias against his people. As in Washington in 1824, the Watchful Fox contrasted the practices of the whites with the conduct they demanded of the Indians. Applause from the assembled chiefs and braves greeted his impassioned, "Why do you not let us fight? You whites are constantly fighting. . . . why do you not let us be as the Great Spirit made us? and let us settle our own difficulties?"

Major Bliss replied hastily that they were not being discriminated against because they were Sacs and Foxes and that not only had the Omahas not asked the United States to punish the Iowa but that the affair was no concern of the Rock River tribesmen. Keokuk's rebuttal was that regardless of the Major's demands the Indians could not force the murderers to surrender, that they must offer themselves. Besides, many of them were hunting far from the villages. This concluded the council, and the tribesmen went back to their hunting.[12]

The Major's optimistic report of the council and the General's own knowledge of Keokuk persuaded Atkinson that the Indians would surrender the murderers, and he and Clark abandoned plans for a meeting to have been held with the red men late in September at Rock Island. St. Vrain, like Bliss, Atkinson, and Clark, believed that the principal Sacs and Foxes had no hostile intentions nor any disposition to act contrary to their treaties. Since it was not practical at the moment to assemble the Indians and he was unaware of a trend in events which favored a resurgence of the Black Hawk band, Atkinson recommended postponing until spring efforts to obtain the culprits.[13]

Following his expulsion from Saukenuk in June, Black Hawk had concluded that resistance to the Long Knives was hopeless. A tired, defeated, old man, the Sac was ready to retire from active participation in tribal affairs. St. Vrain promised to fulfill his request for a corn patch and a small cabin where the elderly brave might live simply. From Davenport, who now owned the land, Black Hawk received permission to be buried in Saukenuk's graveyard among his old friends and comrades-in-arms.

Just as he was resigning himself to passing his remaining

---

12 "Rock Island Council with Sac and Fox," September 5, 1831, in Report of the Indian Bureau, November 19, 1831, 22 Cong., 1 sess., *Senate Ex. Doc. No. 2*, Vol. I, serial 216, 202–204; Bliss to Atkinson, September 6, 1831, enclosed in Atkinson to Colonel R. Jones, September 21, 1821, OAGDF, NA.

13 Atkinson to Colonel Jones, September 21, October 11, 1831, OAGDF, NA; Clark to Cass, September 12, September 22, 1831, Photostat WHS; St. Vrain to Clark, September 22, September 28, 1831, in Clark Papers.

years as a nonentity among those who had thrilled to his exploits and followed him on scores of war parties, the massacre of the Menominees revived his waning hopes. Having acted contrary to the wishes of their chiefs, the Foxes involved in the incident asked Black Hawk's advice. Flattered by their attention the old rebel congratulated them and charged that the President had no right to demand their surrender. Contrasting this reception with that which Keokuk and the other headmen had accorded them, the Foxes threw in their lot with the depleted British Band. As the Indians were preparing to leave their villages for the winter hunt, Neapope returned from a visit to Canada and the Winnebago Prophet. The news that the brave brought restored Black Hawk's confidence and set him to dreaming of expelling the white men from the land of the Sacs and Foxes.

A clever, active brave about thirty years of age, Neapope was Black Hawk's principal lieutenant in the British Band. Although the Sac chiefs disliked his bluster, they respected him as a formidable and eager warrior. In June, 1831, as General Gaines approached Rock Island, Neapope had left Saukenuk for Canada. On his return he reported to Black Hawk that a British agent had informed him that if the Sacs had not sold their village the Americans could not evict them. And, if the Long Knives tried, the British would assist their red brothers! Moreover, Neapope said he had stopped at the Prophet's village and the Winnebago had wonderful news for Black Hawk. Not only had the Potawatomis, Chippewas, and Ottawas agreed to aid the Sacs and Foxes but the British had sent promises to the Prophet of guns, ammunition, clothing, and provisions. If defeated, the Indians could retreat to refuge in the Red River region of Canada. After delivering the message and the Prophet's request that Black Hawk recruit as many Sacs and Foxes as possible, Neapope, his mischief done, returned to the Prophet's village on the Rock.

Elated, Black Hawk spread the news among the Indians and,

for his trouble, was soundly rebuffed by Keokuk. The Watchful Fox called Neapope and the Prophet liars and advised Black Hawk to remain quietly where he was. As Keokuk had requested permission of St. Vrain and Clark to go to Washington and interview the President about their predicament, Black Hawk did abstain from recruiting until he learned that Clark had refused Keokuk's request. Then and there, despite his promises to the contrary, the old Sac decided to return to Saukenuk in the spring. The arrival of discontented Winnebagos, Kickapoos, and Potawatomis to join his ranks strengthened Black Hawk in his decision.

Dissatisfied with the 1819 Treaty of Edwardsville by which their tribe sold their land east of the Mississippi, one band of Kickapoos refused to remove, and in the fall of 1831 many of its members joined the Sac brave. A few Potawatomis were similarly susceptible to the intrigues of Black Hawk and the Prophet. Despite the Prophet's assertion that he could bring the entire Winnebago nation to the aid of the rebels, only the Prophet's band supplied many Winnebago fighting men for Black Hawk's cause.

In the fall of 1831, Clark was earnestly endeavoring to remove both the Kickapoos and the Prophet's followers from ceded land. In July, Shelby County settlers had appealed to Governor Reynolds to oust the Kickapoos accused of the usual depredations. The Superintendent had sent a subagent to persuade the Kickapoos to move, and Colonel Gratiot had been trying all summer to convince the Prophet to break up his village and join the rest of the Winnebagos. That accomplished liar evaded Gratiot as long as possible and when finally cornered denied selling the land around his village, but he finally agreed, reluctantly, to move farther up Rock River.

By the time the ice began to appear on the upper Mississippi, the stage was set for the tragedy to be enacted the next year. Out on the hunting grounds a gullible Black Hawk gathered his followers about him and looked forward to the day when, with the assistance of the Potawatomis, Kickapoos, Chippewas, Winnebagos, and their father across the sea, the Sacs and Foxes would drive the hated Long Knives out of the Valley of the Rock. Meanwhile, in St. Louis, Clark, ignorant of the machinations of the conspirators, recommended to Secretary Cass that the government take steps before spring to protect the Sacs and Foxes from a possible attack by Sioux and Menominees tired of waiting for the white man's justice.[14]

[14] Clark to Cass, December 6, 1831, Photostat WHS.

12. Black Hawk Commits the British Band

DURING THE WINTER OF 1831–32 the tribes on the upper Mississippi exchanged war talks and wampum in preparation for an assault on the Sacs and Foxes. In an effort to gain allies, the Sioux and Menominees approached the Winnebagos. But those Indians, who had lost two warriors to the Sioux during the winter, were in no mood to co-operate.

Out on the hunting grounds the Sacs and Foxes, sheltered from the frigid winds by their winter wigwams, were not prepared to submit quietly to the rumored attack. In the hope of proving their manhood against the best of the Sioux and Menominees, young warriors were honing their scalping knives and eagerly anticipating the end of the winter hunt and the resumption of hostilities. Some of the older heads among their fellow tribesmen were engaged in even more ambitious projects. Expecting war with the whites when they returned to Rock River, Black Hawk and his leading braves were seeking recruits for the British Band.[1] Despite the earnest efforts of

---

[1] St. Vrain to Clark, March 1, 1832, in Clark Papers; John Daugherty to Clark, February 5, 1832, Photostat WHS.

Keokuk and the principal chiefs, the Prophet and Neapope's propaganda swelled Black Hawk's following.

The Watchful Fox no longer hoped that he might plead in person with the Secretary of War and the President. He relied now on his friend George Davenport, visiting in Washington, to appease the British Band and prevent bloodshed. Davenport did not see the President, and his mediations through Congressman Joseph Duncan, who had led the militia the previous summer, were unsuccessful. Old Hickory had resolved to be firm and secure the murderers of the Menominees before the latter and the Sioux mustered their forces for an onslaught.[2] To implement the policy, Major General Alexander Macomb, ranking general of the army, ordered General Atkinson to proceed to Rock Island with the available force at Jefferson Barracks.[3]

Stating that his principal mission was to prevent an attack by other Indians on the Sacs and Foxes, Macomb directed Atkinson to restrain the Sioux and Menominees. Although Henry Atkinson was to use force only if absolutely necessary, he was to permit no temporizing on the part of the Indians.

Unaware of Macomb's orders, Black Hawk confidently proceeded with his plans to return to Rock River in the spring. Emissaries from the British Band tried unsuccessfully to involve the Iowas and Otos in a war against the Americans. This failure did not deter Black Hawk; he still had the backing of the Winnebago Prophet and Neapope's promising statements of British intentions.

By messenger, Keokuk and another Sac chief informed agent St. Vrain that Black Hawk would return to Rock River in the spring. According to other reports, following their winter hunt the British Band expected to rendezvous at the site of

[2] George Davenport to Joseph Duncan, February 11, 1832, in Stock Transcripts; Duncan to President Jackson, March 1, 1832; Elbert Herring to Clark, March 15, 1832; both in Photostat WHS.

[3] Macomb to Atkinson, March 17, 1832, in Letter Books of the Commander-in-Chief, NA.

old Fort Madison and then cross the Mississippi and move up the Rock. After reaching the headwaters of the Rock the warriors would secure their families in that marshy refuge and sally forth to assail the white settlements.[4]

On April 5, as St. Vrain and Major John Bliss conferred at Fort Armstrong, the Prophet appeared unsolicited at Rock Island with a confession. The conspirator voluntarily disclosed to St. Vrain that he had invited Black Hawk's band to join his village. When the astounded agent inquired if the Prophet were aware that the confederated tribes had agreed the previous June not to recross the Mississippi, the deceitful Winnebago replied innocently that he thought the restriction applied only to the mouth of the Rock, not farther up that river. St. Vrain quickly produced the agreement the British Band had signed and read it to the artful Winnebago. The Prophet amiably commented that since they had signed such a treaty they might stay on their own side of the Mississippi. With that the Winnebago left the council chamber, presumably convinced that he should meddle no longer in the differences between the British Band and the United States.

Overnight the Prophet's attitude changed. He had heard that Black Hawk was crossing the Mississippi. When the Major interviewed him the next day, he intimated that the Prophet probably did not care if the British Band recrossed the Mississippi and became involved in a war. "I have nothing to say," retorted the Prophet defiantly. "If you think so, you can make war, those (the Sacs) are my young men, I can call on them, and the Wenebagoes, I am half Sac and half Wenebago." Outraged at the insolence of the Indian, Major Bliss wanted to put him in irons and send him to St. Louis, but St. Vrain and George Davenport advised against it. As the Prophet stalked from the room, the troops at Jefferson Barracks were packing their gear for the move up the Mississippi.

---

[4] Major Bliss to Atkinson, March 30, April 6, 1832, Adjutant General's Office Files, NA (hereafter cited as AGOF, NA).

The first day of April, hardly recovered from the shock of the recent death of a daughter, Atkinson received Macomb's orders. The following day he rode over to St. Louis to see Clark. From his personal knowledge of the Indians and their country, he assured Macomb, "I am persuaded that I shall be able to put your views into effect without much difficulty." But, realizing that this statement left no room for failure, he hedged: "In this, however, I may be mistaken."

Certainly the General had reason to be confident; his record was excellent. Entering the army in 1808 with the rank of captain, he emerged a colonel from the War of 1812, after service which included campaigning under Jackson in Florida. During a long tour of frontier duty, including two expeditions to the Yellowstone and numerous Indian councils, he learned the ways of the redskins well and in 1827 proved it by efficiently suppressing the Winnebago uprising. When Macomb called on him to secure the perpetrators of the Menominee massacre and avert an intertribal war, Atkinson enjoyed a reputation on the frontier equal to that of William Clark.

Believing that the troops would be at Rock Island but a short time, Atkinson ordered his men to take only winter clothing, although he wisely provided that summer uniforms should be readied for transportation if needed. Hardly had the troops had time to execute the order when the General received a warning from Major Bliss that Black Hawk's return was expected. Although he hardly believed that the British Band seriously intended to reoccupy Saukenuk and was sure that if they did he would be there in time to prevent it, Atkinson's confidence was somewhat shaken. "I am apprehensive . . . that I shall have more trouble in settling the difficulties there than I at first expected."

The morning of April 8, 1832, the wives and children of Jefferson Barracks gathered at the river front to see the troops file aboard the steamboats *Enterprise* and *Chieftain* for the move to Rock Island. The afternoon of the third day the *Chief-*

tain reached the lower rapids near the mouth of the Des Moines and met the bearer of bad news. The General learned that five days earlier the British Band, numbering an estimated two thousand warriors, old men, women, and children, had crossed the Mississippi near the mouth of Iowa River, just as predicted, and was between him and Rock Island. Hardly had Atkinson digested this disconcerting item when reports came in that the Prophet had gone bad and would merge his band with Black Hawk's. The worried Atkinson concluded that he did not have a sufficient force to handle the situation and asked Macomb for further orders.

The night of April 11 the *Chieftain* arrived at Rock Island, to be joined the next evening by the *Enterprise*. As General Atkinson came down the gangplank, the British Band, with the exception of one party which had headed directly across country for the Prophet's village, camped on the Mississippi a few miles below the mouth of Rock River. The next morning the Indians, defiantly singing and beating their drums, moved up the Rock. A few miles away in Fort Armstrong, Atkinson, puzzling how to cope with the situation could hear faintly the noisy progress of the British Band.

With only the 220 men he brought with him from Jefferson Barracks plus what he could detach from the garrison at Fort Armstrong, Atkinson felt himself helpless for the moment to interfere with the Indians. The General estimated that the British Band could muster about six hundred warriors, counting about one hundred Kickapoos and a few Potawatomis supposed to have joined them. Fearful of risking an engagement and suffering a defeat which would hearten the British Band and bring it recruits from the wavering and disaffected, Atkinson decided to await developments. Although the Indians had as yet committed no act of hostility, he informed General Macomb that if the situation became more serious, Governor Reynolds would have to call out the militia.

Writing Reynolds himself April 13, Atkinson described the

frontier as being in "great danger." Although he did not ask the Governor for troops—perhaps wishing to avoid the responsibility—the cautious general reported his force inadequate to pursue the British Band. Should he think it necessary he would return to St. Louis to confer with the Governor. Considering the opinions of the men of whom the General had requested information, Atkinson was strangely reluctant to summon the aid of the militia. Traders and agents alike were unanimous in terming the British Band hostile.[5] The one encouraging note was the conduct of Keokuk's followers.

The morning Black Hawk led his loudly defiant band up the Rock, Keokuk and the friendly Sacs and Foxes met Atkinson in council at Rock Island. The White Beaver informed the Indians that he had come to Rock Island to protect them from the Sioux and Menominees and to take into custody eight or ten of the participants in the massacre at Prairie du Chien the previous August. He affected unconcern for the actions of the British Band, which, he said, could be "as easily crushed as a piece of dirt." "If Black Hawk's band strikes one white man," the General fulminated, "in a short time they will cease to exist." Keokuk protested the peaceful intentions of his followers and offered to make one more attempt to persuade the misguided British Band to return. If that failed, he promised that the friendly tribesmen would cross the Mississippi and remain there. Keokuk concluded by attributing all the trouble to the baneful influence of the Prophet. Since Morgan's band was not represented at this council, the General called for another meeting of the friendly Indians to take place April 18.[6]

In the meantime, Atkinson, a thorough if not brilliant officer, visited Galena and Prairie du Chien by steamboat and conferred with leaders in those communities on defense plans.

[5] Nathan Smith to Atkinson, April 13, 1832, BHWP; Thomas W. Taylor to Atkinson, April 13, 1832, BHWP; George Davenport to Atkinson, April 13, 1832, AGOF, NA.

[6] Council at Rock Island, April 13, 1832, BHWP; Johnston's Journal, April 13, 1832, BHWP.

At Prairie du Chien he reviewed the garrison of Fort Crawford and instructed the commanding officer to station five or
six boats in a line across the Mississippi below the mouth of
the Wisconsin to intercept any Sioux and Menominee invaders.
He also ordered the garrison at Fort Winnebago, which domi-
nated the portage of the Fox and Wisconsin rivers, to keep
watch over the Menominees. Similar instructions went to the
agents of the tribes concerned.

En route back to Rock Island the General stopped off at
Galena to see some of the citizens and Colonel Henry Dodge,
the fighting miner from Dodgeville. After discussing problems
of defense with them and authorizing the Galena militia to
draw arms from Fort Crawford should the British Band become more threatening, Atkinson returned to Fort Armstrong
for the second council with the friendly Sacs and Foxes.

The Indians now promised to surrender the next day as
many as they controlled of the warriors implicated in the massacre. Although both Keokuk and St. Vrain had sent word of
the council to the British Band located at the Prophet's village,
none of the rebels appeared. Keokuk's messengers were actually threatened with violence. One of the Menominee murderers brandished a lance, crying that he hoped to break or
wear it out on the Long Knives. Black Hawk observed omi-
nously that he would be prepared to die in twenty days. St.
Vrain was certain that only powder and ball would deter the
growing British Band. Atkinson was convinced and prepared
for a stay of several months.[7]

The simple plan of operations the General outlined for
Macomb and Gaines called for a force of three thousand
mounted militiamen to reinforce his regulars. Since he could
not expect to hear from Gaines or Macomb for at least a week,
if all remained peaceful Atkinson planned to drop down to

[7] Johnston's Journal, April 18, 1832, BHWP; St. Vrain to Clark, April 18,
1832, Photostat WHS; Atkinson to Lieutenant Theophilus Holmes, April 18,
1832, Atkinson's Letter Book, BHWP.

St. Louis to confer with Governor Reynolds. He could only hope that the 250 regulars at Fort Armstrong together with the nearby settlers and the Galena militia would keep the British Band in check until Macomb and Gaines wrote new orders for him. With some misgivings he advised Reynolds to place a few ranger companies on the frontier and await further instructions.

Unknown to Atkinson, then reviewing troops at Fort Crawford, Governor Reynolds had called out about sixteen hundred men April 16 on receipt of Atkinson's letter of April 13. The impetuous Old Ranger also published an electrifying proclamation announcing that Black Hawk's band was in possession of the Rock River country and that the settlers were in "eminent danger." "No citizen ought to remain inactive when his country is invaded, and the helpless part of the community are in danger," trumpeted the Governor. Members of the militia, which included by law all men between the ages of eighteen and forty-five, were asked to volunteer. If they did not volunteer, they would be drafted.

The call came at a poor time for the Illinoisans. A cold, wet spring had delayed plowing and planting; absence from the farm might mean no corn crop. Complicating the situation was a shortage of grain which had left the horses in poor condition, and Reynolds had expressed a preference for mounted men. Despite these handicaps about seventeen hundred eventually answered the Governor's call, although in many cases the draft had to be resorted to.[8] An election was in the offing, and the aspirants for office flocked to the mustering areas to prove their patriotism before the votes were cast. Among the candidates volunteering was one Abraham Lincoln, a long, lean youth from New Salem. Lincoln, a clerk in Denton Offutt's store on the Sangamon, aspired to the Illinois House of Representatives.

Mustering in the communities throughout northern Illinois, the volunteers promptly elected company officers and set

8 *Sangamo Journal*, Springfield, Illinois, April 26, 1832.

out for the rendezvous at Beardstown. On arrival there the volunteers, who looked upon the muster as a big outing, frolicked, drew equipment, and engaged in the serious business of electing battalion and regimental officers. They did it on rations of corn, pork, flour, and whiskey, the staples of diet throughout the campaign. By April 28 the troops were "organized," and the next morning they marched for Yellow Banks on the Mississippi. There the volunteers expected to meet supplies from St. Louis. One day's march from Beardstown the troops met a messenger hurrying to Governor Reynolds.

The day after Atkinson's return from Prairie du Chien and Galena, Keokuk's band proved itself by surrendering three of the Menominee murderers. Of the British Band the General was still uncertain. Until he received orders from his superiors or Black Hawk made a hostile move, the General expected to remain at Rock Island. While waiting he did not relax his efforts to secure the peaceful removal of Black Hawk. Although previous attempts to open communications with the rebellious party had been unsuccessful, on April 24 Atkinson dispatched two young Sacs with a "mild talk." Reminding Black Hawk that he had crossed the Mississippi contrary to the agreement he had signed the previous year, the General cautioned, "It is not too late to do what is right, and what is right do at once." If the Indians did not return, Atkinson threatened to inform their Great Father. "You will be sorry if you do not come back," he chided. The General concluded with the advice that the British Band disregard the "foolish people" asserting that the British would aid Black Hawk.

The reception the British Band accorded the message indicated to the disappointed Atkinson that more than a "mild talk" was now in order. Black Hawk's followers insulted and threatened the emissaries, who returned with the old Sac's reply that "his heart was bad and that he was determined not to turn back."[9] Shortly after the two messengers left the Indian camp, Colonel Gratiot arrived. Accompanied by two other white men he first visited Turtle village, occupying the site of Beloit, Wisconsin. Here the agent learned from the Winnebagos that they had replied unfavorably to war messages from the British Band. To prevent the corruption of a party of Winnebagos going to the Prophet's village and to persuade the Winnebagos there to leave the danger zone, Colonel Gratiot decided to accompany the party.[10]

Gratiot, another white man, and twenty-six Winnebagos reached the Prophet's village April 24. Many of its residents were friendly, but the Prophet appeared sullen. Most of the Indians welcomed Gratiot's advice to move higher up the Rock and merge with the rest of the Winnebagos. All went well until a party of warriors headed by Black Hawk arrived on the scene from their encampment a short distance away. Seeing the white flag which the Winnebagos accompanying Gratiot had hoisted, Black Hawk's followers tore it down. When the Colonel boldly objected, they informed him that he might carry it while marching but he could not raise it in the village. Undaunted, the agent replaced the flag, and the insurgents retaliated by raising a British banner beside it and dancing around the lodge, chanting their war songs and brandishing their lances, tomahawks, and guns.

The white men were becoming concerned for their scalps when the Indians abruptly terminated their hostile demonstration and entered the lodge to talk to Gratiot and the Winnebagos accompanying him. Once inside, however, they resumed their bullying tactics until White Crow, a Winnebago chief

[9] Captain Henry Smith, "Indian Campaigns of 1832," in *Wis. Colls.*, X, 154; Johnston's Journal, April 26, 1832, BHWP.

[10] The account of Gratiot's mission is drawn from the following sources: Gratiot's Journal, January 1, 1832, Stock Transcripts; Gratiot to Cass, April 24, April 26, 1832, Stock Transcripts; Gratiot to Atkinson, April 27, 1832, AGOF, NA; Journal of the Council at Porter's Grove, June 3, 1832, Stock Transcripts; John A. Wakefield, *History of the War Between the United States and the Sac and Fox Nation of Indians*, 11–12.

from Turtle village, bribed the hostile warriors with tobacco. Black Hawk remained a few minutes to confer with the Colonel. The old Sac freely admitted receiving a letter from Atkinson but refused to produce it. After procrastinating a few minutes he promised to return the next day.

The following morning he appeared with the letter and handed it to the agent. Gratiot interpreted it carefully for Black Hawk's benefit. To the "mild talk" the Sac replied curtly that he intended to continue up Rock River. He added that his heart was bad and that if Atkinson sent troops he would fight them. Throughout the interview he was arrogantly contemptuous. The next day the British Band began to move up the Rock and Colonel Gratiot started down the river to report to Atkinson.

The evening of the day that Gratiot reached the Prophet's village, Atkinson had received word from Governor Reynolds that the militia would reach Fort Armstrong about May 10. To co-operate with the army as it moved up the Rock, Atkinson requested that Colonel Dodge raise as many mounted men as possible from the miners in his vicinity. The reports of British Band hostility submitted to Atkinson by the conductors of the "mild talk" and by Colonel Gratiot fortified the General in his resolve to begin operations. "They must be checked at once or the whole frontier will be in a flame," he wrote General Macomb. The same day he assured Governor Reynolds that, "If Black Hawk's Band gains no accessions of strength, they can easily be overcome." Aware of the necessity of impressing the Indians with the futility of resistance, Atkinson added, "Many hands . . . make light work of a job, and there is both safety and economy in adopting such a course." On the morning of May 7 the weary volunteers were straggling into view of the mouth of the Rock, and all the regulars were available for duty except three companies en route from Galena. Atkinson was in a humiliating predicament. He now had to inform the troops that his plans had been revised for a second time. The same day that the volunteers reached the mouth of the Rock, Sacs whom the General had sent to warn the British Band to recross the Mississippi had returned with the perplexing news that Black Hawk was moving up Rock River and not down as Atkinson previously had assured the troops.

After Atkinson's repeated warnings, Black Hawk had realized his position near the Prophet's village was untenable. He had to either conform to orders or escape up the Rock in the hope of obtaining the promised aid of the Winnebagos and Potawatomis. The Winnebago chiefs accompanying Gratiot whispered that they were only professing friendship for the Americans in order to determine their strength. Although these warriors urged Black Hawk to proceed higher up the Rock where he would encounter more friends, their fellow tribesmen among the British Band disillusioned him. They admitted having sent Black Hawk wampum the previous winter inviting him to join them in the spring. However, they now qualified the invitation by stating that the British Band might stay at the Prophet's village and raise corn—if the whites had no objections! Under no circumstances did the Winnebagos want Black Hawk to go farther up the Rock.[11]

Unable to depend upon the Winnebagos for aid and unwilling to admit defeat and submit to the humiliation which must be his lot, Black Hawk gave his band the signal to continue up the river. His only hope now was that the reports of Potawatomi intentions had been true. After the Indians had encamped the evening of the first day's march, their leader summoned his lieutenants and told them privately that Neapope had deceived them with his stories of Winnebago promises. Nevertheless, they would not retreat and would trust that the Potawatomis would assist them. The next morning, to hearten any discouraged members of the band, Black Hawk told his

[11] *Life of Black Hawk*, 136–37.

loyal followers, ignorant of their true situation, that a British detachment would be at Milwaukee in a few days to assist them. Too vainglorious to admit that he had been duped, the old Sac chose to risk the lives of two thousand of his confiding followers at the hands of the undisciplined militia.

When the band reached Dixon's Ferry the morning of April 28—the same day the volunteers were entering state service at Beardstown—John Dixon observed their arrival. In their friendly talks with the old settler the Indians claimed that their only object was to build a town and raise corn on Potawatomi land a few miles east of Dixon's Ferry. Apparently, if the British Band received hospitable treatment from the Potawatomis, Atkinson would have to drive them across the Mississippi.[12]

The General was prepared to do so after May 8 when he mustered into federal service one thousand five hundred mounted and two hundred infantry volunteers. Atkinson gave the command of the 340 regular infantrymen to Zachary Taylor, whom the Sacs and Foxes and a detachment of British artillery had defeated in 1814 when he attempted to destroy Saukenuk and its inhabitants. Although his heavy shock of black hair had greyed over the years, the stocky Taylor was still robust. At a young and active forty-seven years he was in his prime, after years of moving from one frontier post to another. Samuel Whiteside, one of Colonel Taylor's subordinates in 1814, commanded the militia encamped at the old Sac village.

Atkinson was ready to issue movement orders by May 9. Whiteside and the mounted volunteers were to march up the Rock by way of the Prophet's village, while the General, the regulars, and the unmounted volunteers would follow by boat with the supplies. If on arrival at the Prophet's village Whiteside should "be of opinion that it would be prudent to come up with the enemy with as little delay as possible, he will move upon him, and either make him surrender at discretion or coerce him to submission."

12 John Dixon to General Stillman, April 28, 1832, BHWP.

Atkinson erred grievously in permitting the volunteers to advance beyond his effective control. An officer of considerable experience with militia, he must have realized the danger. In remaining with the regulars rather than accompanying the larger force of militia the General nullified his weeks of caution and endangered his entire plan of operations.

Wacomo, the Sac and Fox orator, around 1885. Among his people his eloquence was said to be equal to Tecumseh's, the brilliant leader of the Shawnees. His long flowing hair marks him as one who was outside the warrior group and is unusual among his kind.
Photograph by W. S. Prettyman.

The great frontier photographer, W. S. Prettyman, would probably have chosen this as the best of his pictures. In it are shown all of the remaining full bloods of the entire Sac tribe. Taken in 1884, it shows Pawshepawho standing front center in a white summer robe. In front of him, seated in the place of honor, is his mother, then 107 years old. She remembered the arrival of Lewis and Clark in the northern villages of the Sacs, almost eighty years earlier. The picture was taken four miles northwest of present Davenport, Oklahoma.
Western History Collections, University of Oklahoma Library.

Iowa Sac and Fox delegation to Washington in 1890. Left to
right: Osh-u-ton, Wa-pa-lu-ca, Sho-won, On-a-wat,
and Push-te-na-quah.

Sac and Fox Bark House, 1890.

From a photograph by W. S. Prettyman. *Oklahoma Historical Society.*

13. Blood Flows on a Small Scale Tolerably Fast

THE MORNING of May 10 the volunteer camp at Saukenuk seethed with activity. At the expense of as few votes as possible—the election to be held in August was never very far from the minds of most of the officers—the recently commissioned politicians were trying to coax their friends and neighbors into some sort of marching order for the advance up the Rock. Similar preparations in a more orderly fashion were in progress at Rock Island, and within a few hours the expedition was underway. "I am determined to rid the country of these hostile intruders if it be possible to find them," Atkinson wrote at the end of the first day's march. Supplied with twenty-five days rations for his two thousand men, General Atkinson was certain that the campaign would not exceed that period.

Accompanied by Governor Reynolds and his staff and carrying a few rations in their saddle bags, the fifteen hundred mounted volunteers rode out of the village behind General Whiteside. The General carried orders to halt at the Prophet's village and await the infantry unless the Indians were in striking distance. Bluff Colonel Zachary Taylor commanded the 340 regulars and 165 volunteer infantrymen escorting the supplies loaded in two keelboats and several Mackinaws. Although not burdened with the responsibility for the supply boats, the mounted men had troubles. Horses often mired in the mud, and the cumbersome ox-drawn baggage wagons were constantly in need of assistance. A captured Indian reported the British Band to be but two days march up the river. Unaware that Atkinson had decided to recall his unit, Whiteside determined not to wait at the Prophet's village but to try to overtake the Indians.[1]

After burning most of the lodges in the village, Whiteside and his men marched on. To speed their advance the commander abandoned the baggage wagons. By noon of May 12 the weary, mud-spattered volunteers arrived at Dixon's Ferry, only to learn that the British Band was still twenty-five miles farther up the Rock and, from trail signs, was apparently breaking up into small bands. With only two days' rations at hand the discouraged Whiteside decided to await at Dixon's the arrival of Atkinson and more supplies.

However, two fresh battalions with ample rations were present and craving action. Governor Reynolds had ordered Major Isaiah Stillman's unit to patrol the frontier east from the Mississippi. The other battalion, under Major David Bailey, had instructions to range between Rock River and the settlements on the Illinois. Impatient at their failure to see action, the officers and men of the two units pleaded with Governor Reynolds to permit them to scout ahead of the main force. Exercising his authority as Commander-in-Chief of the Illinois militia, the impetuous Governor ordered Stillman to "cause the troops under your immediate command and the battalion under Major Bailey, to proceed without delay . . . to the head of

---

[1] Atkinson to Whiteside, May 14, 1832, Atkinson's Letter Book, BHWP; Wakefield, *History*, 16; John Reynolds, *My Own Times*, 229; Whiteside to Atkinson, May 18, 1832, AGOF, NA.

'Old Man's Creek' [Kyte River], where it is supposed there are some hostile Indians, and coerce them into submission." The following morning, with 275 men clamoring for combat, Major Stillman was on his way.[2]

That evening, about six o'clock, as Atkinson was composing his order to Whiteside recalling the militia, Stillman prepared to go into camp just north of the mouth of Kyte River. From the standpoint of defense, his choice of a camp site was excellent—a small wood surrounded by open and slightly undulating prairie which could be defended with ease against attackers, who would have to advance against men firing from cover. However, as they hurried about securing their mounts, erecting tents, and sharing their whiskey ration, defense measures were not uppermost in the minds of the volunteers. They had been thus engaged but a short time when the appearance of three mounted Indians with a white flag threw the bivouac into an uproar. Quickly surrounded and rushed into camp, Black Hawk's envoys attempted to deliver their message to the agitated white men.[3]

Disappointed and discouraged at the failure of the Winnebagos to unite with him, yet unwilling to submit to Atkinson, Black Hawk had led his band up the Rock and past Dixon's Ferry in the hope of securing aid and supplies from the Potawatomis. Near the mouth of the Kishwaukee the British Band made camp, and their leader dispatched a message to a nearby Potawatomi village suggesting a conference. The next day a deputation from the Potawatomis appeared and in the presence of the entire band informed Black Hawk that they were unable to supply his people with corn. Disconcerted and not

2 Reynolds, *My Own Times*, 230; Whiteside to Atkinson, May 18, 1832, AGOF, NA; *The Galenian* (Galena, Illinois), May 16, 1832; Reynolds to the Secretary of War, June 4, 1832, Black Hawk War Miscellaneous Papers, NA.

3 The account of the skirmish is based on Henry Smith, "Indian Campaign of 1832," *Wis. Coll.*, 157; Reynolds, *My Own Times*, 231–35; Stillman to Reynolds, May 15, 1832, enclosed in Reynolds to Cass, June 7, 1832, Secretary of War, Letters Received, NA; *The Galenian* (Galena, Illinois), May 23, 1832; *Life of Black Hawk*, 138–42.

wishing to conduct such an unsatisfactory conversation in public, the old Sac asked the Potawatomis to visit him privately that night. They did so, and Black Hawk learned what he had most feared. Not only did they have no corn to share—and the British Band was rapidly exhausting its own scanty supplies—but the Potawatomis denied that the British planned to land a detachment at Milwaukee or send supplies there. Thoroughly rebuffed, the dejected Sacs requested a last conference. Finally, forced to recognize the helplessness of his situation, Black Hawk had decided to surrender if the whites overtook him.

The following day, as Black Hawk and his Potawatomi guests were engaged in a final ceremonial feast, scouts burst in to report that a force of three hundred to four hundred Long Knives was a few miles away. As the visitors departed in haste, Black Hawk, convinced of the futility of resistance, sorrowfully sent three warriors under a white flag to escort the whites to his camp. Should the Long Knives already have encamped, the messengers were to return and guide Black Hawk in person to the American Commander. Not certain of the reception his deputation would receive, the Sac advised five other warriors to follow the envoys and observe developments.

In the midst of the interrogation of the three warriors in Stillman's camp, a volunteer sighted far out on the prairie the other five Indians. The word flashed through the small wood, and a few excited men scrambled on their horses, with or without saddles, and galloped in the direction of the warriors. Others followed, and within minutes a substantial number of Stillman's command, all trace of organization gone, was streaming across the prairie. Alarmed at the torrent of Americans bearing down upon them, the warriors turned to flee. In the pursuit someone opened fire, and the volunteers joined in a ragged volley which downed two of the Indians. Back at the bivouac the sound of the firing increased the confusion around the the three bearers of the white flag and incited the frenzied whites to attack the deputation. Two of the Indians escaped, leaving the other dead in the camp.

The surviving Indian scouts raced for Black Hawk's camp. Dashing in on the old warrior they breathlessly described the treacherous attack of the pursuing whites. His peace overtures apparently rejected, Black Hawk valiantly summoned the forty odd warriors with him, most of his band being several miles away, to sell their lives dearly. Concealing his men behind some bushes, the veteran of many an ambuscade allowed the leading horsemen to approach within a few feet of his warriors before springing the trap.

Emitting piercing war whoops the Indians leaped from their concealment. Panic-stricken at this unexpected turn of events, the leading whites, outnumbered for the moment, wheeled their mounts and fled as rapidly as they had come. In the gathering darkness every shadowy object assumed alarming proportions. As the frantic whites first encountering the Indians raced back toward camp, they carried their comrades with them. The retreat rapidly degenerated into a rout. With the exception of a few brave men who attempted to make a stand and were overwhelmed, each panic-stricken volunteer was concerned only with putting as much distance as possible between himself and the hatchet-swinging redskins. Despite the defensive strength it offered, the fleeing volunteers never halted at their camp but continued their mad course until they reached Dixon's Ferry. Those who had remained at camp, unable to gauge the strength of the attackers in the darkness and unnerved by the hysterical warnings of their terrified fellows, were swept along with the retreat.

Shortly after midnight the volunteers with the fastest horses began to arrive at Dixon's Ferry. They horrified soldiers there with their tales of a disastrous defeat inflicted by an Indian force numbering at least one thousand warriors. Each of the early arrivals was certain that he was one of but few survivors.

Many of them were interrupted in their description of the horrible fate of a comrade by the appearance of said victim, exhausted, weaponless, and distraught, but without a scratch on him inflicted by the murderous horde. Reynolds and Whiteside at first feared that Stillman's detachment was virtually destroyed, but, as survivors continued to straggle in, they revised their estimate of American losses. By morning all but fifty-two men had appeared, and forty-one of these eventually reported in.

Aware of discontent among the troops with regard to their officers, Governor Reynolds considered it improbable that the present demoralized force would remain intact long enough to crush the British Band. As Stillman's men stumbled into camp that night, the quaking Governor wrote Atkinson and Henry Dodge informing them of the catastrophe and composed a proclamation to the Illinois militia. The Old Ranger declared that the Indians had overpowered Stillman and that he considered the Potawatomis and Winnebagos active allies of the Sacs and Foxes. The Governor called for at least two thousand men to rendezvous at Hennepin June 10.

Crippled by a ration shortage, all that General Whiteside could do was march his men to the scene of the battle and provide the slain Americans a decent burial. The evening after the battle the sobered troops reached the battleground, where a gruesome sight confronted them. Although the volunteers found the bodies of only eleven of their comrades, the Indians had mutilated these by hacking off limbs, heads, hearts, and genitals. After burying the maimed corpses the shaken troops went into camp and returned to Dixon's the next day.

For three days after the engagement stragglers from Stillman's unit continued to arrive at the ferry. By the final count the American casualties consisted of eleven killed and several wounded. However, it was the earlier reports of fifty-two killed which circulated widely and terrorized the frontier. Few of the hardy souls who, on hearing of Stillman's fate, had scorned to seek safety with neighbors in a temporary fort, remained in their isolated cabins after hearing of the massacre at Indian Creek.

When a band of nearly forty warriors, mostly Potawatomis, attacked the Davis farm May 21, the men were working in the fields and the blacksmith shop while the women and children busied themselves around the house. The whites, representing several families, could put up no effective resistance, and the slaughter was but the matter of a few minutes. Nine men managed to elude the war party, but the Indians killed and scalped the remaining whites, except for two young girls whom the warriors took prisoner. As the Indians rushed Rachel and Sylvia Hall from the cabin, the horror-stricken girls saw one warrior pick up a child by his feet and brain him against a stump and saw two other warriors hold a squirming small boy while a third Indian shot him.

Placing the girls on horses, the warriors traveled rapidly until they rejoined the British Band after nightfall. For nine days, Sylvia and Rachel Hall lived unmolested with Black Hawk's people, although they had the harrowing experience of witnessing a dance featuring their parents' scalps. When Winnebagos dispatched by Colonel Gratiot came to ransom them, the Sacs and Foxes declared that they had lost too much blood to give up both girls. However, they finally agreed to release both Sylvia and Rachel in return for more horses. At Blue Mound June 1 the Winnebagos turned the girls over to Colonel Dodge.

A ghastly sight met the eyes of the troops who went to bury the fifteen friends and relatives of the Hall girls. As after Stillman's defeat, the Indians had butchered the bodies. They had strung the women up by their feet and had practically chopped the children to pieces. A thrill of horror invaded every cabin as the report of the massacre on Indian Creek spread. "The alarm and distress on the frontier, cannot be described; it is heart rending to see the women and children in an agony of fear, fleeing from their homes and hearths, to seek what they imagine is but a brief respite from death," wrote one of Atkinson's officers. Unable to hunt or fish for fear of marauding Indians the settlers on the Illinois were rapidly exhausting their meager food supplies.

In the isolated lead-mining district all was in turmoil. Women and children from the outlying communities rushed to Galena to escape by steamboat, and the men formed volunteer companies. Choosing to remain, some miners and their families "forted" at a number of places throughout the mining district, hurriedly throwing up a stockade with a blockhouse or two or just reinforcing a large cabin. The editor of the *Galenian* called for a "war of extermination until there shall be no Indian (*with his scalp on*) left in the north part of Illinois." To man the defenses of Galena, five companies were organized. Also included in the community's defense plans were Colonel Henry Dodge and his company of miners.

Meanwhile, on May 17, at Dixon's, for the first time since he had left the mouth of Rock River one week earlier, General Atkinson reunited his army. The General was still confident that he had sufficient troops to conclude the campaign. Ten days later, Atkinson had at his disposal only 300 volunteers and his original 340 regulars. After a futile advance along what was supposed to be the Indians' line of retreat, the overwhelming majority of the militia command had insisted on returning home. Governor Reynolds, no man to ignore the wishes of the enfranchised, discharged the men. Three hundred volunteers, among them Abraham Lincoln, agreed to remain in service until another levy could be inducted. Before learning of the release of the other volunteers the General had anticipated such an eventuality and revised his plans. The arrival of dispatches from Washington spurred him to greater efforts. Writing before he had heard of Stillman's rout, General Macomb bluntly informed Atkinson that Andrew Jackson wanted decisive action. More helpful was Secretary Cass' approval of the use of Illinois militia if necessary. Thus fortified, Atkinson dispatched orders to Governor Reynolds, who was moving south from the Potawatomi village toward Ottawa, to call out two thousand more militiamen if the force under Whiteside refused to remain in service. To recruit a corps of auxiliaries and scouts from among the Sioux and Menominees, Atkinson dispatched Colonel Hamilton to Prairie du Chien. He also summoned two companies from Fort Winnebago and requested the services of Brigadier General Hugh Brady. A rugged old veteran, Brady had offered to take two mounted infantry companies and "whip the Sauks out of the country in one week."

The location of the British Band was at the time unknown to the Americans. A number of trails had led north from the Potawatomi village, but the homesick volunteers had not chosen to continue the pursuit in that direction. Had they persevered they would have overtaken the Indians, who, encumbered by women and children, were moving slowly. The morning after he routed Stillman, Black Hawk had visited the volunteers' camp and looted it. A number of whiskey barrels, mostly empty, especially attracted his attention. Black Hawk later commented sarcastically that the barrels were a surprise to him, as he "had understood that all the *pale faces* belonged to the *temperance societies!*"

After thoroughly plundering the bivouac, mutilating the bodies of the slain whites, and burying the few warriors who had fallen in the engagement, the jubilant Indians returned to their camp. Aware that the whites outnumbered him, Black Hawk decided not to risk another battle. Solicitude for the safety of the women and children and extravagant hopes engendered by the defeat of Stillman prevented him from making another surrender offer. The only course open was to retreat. The headwaters of the Rock offered advantages as a refuge, and Black Hawk chose to go by way of the Kishwaukee in order to confuse the pursuers.

Winnebagos whom the British Band encountered as it approached the head of the Kishwaukee congratulated Black Hawk on his defeat of Stillman. They offered to guide the Sacs and Foxes to a place of safety in the vicinity of the Four Lakes, in present-day Dane County, Wisconsin. Black Hawk accepted and, to cover his retreat and secure supplies, loosed scalping parties on the settlements.

One war party consisting of about thirty Winnebagos intercepted seven whites carrying dispatches for Atkinson from Dixon's Ferry to Galena. The Indians killed four of the party, including the agent Felix St. Vrain. The Sacs and Foxes lost a friend when the Winnebagos lifted the agent's scalp. He had consistently advocated a policy of peaceful persuasion with regard to the red men. As in the case of the Indian Creek massacre the whites credited the Sacs and Foxes with crimes other tribesmen committed. Reporting St. Vrain's death, the *St. Louis Beacon* cried, "The blood of the murdered victims of Indian ferocity can admit of but one atonement;—the lives of a hundred Indians is too small for that of *each* of their fallen victims."

Although the Kickapoos and Rock River Winnebagos, enthused by Stillman's defeat, furnished many recruits for the hostiles, only the Potawatomis among the other tribes furnished any aid at all. It was General Street's assurance that the Winnebagos north of the Wisconsin, the Sioux, and the Menominees were all friendly to the United States that induced Atkinson to send Colonel Hamilton to recruit the force of Indian auxiliaries. The peaceful intentions of Keokuk's band seemed equally dependable.

The Watchful Fox had done well in his effort to keep his band out of the war. When the militia had reached Yellow Banks from Beardstown early in May, Keokuk had entertained the whites with a war dance. Not only had he protested the peaceful intentions of his band but he even offered to serve against Black Hawk![4]

Later in the month rumors circulated among the nervous whites that his band intended to attack Fort Armstrong, and the Watchful Fox appeared personally before the fort's commanding officer and squelched the rumors. Keokuk's people were in an unenviable position. The hostile Indians threatened them for their refusal to fight the Americans, and a number of militiamen made no secret of the fact that they considered the only good Indian a dead Indian. General Atkinson was having his troubles too.[5]

By the end of May the campaign appeared to be a failure. The army, which May 10 had marched so hopefully from the mouth of Rock River, had disintegrated, leaving barely enough troops to guard supplies and conduct rudimentary patrols. Henry Atkinson, after a long and honorable army career, was faced with the galling possibility of failure to accomplish a mission. As one of his officers had pointed out early in the campaign, "This Country will not sustain a man who suffers defeat from Indians no matter what may be the disparity in numbers."[6] His professional career at stake, the General was careful not to underestimate his difficulties to his superiors. "Perhaps there have not been at any time stronger grounds for apprehending a combined war on the part of the Indians, nor could there be a greater alarm or more distress on the frontier," he advised General Macomb.

Learning that Governor Reynolds was discharging the volunteers at Ottawa, Atkinson rode over to consult with him and Colonel Taylor. Although some observers criticized Atkinson as being too conservative in his tactics, none questioned the General's personal bravery. Accompanied only by his staff, Atkinson risked possible ambush, but he reached Ottawa safely.

After consulting with Reynolds at Ottawa, Atkinson directed

4 Wakefield, *History*, 14.
5 George Davenport to Clark, May 27, 1832, Stock Transcripts; Clark to Cass, May 30, 1832, Clark Papers.
6 Lieutenant Reuben Holmes to Major I. H. Hook, April 16, 1832, in Quartermaster Historical File, NA.

the Governor to call out one thousand more troops in addition to the two thousand he had requested May 25. To strengthen his detachment of regulars the General summoned two infantry companies from Fort Leavenworth. To supply the new army, Atkinson ordered rations for three thousand men for sixty days, horses to pack them, and ordnance and medical supplies. The meticulous commander found time to display concern over the fact that one detachment of militia was receiving an unauthorized sugar and coffee ration and to direct that more damaged pork than good should be included in the rations to friendly Indians. The General had no objection to feeding destitute settlers, but he did not want them encouraged to depend on army rations.[7]

Unable yet to resume offensive operations, Atkinson guarded his precious supplies and sent out patrols. To command at Dixon's Ferry he sent Colonel Zachary Taylor, who commented bitterly, "The more I see of the militia the less confidence I have in their effecting any thing of importance; and therefore tremble not only for the safety of the frontiers, but for the reputations of those who command them."[8] The Colonel's pessimism was well founded. In the several skirmishes that occurred within the next three weeks, the Illinois militia gained no laurels, although Dodge's men acquitted themselves well on one occasion. "Blood flows here on a small scale tolerably fast," observed Governor Reynolds.[9]

Dodge, convinced that "we are not to have peace with this bandit collection of Indians until they are killed up in their dens," had just returned from a visit to Atkinson's headquarters when he learned of hostiles on the Pecatonica.[10] Dodge

[7] Atkinson to Colonel Mathews, June 22, 1832; Atkinson to Major Horne, June 2, 1832; both in OAGDF, NA.

[8] Taylor to Atkinson, June 2, 1832, BHWP.

[9] Reynolds to N. Edwards, June 22, 1832, in Washburne, *Edwards Papers*, 589–90.

[10] Dodge to ———, June 14, 1832, in *Scioto Gazette* (Chillicothe, Ohio), July 10, 1832.

immediately ordered a detachment of his men to locate the war party.

The morning of June 16 the Colonel left his camp near Fort Hamilton and, accompanied by two men, went on to the fort. En route they passed a white whom Indians had ambushed before the Colonel reached the fort. Within minutes, Dodge had twenty-nine men in hot pursuit of the war party. Cornering the eleven warriors in a bend of the Pecatonica, Dodge dismounted his men and led twenty-one of them against the Indians, who were concealed under the bank of a small lake. The warriors fired first and severely wounded three men, but the miners charged and dispatched the entire party in less than a minute. About an hour after the whites had scalped the last warrior, Colonel Hamilton arrived on the scene with a party of Sioux, Menominees, and Winnebagos, who literally cut the bodies of their dead enemies to pieces. The "Battle of Pecatonica" eventually assumed an importance out of all proportion to the numbers involved. After a demoralizing series of setbacks the victory was a veritable tonic to the frontiersmen.

While the skirmishing was going on between Dixon's Ferry and Galena, General Atkinson was organizing the incoming militia as the men gathered at Fort Wilburn, the supply depot at the rapids near the mouth of Vermilion River. William Cullen Bryant, the New York poet and editor then touring Illinois, met some of the militiamen en route to the rendezvous. "They were a hard-looking set of men, unkempt and unshaved," he observed. Bryant also noted that the settlers complained that the citizen soldiers were making war upon pigs and chickens as well as upon Indians.

At Fort Wilburn the competition for commissions was lively as prominent men from all walks of life sought rank commensurate with their personally estimated worth. Fortunately, the Old Ranger, who had found it both politically and financially expedient to accompany the troops in his capacity of commander-in-chief of the Illinois militia, was able to place many of them on his staff. By June 22, Atkinson had organized and mustered into federal service three brigades, each with its spy battalion, and one independent spy company.

Meanwhile, news of Indian depredations on Bureau Creek several miles to the west prompted Atkinson to speed Alexander Posey's First Brigade and John Dement's battalion to Dixon's Ferry. Potawatomis and Winnebagos had reported that Black Hawk was in a triangle of land above Lake Koshkonong, and the General planned accordingly.[11] He proposed to move all three brigades to Dixon's and join Taylor and the regulars there. From Dixon's, Atkinson would move troops up both banks of the Rock. The General believed that he could overtake the Indians in seven or eight days. A week earlier, Atkinson had been confident that his militia force of three thousand, bolstered by four hundred regulars and a few hundred Indian auxiliaries, would be able to cope with the British Band. "I cannot fail to put an end in a short time, to the perplexed state of Indian hostilities in this quarter," he wrote Macomb June 15. However, now the General was more cautious. He reminded Macomb that his force consisted almost entirely of new levies and that "it is difficult to say with certainty what will be the result of my efforts."

Atkinson had to effect something quickly or suffer the stigma of losing his command. In Washington the administration was pressing for re-election and could not afford further embarrassing delays in punishing Black Hawk. A quartermaster officer had originally estimated the expense of the pay, subsistence, and transportation of the militia at $88,500, and Congress granted $150,000 for the entire operation. But, by the end of May, Secretary Cass felt it necessary to ask for $150,000 more. Old Hickory's patience was at an end. Early in June he directed John Robb, acting Secretary of War in Cass' absence, to reprimand Atkinson for inactivity and failure to report. Robb complied with a caustic letter which closed with the ominous obser-

[11] Atkinson to Macomb, June 15, 1832, Atkinson's Letter Book, BHWP.

vation, "Some one is to blame in this matter, but upon whom it is to fall, is at present unknown to the Department."[12]

When news finally reached Washington that Atkinson would have to suspend operations until he could organize the second levy of militia, Jackson decided that the time for half-way measures was past. He proposed to collect a formidable force at Chicago, place it under Major General Winfield Scott, and catch the British Band between Scott's force and that of Atkinson. The President gave Scott command of the joint operation, for which the orders were issued June 15. They provided that he should not suspend operations until he had "effectually subdued" the British Band. To carry out his mission the Secretary assigned the General, in addition to Atkinson's force, eight hundred regulars, the six ranger companies recently authorized, and any militia he might need.

Andrew Jackson was not alone in his criticism of Atkinson's conduct of the campaign. General Gaines complained of Atkinson's failure to report his movements, and a Congressman referred bitingly to the "sunshine soldiers." Addison Philleo, the fighting Galena editor, declared it was "an unpleasant task to have to censure the conduct of an individual in the decline of his life," but that Atkinson's "ill contrived movements" jeopardized ten thousand inhabitants of the area. The editor challenged his readers to prove their bravery by bringing in Indian scalps. "If one would show that his steel had been dyed with human blood, let him boast that it came from the heart of a Sac," the belligerent Philleo clarioned.

Galenians had their opportunity when Black Hawk and two hundred warriors attacked a fort on Apple River, about fourteen miles east of their town. Only twenty-five men defended the fort which the local settlers had constructed, but the women and children loaded rifles and cast balls. Repulsed in their initial assault the Indians took shelter in the cabins

12 John Robb to Atkinson, June 12, 1832, Letter Books of the Secretary of War, NA.

near the fort. For over twelve hours the Indians besieged the defenders, who were suffering from thirst when Black Hawk providentially gave up the siege and retreated. The war party took with it livestock and provisions, after inflicting only two casualties on the tough garrison.[13]

As the warriors retreated with their plunder, they left a trail which attracted pursuit, but they ambushed the whites who violated orders to pursue the war party. As Governor Reynolds indicated disarmingly, the men shared the common failing of the militia: "Their only misfortune was the want of discipline and organization." This time they extricated themselves from an embarrassing situation only through the aid of of a column rushed to their relief. Black Hawk, having already lost four warriors in the engagement, declined to wait for the Long Knives to bring overwhelming force against him. Although the Indians had failed to achieve any sensational success, their attack served to delay Atkinson's pursuit for two days. He had expected to march up Rock River without halting at Dixon's, but the harried General was now forced to revise his plans to cope with the emergency.

Atkinson, who had arrived at Dixon's the morning after the initial skirmish, had the problem of evaluating the two attacks. Did they mean that the British Band was moving toward the Mississippi or were they only the work of war parties? The main advance was delayed until Atkinson concluded that these were merely diversionary in intent.

[13] Wakefield, *History*, 33; Reynolds, *My Own Times*, 243; *Life of Black Hawk*, 148–49.

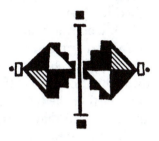

14. Death on the Wisconsin and the Bad Axe

AT NOON on June 28, General Atkinson moved out of Dixon's and up the left bank of the Rock with General Hugh Brady's First Division, consisting of James D. Henry's Third Brigade and the regulars. Joined the next day by seventy-five well-armed Potawatomi warriors, the General was confident once more that he had "an army in the field sufficient to rid the country of all hostility."

For the next two days the column trudged across the broad, rolling prairies, through coarse, high grass interspersed with a few flowers. Only an occasional tree or small grove broke the monotony of the sea of grass. The volunteers encountered nothing more dangerous than the green-headed prairie flies which made life miserable for the horses.

By July 1 the force had reached deserted Turtle village, which Gratiot had visited to parley with the Winnebagos, and camped a mile beyond on the open prairie near the Rock. The troops, who had as yet seen only friendly Indians, found indications that the British Band had been in the vicinity shortly before. That night Atkinson had the camp prepared for attack.

Although nervous sentries fired several times at shadows and strange sounds kept the camp in turmoil, the Sacs and Foxes failed to appear.

The troops had marched but two or three miles the next morning when they sighted an Indian, presumably hostile, on a high prairie beyond the Rock. A thrill of excitement ran through the column as the men viewed the lone warrior. A few miles farther the troops passed with quickened steps through an abandoned camp of the British Band. Even the most apathetic volunteer checked his priming when a scout hurried back with the report that a fresh Indian trail lay ahead, but no contacts were made that day.

On the morning of July 3 scouts rushed in with the electrifying report that they had found the main trail of the fugitives. Then, about a mile and a half below Lake Koshkonong—an expansion of Rock River about four miles wide and six to eight miles long—Atkinson halted his men and sent out more scouts. Although they did not locate the British Band, they did find a deserted encampment which the Indians had apparently occupied for a considerable time. Only a few ornaments, some settlers' scalps, and the bodies of five red men who had succumbed to wounds remained. From all appearances the British Band had moved farther up the lake by trails leading toward the head of Rock River. Atkinson decided to halt until he had further information.

The troops under Atkinson celebrated the holiday by futilely reconnoitering both sides of the lake. That evening, General Milton K. Alexander arrived with his tired and disorganized Second Brigade, after carrying out Atkinson's order to search the country toward Plum River and the Mississippi. He reported a comparable lack of success in coming to grips with the elusive savages.

The patrols explored both sides of Lake Koshkonong again the next day for signs of the phantom band. Scouts on the left bank brought in the only Indian sighted, an old, blind, half-starved Sac. When Atkinson threatened to kill him if he lied, the old man admitted that Black Hawk had passed up the left bank toward the head of Rock River. Although patrols on the right bank traveled about twelve miles, they failed to find even one Indian. The next evening, after a fruitless excursion through the swamps, Atkinson received several dispatches, including copies of Scott's orders to move west with a new army and John Robb's biting letter written at Jackson's direction. Two more days of clinging mire and bloodthirsty mosquitoes followed, as a supply crisis developed. For several days the troops had been going hungry, although the volunteers had started the pursuit with fifteen days' rations and sixty head of cattle, plus a few days' rations of bacon and flour in light wagons. Two of the brigades had wasted their supplies.[1] The situation was now so serious that the disgusted Atkinson was forced to call a halt to the pursuit. Supply trains were presumably on the way, but the need was urgent. The General reluctantly ordered Posey to Fort Hamilton, where he was to remain with his brigade until further orders. Atkinson expected to use part of this brigade to escort supplies and the remainder to guard the mining region and intercept Black Hawk should he head for the Mississippi. At the same time, Atkinson directed Alexander and James D. Henry to march their brigades to Fort Winnebago at the Portage to obtain twelve days' provisions and "return to these Head Quarters without delay."[2] The following day he ordered Dodge to Fort Winnebago for the same purpose. The General also discharged all the ration-consuming Winnebagos except White Crow and his son, whom he retained to guide the troops to the Portage.

On July 9 the volunteers marched away in search of provisions and the regulars moved to the mouth of the Scuppernong and began the construction of Fort Koshkonong. The formidable army which had left Dixon's June 28 had accom-

[1] Atkinson to Scott, July 9, 1832, AGOF, NA.
[2] Order No. 51, July 9, 1832, Atkinson's Order Book. BHWP.

plished exactly nothing. Its only victim in two weeks of campaigning had been the old, blind Sac whom Atkinson had interrogated. Although the General released him with promises of impunity, some of Posey's men murdered the harmless old warrior and took his scalp.

Convinced that the campaign was a failure, many of the volunteers, including Governor Reynolds, two Illinois Supreme Court Justices, and the Secretary of State departed for home. Private Abe Lincoln, his enlistment at an end, also headed for civilization. Years later, while ridiculing the efforts to present Lewis Cass as a military hero, Congressman Lincoln discounted his own, as well as Cass', pretensions to a niche in Valhalla. "If General Cass went in advance of me in picking whortleberries," commented Lincoln sarcastically, "I guess I surpassed him in charges upon the wild onions. If he saw any live fighting Indians, it was more than I did, but I had a good many bloody experiences with the mosquitoes; and although I never fainted from loss of blood, I can truly say I was often very hungry."[3]

As his army disintegrated, General Atkinson sent out patrols and wrote pitiful letters. To Winfield Scott, at Chicago watching his own force dissolve in the face of a cholera epidemic, the harassed commander at the mouth of the Scuppernong predicted that the campaign would probably extend into the winter season. To Macomb, Atkinson complained that so long as Black Hawk's people found it possible to "subsist on roots and fish taken from the swamps and lakes," he would probably never overtake them.[4]

A few weeks earlier the red men had begun to depend on bark and roots. The degree of dependence increased as the Indians left the vicinity of Lake Koshkonong, abounding in

---

[3] *Congressional Globe,* 30 Cong., 1 sess. (1847–48), Appendix, 1042.
[4] Atkinson to Scott, July 11, 1832; Atkinson to Macomb, July 13, 1832; both in AGOF, NA.

pike, bass, and catfish, and pushed into the swamps where game and fish were scarce. The debilitating effect of such a diet soon became apparent. Grieving women saw their papooses fail, and bitter, frustrated warriors stood by helpless as their aged parents faded away. The number who fell by the wayside mounted with each succeeding day. And Black Hawk's losses were not restricted to those dying of starvation. Scores of the Winnebagos, Kickapoos, and Potawatomis took the opportunity to desert the band. The position of the Sacs and Foxes was desperate. Now too far from the white settlements to make raiding for supplies practical, Black Hawk also feared encirclement—if his people did not starve first! Although unaware that the White Beaver's army was temporarily immobilized, the old warrior decided to attempt to break through.[5] Summoning their strength for a final effort, the remnant of the band headed west for the Wisconsin, which they proposed to descend to the Mississippi. Once across this great river they hoped to merge with Keokuk's band or evade pursuit on the great plains. But fate was against them; couriers to Atkinson from Dodge and Henry happened on their trail.

The evening of July 11, as Black Hawk pondered his predicament, Dodge and his miners arrived at Fort Winnebago. The following morning the Colonel ordered the bakers at the fort to prepare bread for his grumbling men. The miners had had rough riding to reach the fort, and they threatened to retire from the campaign if Dodge insisted upon returning by the same route. At this critical point, John Kinzie, son of the Chicago pioneer and a former employee of the American Fur Company, came to the Colonel's assistance. Currently the Winnebago subagent at the Portage, he produced a party of Winnebagos who claimed to know the location of the fugitive band. He also introduced to Dodge an interpreter, Pierre Pacquette, the son of a French trader and a Winnebago woman.

[5] *Life of Black Hawk.*

Through the half-blood the Winnebagos told the Colonel that Black Hawk was camped at the rapids of the Rock, near the site of present-day Hustisford, Wisconsin.[6]

That evening Alexander and Henry marched in with their weary brigades and the leaders conferred on their next move. Atkinson's orders had explicitly directed Dodge, Posey, and Alexander to return without delay, although he had not specified a route. Aware that his unruly troopers would probably desert him if he returned the way he had come and intrigued by the reports of the Winnebagos on the location of the British Band, Dodge urged that Henry and Alexander join him in a march to the rapids. Alexander cautiously declined to risk Atkinson's wrath, but Henry agreed to co-operate with the forceful colonel. Early on the morning of July 15, Alexander marched for Atkinson's headquarters and Henry and Dodge moved east toward the reported location of the British Band.[7]

The combined force leaving Fort Winnebago behind Pacquette and the Winnebagos did not exceed 600 men. Although Dodge had authority to command only the 150 remaining in his squadron, Henry deferred to his general recommendations. As Atkinson's respectful treatment of him indicated, the Colonel was a man of renown and experience on the frontier. Plainly indicative of the relation between Dodge and Henry were their proposed ranks in the newly organized battalion of United States Rangers. While at Fort Winnebago, Dodge accepted a commission as major to command the new unit, whereas the younger and less experienced Henry subsequently was offered a commission as captain to serve under him.[8]

Guided by Pacquette and seven or eight Winnebagos, Dodge

6 Dodge to Atkinson, July 14, 1832, BHWP; Dodge to John H. Kinzie, January 5, 1833, Stock Transcripts.

7 There has been considerable controversy about whether Henry or Dodge deserves the credit for the decision to return by way of the rapids. Generally speaking, the Illinois writers have favored Henry, the Wisconsin writers, Dodge.

8 Dodge to Cass, July 12, 1832, Secretary of War, Letters Received, NA; Scott to Henry, August 10, 1832, BHWP.

and Henry approached the rapids July 18. Contrary to their expectations, the only Indians they found there were a few Winnebagos occupying a small village in the midst of a heavy growth of timber. Dodge anxiously interrogated the Indians, who reported that the British Band was camped on a lake not more than twenty miles north. After consulting with the other officers, Dodge and Henry decided to notify Atkinson of their situation and prepared to march north the next day. The two adjutants from their commands volunteered to carry the message. That same afternoon, guided by a Winnebago, they set out for Atkinson's headquarters. In less than twelve miles they crossed a fresh trail heading southwest.[9]

Judging from the signs that only the British Band could have made the trail, the excited adjutants wanted to continue on to Fort Koshkonong, but the frightened Winnebago guide balked. Night was approaching, and the messengers, unable to proceed without their guide, turned back and all three rode to the camp they had left that afternoon. Although welcomed back by a volley from trigger-happy sentries, they escaped injury and communicated their exhilarating discovery to their delighted commanders. Dodge and Henry agreed that the trail must be that of the main band of hostiles and prepared to take up the pursuit at daylight.

The next morning the troops moved out briskly, leaving behind them the baggage wagons, sutler's stores, and anything else which they could dispense with. A few rugged individuals even left their blankets. The pursuit led the enthused Americans through swamps and thickets, but there were no complaints, although the men were on occasion up to their armpits in mud and water. After two months of frustrating marching and countermarching the enemy appeared within reach. The sight of oaks from which the famished Indians had peeled the bark and holes from which they had grubbed roots cheered

9 Dodge to Atkinson, July 18, July 19, 1832, BHWP; Wakefield, *History*, 62–63; Henry to Atkinson, July 19, 1832, BHWP.

the pursuers. Even a severe thunderstorm which came up before dark did not dampen their spirits. Barely able to light fires to warm their chilled bones and cook their meager suppers, the weary frontiersmen wrapped themselves in their blankets on the damp ground and tried to get a few hours' rest before resuming the chase.

After a hasty breakfast the next morning, Dodge and Henry were on the trail. That day scouts captured a Winnebago who stated that Black Hawk's band was but a short distance ahead. The commanders threw their troops into battle formation and advanced with the expectation of overtaking the fugitives by sundown. When they reached the east end of Lake Monona, the third of a string of four beautiful lakes, the light began to fail. The commanders halted their troops to consult with their guides. Pacquette advised against a night passage between Lake Monona and Lake Mendota. The underbrush was very dense, and Dodge and Henry, not caring to risk an ambush, called off the pursuit for the night.

Up at daylight July 21, the men gulped a little breakfast, rounded up their mounts, and were soon on their way. About ten o'clock in the morning scouts killed an Indian sitting on the grave of his wife, who had died of hunger and exhaustion. Dr. Philleo, the fearless physician and editor, was among those who fired at the grief-stricken warrior and took his scalp. This grim trophy and another like it, Philleo sent to Galena. The *Cincinnati Chronicle* scathingly commented, "We trust that the Galenian is the only paper in the Union that could boast of such a feat, and that its editor is the only one of the fraternity capable of perpetrating so disgusting and cruel an act."[10]

As Philleo and his comrades moved rapidly over the site of

10 The account of the pursuit and battle are drawn from the following sources: Dodge to Atkinson, July 22, 1832, AGOF, NA; Henry to Atkinson, July 23, 1832, in *Sangamo Journal* (Springfield, Illinois), August 3, 1832; Daniel M. Parkinson, "Pioneer Life in Wisconsin," in *Wis. Colls.*, II, 355–57; Wakefield, *History*, 64.

present-day Madison, Wisconsin, at least one of them was struck with the magnificent beauty of the Four Lakes and lamented that they were in an area "not fit for any civilized people to inhabit." However, the rate of pursuit left little time for the contemplation of the beauties of nature. The horses of the soldiers began to show the effect of the rapid pace, and a few began to give out. When this occurred the rider would quickly dismount, unsaddle, and continue on foot. Skirmishers made an increasing number of contacts with the rear guard of the British Band and in one exchange killed two warriors. In the afternoon a chilling rain began to fall and continued until dark. As the whites pressed upon them, the desperate Indians made a series of feints designed to draw off the attackers and delay pursuit. These made it necessary for Dodge and Henry to form battle lines several times, but the eager troops maintained sufficient speed to gain on the half-starved red men. The frequency with which the Americans encountered mats, kettles, and blankets the Indians had strewed along the muddy trail indicated the plight of the retreating redskins and stimulated the frontiersmen.

Shortly before sunset the white column came within sight of the Wisconsin. At this moment scouts who had pursued three Indians to within a mile of the river galloped back with a band of warriors at their heels. Dodge, who, with Major Ewing's scouts, led the column, dismounted his men to receive the charge. The screaming warriors raced to within thirty yards of the flaming guns and then retreated, leaving one dead Indian. By this time, Henry had brought up the remainder of his men, and the battle was on.

The Americans occupied a small plain facing the Wisconsin River bottom. Black Hawk and his warriors infested the hills on their left and from these heights began to pour a hot fire into the white ranks. Leaving their horses behind, the frontiersmen drove the Indians from the hills and down into the high grass and underbrush of the river bottom. It was now about

7:00 P.M., and the commanders debated whether to push their advantage or postpone operations until morning. Concluding that they could not reach the Indian positions before dark, and the idea of a night attack appealing to no one, Dodge and Henry broke off action. They well knew that the nearly forty-mile forced march had exhausted their men and that the rain and mud of the last six hours had fouled some of their flint-locks. About 8:00 P.M. the tired but cheerful troops went into camp, where the battle had opened. They had killed about seventy of Black Hawk's warriors and had lost only one man in return, although eight more whites carried wounds.

In the morning, Dodge and Henry formed their men and led them warily across the marshy bottom toward the river. Black Hawk, however, had pulled out. During the evening and night the Indians had worked feverishly, stripping lengths of elm bark and tying their ends together to make frail canoes. Others improvised rafts from mats and skins. By means of these makeshift contrivances the warriors transferred their dependents to the north bank of the shallow but wide stream and then swam it with their ponies. A few Sacs and Foxes, unable to go farther under their own power, drifted down the Wisconsin in their fragile craft.

Dodge and Henry had dealt the British Band a hard blow, but it was still intact and retreating. Black Hawk could well claim a tactical victory. Although burdened with numerous women, children, and old people, he had effected a river crossing in the face of a superior force. Had the whites crossed the Wisconsin the morning after the battle they would have certainly overtaken the fugitives. But Dodge and Henry, grown cautious, considered the one day's rations at hand and the shortage of tools to make rafts and decided against it. This decision spared the Indians for another twelve painful days.

Instead of marching directly to a supply depot for the needed provisions to continue the pursuit, the jubilant frontiersmen strolled back to their camp and passed the day drying their clothing and equipment and refighting the battle. Some inquisitive souls tired of the mutual eulogizing and ventured from the camp to search for signs of the British Band. Returning late in the evening with reports of smoke across the Wisconsin, they cut short the festivities. A few slept fitfully that night, but many, too apprehensive to relax, huddled around the fires reliving the experiences of the campaign.

About an hour and a half before dawn a loud shrill voice from a nearby hill brought them scrambling to their feet. As they tumbled from their blankets and grasped their weapons, the frontiersmen realized that the speaker was an Indian. As the whites braced themselves for the Indian onslaught, the strident voice suddenly ceased. Although the volunteers did not relax until dawn, no attack materialized. A reconnaissance at daylight in the direction from which the voice had come disclosed that the orator had either been alone or one of a small party. Weeks later the frontiersmen learned the occasion for the frightening experience they had undergone.[11]

Neapope, Black Hawk's principal lieutenant, had returned to try to arrange surrender terms. Speaking in Winnebago he had described the pitiful condition of the women and children of the British Band and proposed that the Long Knives permit the band to retire to the west side of the Mississippi, where they would remain in peace. Unfortunately, Pacquette and the Winnebagos had left Dodge and Henry following the battle the day before. As earlier with Stillman, the whites failed to comprehend an Indian surrender offer. The Great Spirit seemed determined that the tragedy should be played out to the bitter end.

The morning after Neapope's disturbing interlude, Dodge and Henry marched about twenty miles south to the fort at the Blue Mounds, islands in a sea of prairie sixty-five miles east of Prairie du Chien. The following evening, Atkinson

11 Wakefield, *History*, 70; Reynolds, *My Own Times*, 262; Parkinson, "Pioneer Life," 359. Parkinson describes the incident as taking place the night after the battle.

arrived with the regulars and part of General Alexander's brigade, after a hard march from Lake Koshkonong. His force was "broken down with fatigue and privation," but he found some consolation in the belief that his prey was also "much crippled, disheartened and suffering for subsistence."

At least one of Atkinson's men was still full of fire. An aide to the General, William Clark's son Lewis, had conceived a plan by which he might bypass General Scott's ban on scalping. The valiant young officer figured that if he killed a "Red Rascal," before the Indian died he would "have his head off." Then, having his "noodle" and free of any charges of mutilation, he could take the Indian's scalp "with impunity."[12]

The morning after he arrived at Blue Mounds the ingenious young officer marched from the fort with the other regulars and Henry and Alexander's brigades. Within twenty-four hours they arrived at Helena, where the Quartermaster General was preparing for the crossing. While the troops were hastily fabricating rafts from the abandoned cabins, Atkinson planned his pursuit. To ensure the fastest pace possible the General trimmed his force to one thousand three hundred picked men carrying eight days' rations. Although he could strip his army of all physical encumbrances, there was little that Atkinson could do to lift its morale. The men had no stomach for the task that lay before them. Black Hawk would have at least a five-day lead, and the country through which he was now fleeing was totally unknown to the Americans.

Not until noon on July 28 did the anxious Atkinson have his column across the river and searching for the retreating Indians. After proceeding three or four miles, leading elements discovered the trail bearing west. Cheered by the ease with which they had found it, the men ceased their murmuring and strode on with a will. After marching about fourteen miles they encamped for the night where the Indians had turned up the Pine River valley.

12 Lewis Clark to William Clark, July 25, 1832, OAGDF, NA.

The nature of the terrain over which the troops pursued the Indians soon changed. Heretofore, the chase had been over rolling prairies or through the marshes and swamps bordering Rock River. Now the volunteers and regulars encountered extremely hilly ground and an occasional marshy stream running across their course. Although covered with dense forests and thick underbrush, the hills bore but little grass, and the evening of July 29 the horses were tied up without having eaten. The regular infantry, plodding along behind the mounted volunteers for the past three and a half months, now came into their own. Over the rugged terrain the foot sloggers made better time than the mounted men. The trail they followed now ran northwest but did not improve in character. Atkinson finally found it necessary to abandon the light wagon carrying the medical stores. Indians native to the rugged country said their only visitors for years had been their fellow Winnebago tribesmen who had retreated east after precipitating the Winnebago War of 1827. This the frontiersmen had no difficulty believing. After two days on the trail the mounted men found it necessary to cut small saplings to feed their horses. The troops themselves were not suffering from hunger, as they still had beef cattle driven along with them from Helena.

The Indians were in more serious straits. Although aware that they were being pursued and desperately in need of their mounts, the red men were forced to resort to horse meat. On July 30 the troops began to encounter additional evidence of the wretched condition of the fugitives. Indian bodies marked by wounds began to appear along the trail. Other corpses showed no signs of bullet or knife wounds, and their condition indicated death by starvation. More and more traps, kettles, blankets, and mats littered the trail, revealing that the retreat was rapidly turning into a rout.[13] The absence of any delaying action on the part of the warriors, although the terrain was

---

13 Johnston to Captain Loomis, August 1, 1832, BHWP; Wakefield, *History*, 77–79; Johnston's Journal, July 29, 1832; Smith, "Indian Campaign of 1832," 163.

Black Hawk's Route, 1832

WISCONSIN

Bad Axe R.

The Dells
Ft. Winnebago

Wisconsin Heights

Helena
Ft. Koshkonong

Prairie du Chien

Pecatonica
Turtle Village

Galena
Apple River Fort

Stillman's Run

Indian Creek

Ottawa

Chicago

LAKE MICHIGAN

IOWA

Prophet's Village
Dixon's Ferry
Ft. Wilbourn

Illinois River

Yellow Banks

ILLINOIS

Beardstown

●	Town
■	Fort
▲	Battle or Skirmish
⌐	Black Hawk's Route
░	Route uncertain

MISSOURI

Missouri River

St. Louis

well suited to it, manifested the loss of morale. By the evening of July 31 the troops were only about twenty miles behind the British Band.

Guided by several of the Prophet's Winnebago relatives from the Mississippi, Black Hawk and not more than five hundred of the original British Band arrived at the great river the morning of August 1, at a point just below where the Bad Axe emptied into the Mississippi about forty miles above Prairie du Chien. The hundreds of others who had constituted the band in May had either starved, deserted, or lost their scalps. The desperate survivors were disappointed to find no canoes on the banks of the river. Black Hawk called a council and advised going up the Mississippi and secreting themselves among the Winnebagos. He found practically no support for his suggestion. The suffering they had undergone the past weeks had disillusioned the Sacs and Foxes and their allies. Most of the band disregarded Black Hawk's advice and began making preparations for crossing the river. For several hours they worked feverishly, improvising rafts and canoes. By swimming and paddling their crude craft a few of the strongest had reached the sanctuary of the west bank when the steamboat *Warrior* appeared, to the great consternation and dismay of the Indians.[14]

Loaded with a detachment of troops and an artillery piece, the boat turned toward the shore and anchored.[15] Aware of the futility of resistance, the Indians raised white flags and hailed the whites with surrender offers. However, the interpreter on the *Warrior* reported them to be Winnebagos requesting that the whites land. Naturally suspicious of their actions in view

[14] Prisoner Testimony, taken August 20, 1832, Black Hawk War Miscellaneous Papers, NA.

[15] The account of the skirmish is based on a letter from Captain John Throckmorton to his brother, August 3, 1832, in *The New York Mercury*, August 29, 1832; Lieutenant James W. Kingsbury to Major Hook, August 8, 1832, Quartermaster Historical File, NA; Lieutenant Reuben Holmes to Atkinson, August 5, 1832, BHWP; *Life of Black Hawk*, 157–58.

of the information he had received, Lieutenant James W. Kingsbury, the boat's commander, refused and demanded that the Indians send two men aboard. Now it was the turn of the Sacs and Foxes to misunderstand, and they failed to comply. To the jittery men on the *Warrior* the Indians appeared to be priming their guns and seeking cover. Assured by an Indian woman aboard that the Indians were Sacs and convinced that they were playing for time, the Lieutenant gave the order to open fire. The storm of lead blasted a number of the dumfounded redskins, but the survivors took shelter and returned the fire. For about two hours the exchange continued, but the Indians suffered few casualties after the first surprise volley and the whites had but one man wounded. As the steamboat exhausted its fuel, Kingsbury had to break off the engagement and drop down to Prairie du Chien for more wood.

The twenty-three Indians killed in the engagement were a serious loss to the British Band, but the delay in crossing the river was a disaster. During the hours of daylight which the battle had consumed, many of the band could have crossed, and the remainder would have been ready for the attempt at dawn. After the *Warrior* left, Black Hawk reiterated his plea that they turn north instead of attempting the crossing. Only four lodges, including the Prophet's, followed the discredited leader out of camp that night. A few more Indians managed to reach the west bank under cover of darkness, but most of the band chose to wait until dawn for the crossing. The enterprise of a few whites had been their undoing.

The morning after the battle of Wisconsin Heights, Henry Dodge had advised the commanding officer of Fort Crawford, Captain Loomis, to place artillery in position to command the mouth of the Wisconsin, to prevent the escape of the Indians down the river. The resourceful captain went further than Dodge had suggested. He stationed the detachments on the river and also ordered the Winnebagos above Fort Crawford down to Prairie du Chien. By thus removing them from any possibility of aiding Black Hawk and by destroying or bringing in all their canoes, he succeeded in impeding the British Band's passage of the Mississippi. As an additional precaution he kept the steamboat *Enterprise,* armed with a cannon, running up and down the river above Prairie du Chien. In all this the industrious Captain had the co-operation of General Street, the Indian agent at the Prairie.

Loomis' and Street's enterprise brought results even before the *Warrior* episode. The night of July 28 the first flimsy canoes, loaded with starved and tattered members of the British Band, attempted to escape from the Wisconsin into the Mississippi. From a flatboat stationed at the mouth of the Wisconsin, troops fired on the fugitives and claimed the destruction of three or four canoes, but the attempts continued. Street assigned Menominee and Winnebago warriors to aid the troops on the Wisconsin, and they also had good hunting. By daylight and torchlight they ferreted out the miserable beings seeking safety across the Mississippi. In the period from July 29 to August 2 the Indian auxiliaries took nine scalps and thirty-four prisoners, mostly women and children. The pitifully emaciated condition of the captives moved even the fierce Winnebagos to entreat Street to clothe and feed them. Although he despaired of being able to save some of the children, the agent drew generously from government stores to aid the pathetic prisoners.[16]

Meanwhile, Captain Loomis had decided to employ Chief Wabashaw's band of Sioux against the Sacs and Foxes. To contact the Sioux he sent a half-blood interpreter aboard the *Warrior,* which carried a complement of twenty-one regulars and orders to engage any hostile Indians it might intercept. The steamboat encountered no hostiles on the trip upstream. Wabashaw, a short, elderly, sinister-looking chief with a black

[16] Lieutenant Joseph Ritner to Captain Loomis, July 29, 1832, BHWP; Atkinson to Scott, August 5, 1832, AGOF, NA; Street to William Clark, August 1, 1832, Photostat WHS; Captain Loomis to ———, August 2, 1832, in *Sangamo Journal,* August 18, 1832.

patch covering a mutilated eye, welcomed the Americans and Loomis' call to arms. One hundred and fifty warriors immediately painted and armed themselves to descend the river and patrol its banks. On the *Warrior's* return trip it came upon the Sacs and Foxes as they prepared to cross the Mississippi. Meanwhile, Atkinson was drawing near.

The frequency with which the Americans encountered Indian bodies and possessions strewn along the trail spurred them on. That evening they passed the body of a chief whose loyal friends and relatives had risked their lives to bury him with some little ceremony. Painted and decorated, he lay in a crypt of logs covered by leafy branches. A little farther on scouts found a disabled warrior abandoned to his fate by his more realistic fellows. He informed the white men that the Indians would reach the Mississippi that day and cross the next morning.

About 8:00 P.M., Atkinson halted the column and the exhausted men went into camp. To obtain water they had to lower their tired and aching bodies down a precipice and clamber painfully back with full canteens. The men were just preparing to eat when Atkinson's order to be ready to march at 2:00 A.M. jolted them. Henry and Alexander's Illinois volunteers heard it only after they had turned their horses out to graze. With the prospect of only a few hours' rest and then perhaps an arrow or a musket ball in their breast, the men hurried their meager supper and crawled into their blankets. By 10:00 P.M. only the sentries in the camp were stirring.

Two hours later the strident notes of a bugle roused the men. Groping around in the darkness, they tried to secure their mounts and get a little breakfast before moving out. The regulars and Dodge's men, who had received Atkinson's order the previous evening before loosing their horses, left camp while many of the volunteers were still rounding up their mounts. After riding about three miles, Dodge's scouts in the van contacted a small party of Indians. They dispatched eight of the warriors, and the others retreated toward the river and to the right. Mistaking the rear guard for the main body, Atkinson made what was almost a grave error by halting and forming for battle. Dodge occupied a position on the left of the regulars, who were drawn up in extended order. When Posey came up, Atkinson placed him on the right of the regulars. When Alexander came into line he formed on Posey's right.[17]

As these troops advanced slowly, Henry's brigade, the last to leave camp, came up fortuitously some distance to the left of Dodge's men and on the trail leading to the main Indian force. These troops and a few of Dodge's scouts, sent by Atkinson to reconnoiter on the left when he failed to encounter any more Indians in front of him, opened the battle. The feebly resisting Sacs and Foxes retreated across several sluices and through the fallen timber, underbrush, and high brush covering the river bottom. The regulars, the rest of Dodge's men, and a detachment of Posey's brigade hurried over to assist Henry, but only two companies of Alexander's men got in the battle. Together the troops drove the dispirited and outnumbered Indians from the river bottom and onto several small willow bars.

The warriors were able to put up only a token resistance, and after the initial exchange the "battle" was little more than a massacre. The troops did not discriminate in the confusion and made the most of this opportunity to retaliate against the murdering redskins. Firing at anything that moved, they slew many women and children as they cowered in the underbrush, hid behind logs, burrowed in the sand, or attempted to escape by swimming. Retreating before the whites, a few Sacs and Foxes from the willow bars crossed to two larger islands nearby

---

[17] The account of the battle is based on the following: Atkinson to Scott, August 5, August 9, 1832, AGOF, NA; Alexander to Atkinson, August 4, 1832, BHWP; Taylor to Atkinson, August 5, 1832, BHWP; *Life of Black Hawk*, 159–60; Wakefield, *History*, 84–85.

and climbed trees. At this point, the *Warrior,* which had been delayed by a heavy fog, reappeared.

Atkinson placed the regulars and a company or two of the volunteers on the boat and ordered them to clean out the islands. After the *Warrior* had raked them with its cannon, the troops routed the remaining Indians from the trees and drove them into the river, where they drowned or were shot by the troops lining the banks. More than eight hours after Dodge's men opened the engagement, the last shot was fired. The losses of the Indians could only be estimated at 150, as most of them had died in the water and the bodies were not recovered. The whites took thirty-nine prisoners, all women and children. Atkinson lost eleven men, and sixteen were wounded, of whom three subsequently died.

While the surgeons dressed the wounds of the soldiers and the Indian survivors, Atkinson decided against further pursuit. The volunteers' horses were exhausted, and the infantry was without shoes. It seemed unnecessarily cruel to the General to shed more blood until he discovered if the remnants of the band would surrender. Accordingly, he loaded his prisoners and wounded aboard the *Warrior* and sent them down to Prairie du Chien, while the troops went into camp at the scene of the battle. The steamboat, which descended the Mississippi in company with numerous Indian corpses, horses, and equipment, returned the next morning. That day, Wabashaw and his 150 Sioux reported to Atkinson.

From prisoner interrogation, Atkinson had learned that Black Hawk had no more than fifty followers, including women and children, when he left the main band and moved north. The approximately one hundred who had escaped across the Mississippi, the General expected to seek safety in Keokuk's band. Soon after the battle, Atkinson sent a message for Keokuk to deliver to these fugitives. If the hostile Indians would surrender it was promised that all but a few hostages would be released. Unfortunately, the message did not reach the survivors before Wabashaw and his Sioux were among them with tomahawk and scalping knife. Atkinson's concern for the Sacs and Foxes had not led him to recall Wabashaw's bloodthirsty warriors, whom he had deputized to search for the members of the British Band. When the Sioux overtook the starving and practically defenseless fugitives, they spared only twenty-two of the women and children. Sixty-eight Sac and Fox scalps bore mute testimony to the massacre the Sioux perpetrated.[18]

The troops remained on the battleground at the mouth of the Bad Axe for a day and a half. Then the *Warrior* transported the regulars down to Fort Crawford and the volunteers rode overland for the same destination. When the frontiersmen reached Prairie du Chien, one of the last shocking scenes of the Black Hawk War met their eyes. Menominee women had obtained the scalps of women of Black Hawk's band and were engaged in a scalp dance of their own.[19]

Volunteer interest in the scalp dance dissipated rapidly when they heard Atkinson's good news for them. The following morning most of them would march for Dixon's to be discharged. Atkinson had learned from General Scott, who had arrived in Galena on August 3, that he would depend entirely on the rangers and the infantry for any further operations. The morning after the happy volunteers marched for home to begin the legend of the Black Hawk War, General Scott arrived at Prairie du Chien. Six harrowing weeks after leaving New York to take command of the operations against Black Hawk, Scott was finally ready to take over. Although he had not seen a hostile Indian in that time, the General had met in the cholera a more formidable foe than the aging Black Hawk and his tattered legion.

[18] Atkinson to Scott, August 5, 1832, AGOF, NA; Scott to Cass, August 16, 1832, Secretary of War, Letters Received, NA; Street to Scott, August 22, 1832, AGOF, NA.
[19] Wakefield, *History*, 91.

15. The Power to Dictate

W ITH THE BRITISH BAND destroyed as a fighting force, Scott turned his attention to concluding
the campaign by capturing the principal Indian
leaders and negotiating treaties with the tribes involved. Henry
Atkinson was pleased to receive orders from Scott to return to
Jefferson Barracks and his family. He was fortunate to be returning home victorious, as his conduct of the campaign was
open to criticism. Except for the pursuit from the Wisconsin
to the Mississippi, the General had consistently lagged behind
with the regulars when he should have been operating aggres-
sively with the more mobile mounted part of his command.
As he descended the Mississippi, columns of Illinois militia,
tired but happy, wended their way toward Dixon's Ferry and
discharge. They also had little for which to congratulate themselves. Their lack of discipline and training had unnecessarily
protracted the campaign.

Before surrendering his command to Scott, Atkinson had
posted rewards for the capture of the British Band leaders,
and parties of Sioux, Menominees, and Winnebagos scoured
the countryside, bringing in scalps and prisoners. The same
day that Scott reached Fort Crawford, friendly Indians brought

in the two Winnebagos, both badly wounded, who had guided Black Hawk to the Mississippi. Imprisoning these warriors, Scott turned to negotiating with their tribe on the issue of the crimes of these Indians and other Winnebagos participating actively as members of the British Band. As Rock Island was more centrally located to receive the ranger companies and troops due from Chicago, the General moved down to Fort Armstrong to conduct negotiations and to be prepared to strike in any direction.

Scott's original orders had included the responsibility for concluding a peace, with specific instructions on the terms to be imposed. All hostile Indians were to remove west of the Mississippi. If a major part of a tribe had fought against the Americans, the General was to demand all that tribe's land east of the Mississippi. If less than a majority of the tribe had taken up arms, he was to demand a proportion of its land equal to the proportion of the tribe which was hostile.[1] If the principal leaders of the Sacs and Foxes were involved, Scott was to secure the cession of a forty to one-hundred-mile-wide strip of their land along the west bank of the Mississippi. In the opinion of the shortsighted Secretary of War, regardless of the degree of Indian guilt, Scott should try to obtain the cession of all Sac and Fox land fronting the river, thus blockading them from contact with the whites.

Although originally Scott alone held the commission to conduct peace negotiations, Secretary Cass later delegated Governor Reynolds as co-commissioner. The Old Ranger, always willing to supplement his salary from the state, accepted the appointment with alacrity. However, Scott was to be the directing force in the treaty making.

Having decided to deal with the Winnebagos first, the General summoned them to meet him by September 10 in council at Fort Armstrong. Meanwhile, troops from Chicago and Detroit began to straggle in, and on August 26 cholera ap-

[1] Cass to Scott, June 15, 1832, Letter Books of the Secretary of War, NA.

peared among rangers who had visited Fort Dearborn contrary to Scott's orders. The disease ran its dreadful course quickly and, after striking down four officers and over fifty men, subsided. Scott was then able to turn to the serious business of peace negotiations.

The General had asked one young officer, as a Christian, to examine and comment on the treaty he proposed to present to the Winnebagos. Scott observed that he did not wish to blush later for anything he might then do. Unfortunately, the General was not so careful about insuring the presence of all Winnebagos concerned. None of the tribesmen residing on Fox River or Lake Winnebago were consulted, although their lands were forfeited by the treaty. In addition, the Winnebagos agreed to surrender nine specified warriors for crimes committed during the outbreak.

Neapope was the first of the principal conspirators delivered to Scott. Before the cholera erupted at Rock Island, Keokuk produced him and several other survivors of the British Band.[2] Black Hawk and the Prophet were more elusive. Nothing had been heard of them since their party left the main band after the *Warrior's* attack on the evening of August 1. Various reports had Black Hawk dead, heading toward Milwaukee, fleeing up the Mississippi toward the Chippewas, and escaping toward Canada.[3] None of these reports was true. Black Hawk learned of the fate of the British Band from a warrior who escaped the carnage, and the old Sac, the Prophet, and their small party of faithful followers pushed northeast into Winnebago territory.[4] Inspired by the possibility of earning the reward of $100 in cash and twenty ponies and the hope of redeeming their nation in the eyes of the Long Knives, a party of Winnebagos trailed Black Hawk and his party to a point

[2] Pilcher to Clark, August 23, 1832, Photostat WHS.
[3] A. S. Johnston to Samuel C. Stambaugh, August 7, 1832; Samuel C. Stambaugh to George Boyd, August 28, 1832; Scott to Samuel C. Stambaugh, August 17, 1832; all in Photostat WHS.
[4] *Life of Black Hawk*, 160.

near the Wisconsin Dells.[5] After keeping the fugitives under observation for two days, on the morning of the third day the Winnebagos surprised them as they slept. Black Hawk and his people surrendered without striking a blow.[6]

One-Eyed Decorah and Chaetar, the Winnebagos who led the captors, delivered their splendidly attired prisoners to General Street at his agency. The subdued Sac leader denied that he had provoked the war and even maintained earnestly that he had tried to stop it once begun but had been overruled by a faction of chiefs and braves in the British Band.

Although Black Hawk petitioned humbly to be released to join Keokuk, the agent turned him, his two sons, and the Prophet and his son over to Colonel Zachary Taylor at Fort Crawford. Taylor entrusted the Indians to a guard under Lieutenant Jefferson Davis, his future son-in-law, and dispatched them by steamboat to Jefferson Barracks.

The trip down the river was uneventful. A gallant young Mississippian who had just returned from leave in the South, Lieutenant Davis treated the Indians with consideration. "He is a good and brave young chief, with whose conduct I was much pleased," observed Black Hawk. The boat did not stop at Rock Island for fear of the cholera, and a rather ludicrous scene resulted. When Winfield Scott came out in a small boat to see the men who had caused him so much trouble, the Captain stoutly refused to let him come aboard. Leaving Fuss and Feathers fuming, the boat continued downstream.

With Black Hawk, the Prophet, and Neapope behind bars, Scott and Reynolds were able to turn to negotiations with the Sacs and Foxes. Scott, resplendent in full uniform, delivered

[5] Wakefield, *History*, 97.

[6] There is much conflicting testimony concerning the circumstances of the capture of the fugitives. After he was released the next summer, Black Hawk attempted to recover from the Winnebagos the forty horses, kettles, and other equipment they had taken from his party at the time of the capture. This would appear to substantiate the story that Black Hawk and the Prophet had a small party of followers with them. See Street to Elbert Herring, August 1, 1833, Photostat WHS.

the demands of the United States at the opening session September 19. After some slight modifications desired by the Indians, the treaty was acceptable to both parties. Scott and Reynolds accurately observed, "The power to dictate was very much in our own hands."[7]

Although the commissioners described the treaty as being formulated on the "blended grounds of conquest and contract," it savored more of the former. The preface of the treaty spoke of "a formidable band" under "certain lawless and desperate leaders" which, "in violation of treaties, commenced an unprovoked war upon unsuspecting and defenseless citizens of the United States, sparing neither age nor sex." From the Sacs and Foxes, "partly as an indemnity" and "partly to secure the future safety and tranquility of the invaded frontier," the United States extracted an extremely valuable cession.

The Indians ceded a strip of land fifty miles wide running almost the length of the Mississippi frontage of the present state of Iowa. The commissioners estimated that this tract, in which the Sacs and Foxes retained a small reservation, contained six million acres of land. And they gleefully predicted that within a period of thirty years, during which time the United States would have paid the tribesmen $660,000 for the cession, it would be worth more than $7,000,000. To ensure that this transaction would not occasion the trouble of that of 1804, Scott and Reynolds carefully stipulated that the Indians were to remove before June 1, 1833, and never again "reside, plant, fish, or hunt, on any portion of the ceded land."

Some articles of the treaty found favor with the Indians by providing that the United States furnish the tribes an additional blacksmith and gunsmith's shop and supply annually quantities of tobacco and salt. As Gaines had done the previous year, Scott and Reynolds consented to deliver provisions to help the red men through the winter. In addition, the com-

[7] Scott and Reynolds to Cass, September 22, 1832, Stock Transcripts.

missioners agreed to pay the firm of Farnham and Davenport $40,000 the Sacs and Foxes owed these traders.

As acting agent for the tribes, Joshua Pilcher objected to this payment. However, he had already been replaced by Marmaduke Davenport, who was on his way to Rock Island to assume his duties. And, as George Davenport slyly observed, the commissioners were quartered at his house and the Indians had employed him to handle the negotiations between them and the United States. For his interference, Pilcher was pungently described by the semiliterate Davenport as "an evill Genious equel to the Cholra if he had the same pour to scourge mankind."

During the negotiation of the treaty, Keokuk was at his old post of spokesman for the Sacs and Foxes. The commissioners were, of course, pleased to work with him. To increase his influence among the tribes they proclaimed him civil chief, a hereditary rank entirely out of their giving. Hitherto only a war chief, although, of course, a most influential one, Keokuk accepted the dubious title. In fulfilling his greatest ambition he met no opposition from his old rival Black Hawk. The latter was in no position to protest.

In reporting the negotiations to Secretary Cass the commissioners recommended that the prisoners at Jefferson Barracks be held for at least ten years. A few weeks later, Scott qualified this with the advice that all but Black Hawk, the Prophet, and their sons be released. These he regarded as "turbulent spirits" considering themselves "British Indians" and, if released, likely to cause trouble. Moreover, they should be removed to Fort Monroe, on Chesapeake Bay, where there would be no necessity of keeping the Indians under such close surveillance as was obligatory at Jefferson Barracks. The Secretary of War, not a harsh man, agreed and ordered Atkinson to release the less important hostages to Keokuk's custody.

The following March the Watchful Fox, resplendent in a

brightly colored calico shirt and a green blanket, a figured handkerchief around his head, gleaming brass rings encircling his neck and wrists, and a large United States medal on his breast, led a delegation to St. Louis to intercede in behalf of the hostages at Jefferson Barracks. In a council with the Indians in his museum, Clark, already aware that Atkinson had orders to release the prisoners, promised Keokuk that he would intercede in their behalf if the delegation would agree to be responsible for the warriors to be liberated. He then took them down the river in the *Warrior,* the same craft which had been Black Hawk's undoing, to interview the old Sac at Jefferson Barracks.

General Atkinson arranged the meeting and produced the prisoners, Black Hawk and the Prophet wearing a ball and chain. Unpainted and melancholy after a long, gloomy winter the dejected captives appeared before their gaily-appareled fellow tribesmen. When the prisoners perceived that Keokuk was interceding for them, they brightened but soon learned that not all were to gain their freedom. As Scott had recommended, Black Hawk, the Prophet, Neapope, Black Hawk's eldest son, and two others were soon on their way east to safer prisons.

Accompanied by an interpreter and an armed guard, they reached Washington late in April, and President Jackson granted them an interview. Old Hickory was surprisingly cordial to the prisoners. He showed the Indians clothes they were to receive and declared that the length of their confinement would depend on the conduct of their fellow tribesmen back on the frontier. The redskins were impatient of restraint and ready to promise anything to be released. The ill-tempered Prophet, his long, unkempt hair matched by a scraggly mustache, asked to be returned immediately and blamed the outbreak of hostilities on the British Band's efforts to raise crops. A hollow-cheeked Black Hawk, his countenance marked with sorrow, naïvely suggested that like Keokuk they had come to visit their Great White Father and like Keokuk should be permitted to return. To the War Department officials the prisoners appeared humble and contrite. Cass resolved to retain the Indians only until Atkinson and Clark decided it was safe for them to return. At Fort Monroe, to which the guard delivered the prisoners after their interview with Jackson, the Indians had the freedom of the post.

In May, Clark advised releasing the hostages to the custody of Keokuk, an act calculated to strengthen the Watchful Fox's influence among the tribesmen. Atkinson added his recommendation of clemency, but it was not needed. On the receipt of Clark's letter, Cass had decided to release the hostages, and on May 30 the Secretary issued orders to Major John Garland to escort the captives back to their people by way of Norfolk, Baltimore, Philadelphia, New York, Albany, and the Great Lakes. The red men were to see first hand the power of the pale faces.

At Norfolk, en route home, Black Hawk was properly awed by the seventy-four-gun *Delaware,* and he and the Prophet made balcony appearances for the crowds that thronged to see them. In Baltimore the Indians competed successfully with President Jackson for attention, and their mob appeal there and at Norfolk was duplicated at every stop along the journey. A New Yorker presented Black Hawk with earrings for Singing Bird, and several impulsive women kissed Black Hawk's eldest son, whom a Washington correspondent described as "a noble specimen of physical beauty." More interesting to the other Indians were the amazing ascent of a balloonist and spectacular fireworks displays in New York.

At Albany the curious thronged in such numbers that the party could not land for an hour after it docked at the river wharf. Not all Americans looked kindly upon these demonstrations. *Niles Weekly Register,* in reporting the reception accorded the Indians in the various cities, sneeringly attributed it to the great American love for "sights." "Even a hanging match has brought 20 or 30,000 of them together." The irritated editor of *National Intelligencer* expressed his opinion of the demonstrations by means of a "letter" from Black Hawk to his wife. In it the red man purported to explain his popularity to his "having killed a few Long Knives, and burnt up some of the women and children in their wigwams."

Although flattered by the attention they received, the tour had a sobering effect on the Indians. The wonders of the white man's world strongly impressed them. The well-stocked arsenals led the Indians to believe that the United States was preparing for war. At Philadelphia the rapidity with which the mint turned out coins and medals gave them an impression of inexhaustible American wealth. In the railroads and canals, Black Hawk saw that the Long Knives had the means of assembling enough warriors to exterminate all the Sacs and Foxes on the frontier. In a speech to a Seneca chief encountered on the trip home, Black Hawk neatly summarized the Indians' reaction: "Brothers, we have seen how great a people the whites are. They are very rich and very strong—it is folly for us to fight them." The tragedy is that he had not accompanied one of the earlier Sac and Fox deputations to Washington. Had he done so, there probably would never have been a Black Hawk War.

When Major Garland and his party reached the Mississippi after a passage through the lakes and down the Fox-Wisconsin waterway, the Major released the Prophet to the Winnebagos at Prairie du Chien. From Rock Island, messengers summoned Keokuk and the head men of the Sacs and Foxes to receive the hostages from their tribes. Early in August, Keokuk and his retinue arrived at Fort Armstrong for the transfer of the prisoners. There, in sight of the beautiful Rock River Valley for which he had fought, Black Hawk tasted the bitter dregs of defeat. Major Garland opened the council with an address from President Jackson. Old Hickory made it crystal clear that the United States recognized Keokuk as the head of the

Sacs and expected the aged Black Hawk and all his fellow tribesmen to regard the Watchful Fox as such. Considerably agitated at this pronouncement, Black Hawk rose in protest. Denying vehemently that the President had informed him of any such arrangements, Black Hawk cried that he refused to be advised by anyone. Overcome by emotion he sank to his seat. The commanding officer of Fort Armstrong curtly reminded the old man that the treaty provided for just such an arrangement. Kindly and tactfully, Keokuk soothed Black Hawk and asked the white men to overlook the outburst, promising to be responsible for the old warrior's good behavior. Keokuk's handling of this awkward situation demonstrated once again the wisdom of the white men in choosing him as their agent.

When he regained his composure, Black Hawk realized his mistake and, no longer the haughty, imperious brave of old, begged permission to retract his statements before they reached the ears of the President.[8] This abject capitulation marked the end of the Black Hawk War. In the few years that remained to him the old warrior was content to reflect on past glory. Never again did he attempt to rally his people to stem the tide of the Long Knives. He had fought his last fight against the trend which had its inception at St. Louis in 1804 when Quashquame and the other Sac and Fox delegates signed the treaty of cession at the request of William Henry Harrison.

The romance of the Black Hawk War lived long after the death of its leaders and the western exile of the tribesmen. As the last Indian war in Illinois and Wisconsin, its memory was cherished by all its veterans, and many frontiersmen profited socially and politically from their brief participation in the campaign. The subsequent rise to fame of Abraham Lincoln, Jefferson Davis, Zachary Taylor, and a host of others who fought red men and mosquitoes across the prairies, through the swamps, and over the hills, cast a nostalgic glamour over the miserable little campaign.

8 *Life of Black Hawk*, 176–77; *Niles Weekly Register*, October 5, 1833; Major Garland to Cass, October 5, 1833, Photostat WHS.

In addition to the politically inspired romances, several controversies arose out of the war and each spawned a considerable body of polemic literature. Partisans discussed with fervor the respective roles of the troops of Illinois and Wisconsin. The Illinoisans hailed James D. Henry as the real hero of the war, while Badgers praised their own Henry Dodge.

By 1850 a number of reminiscences had appeared which purported to describe in detail, sometimes minute, the events of particular skirmishes or marches which had occurred twenty years earlier. Seldom did the narrator play a minor or unheroic role in the account. Each narrative in turn gave rise to more controversies among veterans as they squabbled over their respective parts in the defeat of Black Hawk and his people. Unfortunately, there was too little glory in the campaign to allow of much division. After 1861 many veterans, undeterred by the fact that Jefferson Davis was on leave in the South until Abraham Lincoln left the army, interested themselves in creating imaginary situations in which Captain Lincoln, or sometimes Private Lincoln, and Lieutenant Davis were brought face to face.

The net result of this body of literature was the creation of a war which never took place. Too, it served to divert attention from the operation of the federal Indian policy during a vital thirty-year period and the inexorable retreat of a native race before a more advanced civilization. To understand the Black Hawk War one cannot concentrate alone on the events of the summer of 1832.

Neither the romances nor the polemics, however, succeeded in metamorphosing the actors in this frontier farce into shining heroes or bloody villains. Among the white men, Henry Atkinson, William Clark, Thomas Forsyth, and John Reynolds, to name only a few, possessed more than average ability, but they had, as well, their full share of human frailty. Among the Indians perhaps only the Prophet deserved the opprobrium heaped upon him.

Black Hawk, whom romancers strove to make into a striking hero of a noble cause, was hardly comparable to Pontiac, Tecumseh, or even the later Sitting Bull. The Sac brave had little organizing ability or political acumen. It was the cause and not the man which swelled the ranks of the British Band and made him a hero among the conservative faction in Oklahoma a century later. Indeed, Black Hawk was unusually susceptible to influence and flattery. Neapope and the Prophet manipulated him with ease. Despite his often proclaimed devotion to the cornfields and graves of his ancestors in the valley of the Rock, Black Hawk was probably motivated as much by jealous resentment of Keokuk's rise in the tribal councils.

Keokuk, on the other hand, was a consummate politician and an extremely effective orator. After the War of 1812 he shrewdly realized that armed resistance to the Americans was futile, a fact which the stubborn Black Hawk, to the tragic misfortune of his followers, either did not comprehend or refused to admit. Vices Keokuk certainly had; he was inordinately ambitious and was influenced by the gifts and honors heaped upon him by the grateful and calculating whites. Yet he was an able defender of his people's rights, and perhaps no other Sac or Fox could have done better. Certainly Black Hawk led a lost cause, a fact which he was either too ignorant or too proud to admit.

From the day in 1804 when the Sacs and Foxes signed Harrison's treaty in St. Louis, their doom was sealed. However, even if Governor Harrison had acted more scrupulously or the chiefs less rashly, there would have been little difference in the ultimate fate of the Indians. Treaty or no treaty, the frontiersmen who each year settled their families nearer to Saukenuk would have accomplished the removal of the Sacs and Foxes. Had Black Hawk had the genius of a Tecumseh and still elected to fight, his fate would have been the same. That the wickiup should give way to the log cabin was inevitable. Ahead of the Sacs and Foxes were years of frustration, misery, and disappointment as the authorities in Washington labored to strip them of their native culture—and land—and convert them into American citizens.

The "Old Store" at the Sac and Fox Agency, located near present-day Stroud, Oklahoma, as it appeared in 1875.
Western History Collections, University of Oklahoma Library.

The Sac and Fox Boarding School was opened in 1872 at the Sac and Fox Agency.
Western History Collections, University of Oklahoma Library.

"The Agent's House," undated, shows Frank Olsmith
(gunsmith), Clarkson Pickett (clerk), Eliza Perkins, Anna
Pickett (wife of Clarkson), Maomi Gibbs (in window),
Eva Gibbs, and Aunt Mary Pickering (agent's wife).
Western History Collections, University of Oklahoma Library.

A group of Sac and Fox Indians and whites standing on the porch of the trading post on the Sac and Fox reservation, Indian Territory, around 1889.
Western History Collections, University of Oklahoma Library.

Sac and Fox Indians in front of the frame and bark-roofed
summer house on the Sac and Fox reservation east of
Oklahoma City, 1889.
Western History Collections, University of Oklahoma Library.

*This photograph of Wampashka, a Sac and Fox teenager,
was taken by J. K. Hillers sometime before 1896.*
Western History Collections, University of Oklahoma Library.

16. Iowa Interlude

FROM 1804 to 1833 the possibility of one thousand Sac and Fox warriors' donning war regalia and heading for the nearest settlement was a factor in policy making in Washington and in the frontier capitals. However, the end of the Black Hawk War marked the beginning of a new period for the Sacs and Foxes. Following the crushing defeat inflicted on the recalcitrant element among the tribes, any idea that the Indians could effectively resist the white advance evaporated. This is reflected in actions of the tribesmen themselves and in the policies and attitudes of Americans toward the Sacs and Foxes. The tone adopted in dealing with the Indians became increasingly one of condescending paternalism.

During their thirteen-year tenure in Iowa the Sacs and Foxes deteriorated considerably. Their decline was manifested not only in the attitude taken toward them by the government but also in the rapid reduction in population. As Governor Robert Lucas of Iowa Territory commented in 1840, "The Sac and Fox Indians, from once being warlike and a terror to their enemies, are fast progressing toward extermination." Allowing for losses during the 1832 hostilities, they numbered nearly six thousand in 1833. When the removal from Iowa took place, the agent reported a total of 1,207 Sacs and 1,271 Foxes. This represents approximately a 50 per cent population loss during a period of thirteen years, and a closer look at the record compiled by the Sacs and Foxes tends to support the figure. Not only were the tribes torn by schism, but their way of life underwent a rapid change due to growing scarcity of game and mounting pressure from the whites, who were introducing liquor and disease among the tribesmen as well as coveting their land.

Throughout the Iowa interlude the Indians attempted to pursue their traditional way of life. They located themselves in several villages and followed the same cycle of hunts interspersed with visits to the village to plant and harvest crops. In Iowa the Sacs and Foxes hunted and trapped deer, muskrats, beaver, otter, and raccoons. And, as they had done for years, they annually sent hunting parties out to the plains to trail the buffalo herds. But as years passed their hunting proved less profitable. The concentration of Indians beyond the Mississippi and the growing number of white hunters were making severe inroads on the supply of game.

Instead of the winter hunt some bands began the practice of wintering among the white settlements. This contact with the whites was unfortunate, as the Indians encountered normally the more unscrupulous elements. The relatively large annuities being received by the Sacs and Foxes relieved some tribesmen of the absolute necessity of making the most of their hunting and led to competition among the few legitimate traders and the many liquor vendors. The latter posed for the Sac and Fox agents one of their most pressing problems.

Time and time again the agents protested about the activities of the numerous unscrupulous whites. One agent in Wisconsin claimed that two-thirds of the frontier population was engaged in trading with the Indians with whiskey as the bait. Considering that the Indians were prepared to exchange anything for the liquor—traps, guns, horses, furs, and even the clothing they were wearing—it is understandable why so many whites succumbed to the temptation to profit from the situation. Not content with the normal high level of profit from such a transaction, some of the traders tried to increase the profit by diluting the whiskey after the Indian had passed the stage of perceptiveness. This inevitably led to trouble. For if drunken Indians did not turn on the whites who had defrauded them, in their intoxicated condition they might vent their spleen on any white they encountered.

The magnitude of the problem appeared to dismay the officials. John Beach, agent during much of the Iowa interlude, stated that except when the warriors were hunting far from white contacts Sac and Fox camps presented a "continual scene of the most revolting intoxication."[1] Iowa's Governor Chambers classified the leaders of the tribes as "inveterate sots,"[2] and even Keokuk, his favorite, was incapacitated for a time by a stab wound suffered in a drunken brawl. Although liquor seems to have caused the brawl, relations among the various bands of Sacs and Foxes might well have occasioned the trouble.

In the decade following the Black Hawk War at least two lines of cleavage divided the Sacs and Foxes into a bitter, quarreling people. One line divided the two tribes into pro- and anti-Keokuk factions, while another accentuated the tribal differentiation as the Sacs and Foxes drifted apart. These were just the forerunners of later schisms which would ultimately result in the splitting off of another faction, just as the Missouri Sacs had parted company with their fellow tribesmen during the War of 1812. Mutual recriminations over respective roles in the hostilities of 1832, Keokuk's position within the tribes, the method of payment of annuities, and additional land ces-

1 Annual Report of John Beach, September 1, 1842, 27 Cong., 3 sess., *House Ex. Docs.*, serial 418, pp. 416–19.

2 Annual Report of John Chambers, September 27, 1844, 28 Cong., 2 sess., *House Ex. Docs.*, serial 463, pp. 412–15.

sions also played a part in breaking up what had once been a strong confederation.

Inevitably, the Sac and Fox agents found themselves drawn into the controversies as their activities, by design or otherwise, strengthened one faction or the other. Marmaduke S. Davenport served as agent for the tribes until a reshuffling of agencies brought Joseph Street to Rock Island in 1834. An old acquaintance of the Sacs and Foxes, he served them faithfully until his death in 1840. Street was succeeded by his son-in-law, John Beach, a retired army officer who pursued approximately the same course in the confused, often angry, and always perplexing Indian-American relations.

As usual, the agents had to contend with the intertribal wars in which the Sacs and Foxes became involved. The removal of the Sacs and Foxes from the Mississippi River intensified their troubles with the Sioux. Forced finally on to less fertile soil, the confederated tribes became more dependent on the chase. The decline in the animal population forced the Indians to range farther, increasing the possibility of their contacting Sioux parties.

Even the Sacs and Foxes who remained neutral in 1832 longed for Sioux scalps when the survivors of the band driven over the hills and across the prairies recounted how Wabashaw's Sioux had fallen upon them at the height of their defenseless misery. The Menominees and Winnebagos also lost scalps to the Sacs and Foxes for these and other reasons. Even in their decline the Sacs and Foxes were a match for most tribes they would encounter, although they were forced to recognize white supremacy.

In the 1830's and 1840's settlers poured into the Mississippi Valley, and their insatiable appetite for Indian land ultimately led to the exclusion of the Sacs and Foxes from Iowa and their location south of the Missouri River. When Scott drew up his treaty for Sac and Fox signatures in 1832, he required cession of all their land along the Mississippi. Aside from its significance as a penalty, the cession was supposed to benefit the Indians by excluding them from ready contact with the whites. Assuming that this was a genuine consideration and not a mere rationalization by land-hungry Americans, the most charitable thing that can be said is that it was an extremely shortsighted viewpoint. There was no relief for the Indians from white pressure.

By August, 1833, when Black Hawk and his associates were turned over to Keokuk's party, there had already appeared the general themes which would dominate Sac and Fox relations with the United States during the Iowa interlude. Keokuk, at the head of a large delegation, had negotiated with Clark in St. Louis on problems concerning the Sioux and the tribes' annuities. He demanded the return of prisoners held by the Sioux and cessation of Sioux intrusions on Sac and Fox land. The payment of annuities to the chiefs instead of to individuals, as was customary, was also insisted upon by Keokuk. To support his argument for this mode of payment, he could cite Scott's assurance along these lines during the 1832 negotiations. For the moment, Keokuk won his point on annuities; they would be paid to the chiefs, which would mean, in effect, to Keokuk.

By his control of tribal finances, Keokuk punished his enemies and rewarded his friends. Black Hawk might be once again among his people, but any Indian who was so foolish as to challenge Keokuk's authority would find himself excluded from the annuity payment. Not that the annuity after division represented much for the individual; most of it went to the traders who had advanced credit to the tribes. With the traders and with the agents Street and Beach, Keokuk's stock was very high, but with his fellow tribesmen and the Foxes it was a different story. The Sacs were dissatisfied with his handling of the money and the Foxes regarded his policy as completely unjust. To Street, Keokuk might be "a very extraordinary man of a high order of talent."[3] A white man representing the dissident Foxes described him as a half-blood, not a chief, who expended Sac and Fox funds for "fine horses, good *Brandy, Horse Racing, Steam Boat fare, etc.,* etc., whilst there are hundreds who receive nothing but what they get by hunting."[4] In May, 1836, the opposition to Keokuk was expressed in a council the Indians had with Street. Had the agent not stood by his friend Keokuk, the latter would have been supplanted by Hardfish, who could claim hereditary right to Keokuk's post and boasted a wound gained while serving against the whites in 1832.[5]

On the score of opposition to the Sioux, Keokuk's record was much better from the Sac and Fox viewpoint. Although he co-operated in surrendering Foxes who had penetrated Sioux territory and taken scalps. Keokuk pleaded the Sac and Fox cause against the Sioux very effectively. All he asked of the whites was that they step aside and let the Indians fight it out. In council, the Sacs and Foxes even requested that any Sioux imprisoned for crime against them be released so that the Indians might revenge their dead in the time-honored fashion. And if the Sacs and Foxes slew Winnebagos by mistake and took Menominee scalps by design, it was hardly a novel development.

It is remarkable that a few whites did not lose their lives, as the Indians certainly had some legitimate complaints. Some whites hunted on Indian lands, and others, scenting an approaching land cession, scouted out the best land and occasionally squatted on it and began to clear choice tracts. As a spokesman for the Missouri Sacs pointed out, even Keokuk, with his silver saddle, would be unable to stem "the great fog of white people which is rolling toward the setting sun."[6]

[3] Joseph Street to William Clark, October 7, 1835, Sac and Fox Agency File, National Archives (hereafter cited as S–F File, NA).

[4] J. B. Patterson to Elbert Herring, June 20, 1835, S–F File, NA.

[5] Report of Sac and Fox Council, May 29, 1836, S–F File, NA.

The first cession following the Black Hawk War was suggested by Keokuk himself, probably with the consent of most of the Sacs and Foxes. To reduce friction with the whites the Watchful Fox urged the United States to buy the four-hundred-square-mile reserve which enclosed his village on the Iowa River. He also requested that the agency be moved from Rock Island to the Sac and Fox country. Certainly this was advisable, as tribesmen wishing to talk to their agent had to cross a belt of settlement along the Mississippi and this made for trouble with the whites. But when the commanding officer of Fort Armstrong tried to pin the Indians down to precise terms, they were evasive, and Keokuk proposed sending a delegation to Washington to settle the matter.[7]

The Indians were obviously learning to appreciate these excursions; on one occasion a party of chiefs insisted on first class accommodations by steamboat to St. Louis because deck accommodations were not fitting for chiefs and headmen! In addition, there was the added advantage of dealing directly with the men who made the decisions. As they had once liked to travel to St. Louis and by-pass Forsyth to talk with William Clark, they now liked to by-pass Clark and deal directly with the Commissioner of Indian Affairs or the Secretary of War. However, this time the Indians would have to content themselves with talks near Rock Island.

Representing the United States on the right bank of the Mississippi, opposite Rock Island, in September, 1836, was Henry Dodge, the hero of Pecatonica and now governor of Wisconsin Territory. Seated at one end of the council lodge and surrounded by Agent Street and representatives of the military, Dodge faced a delegation of traders flanked by the Sacs and Foxes. The central position of the traders reflected their stake in the negotiations.

6 Missouri Sac Council at Fort Leavenworth, June 12, 1836, S–F File, NA.
7 Keokuk and Chiefs to Joseph Street, August 19, 1834; Colonel M. Davenport to William Clark, January 12, 1835; both in S–F File, NA.

Governor Dodge opened the sessions with a sweeping proposal. He asked the Sacs and Foxes to sell not only the four-hundred-square-mile reserve but also their entire holdings in Iowa and to remove south of the Missouri to an area which he pictured as a land of mild climate, good corn land, proximity to buffalo, and no whites. Speaking for the Indians Keokuk declined this invitation with a vague reference to previous unsatisfactory treaties. Dodge believed the Indians' reluctance to sell more land could be explained in terms of trader desire to keep them in Iowa, coupled with Sac and Fox appreciation of the potential value of their land.

For the 256,000 acres on the Iowa River which the Indians were prepared to sell, Keokuk asked $1.25 an acre. The Colonel offered 75 cents an acre and this is approximately the figure the Indians finally settled upon. Considering the average price paid Indians for land, the Sacs and Foxes had made a good bargain, but, as Dodge himself pointed out, the land could be readily sold to settlers for three dollars an acre.[8] Dealing from strength with relatively unsophisticated Indians had its advantages.

Throughout the negotiations, Keokuk was the principal spokesman for the tribesmen. He was attired in white buckskin leggings and a blanket, and for decoration he had a string of bear claws encircling his neck and a large snake skin dangling from his right arm. As he gestured to emphasize points, small bells attached to the snake skin tinkled an accompaniment to his forceful and graceful periods. In marked contrast with Keokuk's commanding presence was Black Hawk's appearance; denied any part in the maneuvering, the old warrior standing on the outskirts was clad in a shabby frock coat. Also present were Neapope and the Prophet, and when the former tried to participate, Dodge declared Black Hawk's lieutenant to be out of order.

[8] Henry Dodge to C. A. Harris, October 29, 1836, Prairie du Chien Agency File, NA.

Iowa Interlude

The treaty was signed September 28 after several days of bargaining, and it provided that the Indians would evacuate the reserve by November 1 and would never return to hunt, fish, or plant. It is interesting to note that those whites, primarily traders, with claims against the Indians received about one-fourth of the purchase price paid the Indians. Like most treaties being negotiated with tribes during this period, this one included a clause calling for expenditure of funds for civilizing the Indians. Despite this, the Sacs and Foxes still stood steadfast in their refusal to be converted into Christian agrarians.

If anything, the Sac and Fox resistance to civilizing influences stiffened. Although four of their boys had attended Choctaw Academy in Tennessee prior to the Black Hawk War, there is no evidence that they stayed long or ever returned to spread enlightenment among their people. No schools were introduced among the Sacs and Foxes, and when the government tried to put into effect the clause in the treaty authorizing the president, at his discretion, to spend Indian funds for education, the Indians protested vigorously and successfully.[9]

Again, in 1842, the Indians resisted an effort to include a provision for education in a treaty. T. Hartley Crawford, the commissioner of Indian affairs, regarded the establishment of a manual labor school among the tribesmen as fundamental to any effort to civilize them, but the Indian attitude was expressed by Keokuk in abortive negotiations in 1841. "As to the proposal to build school houses," said the Watchful Fox, "we have always been opposed to them, and will never consent to have them introduced into our nation."[10] Some of the opposition could be attributed to the status of Indian youths who returned to their tribes after exposure to the white man's culture. In their native habitat they found themselves ridiculed

9 Copy of Street to Governor Lucas, August 17, 1839, S–F File, NA.
10 Minutes of a Treaty held at the Sac and Fox Agency, October 15, 1841, 27 Cong., 2 sess., *Senate Docs.*, serial 395, pp. 270–75.

and derided by their fellow tribesmen. Agent John Beach summed up the Indian attitude well: "Our education seems to consist in knowing how most effectually to cheat them; our civilization in knowing how to pander to the worst propensities of nature, and then beholding the criminal and inhuman results with a cold indifference—a worse than heathen apathy while our religion is readily summed up in the consideration of dollars and cents."[11]

The Sacs and Foxes were unenthusiastic about Christianity as well as education. Attempts to locate missions among them were in vain. Although in contact with white men for two centuries, the Sacs and Foxes in Iowa were thoroughgoing pagans. This would appear to indicate not only a considerable attachment to their own religion but a lack of Christian missionary zeal.

Most of the early programs for civilizing Indians stressed religious education. However, by the 1830's the responsible authorities were shifting the emphasis to manual labor schools. In these the Indian would be taught to read and write and do simple calculations, but the primary purpose would be to prepare him for a career in agriculture. Supplementing the manual labor schools were pattern farms and assistance in breaking and fencing land, reminiscent of the mission of the incompetent and corrupt William Ewing around 1806.

Although the Sacs and Foxes did depend in part upon agriculture, the hope of converting their warriors into farmers was not a realistic one. The agency pattern farm was maintained industriously by the white employees, but only its watermelon crop seems to have inspired much interest in the Indians. As had been the case for generations, the Sac and Fox women tended small corn and vegetable patches near the lodges where the horses could be kept from devouring the produce. The agents did provide labor to plow and fence in

[11] Annual Report of John Beach, September 1, 1845, 29 Cong., 1 sess., *Senate Docs.*, serial 470, pp. 483–86.

large fields to be tilled in common by each band, but the Indians were unwilling to take advantage of them or even be instructed in agriculture beyond what might be learned by casual observation. If the Sacs and Foxes were not prepared to take full advantage of the splendid Iowa soil, the whites would be happy to remove them.

During the 1836 negotiations, Colonel Dodge had attempted to persuade the Indians to cede their entire claim to Iowa, but failing in this he had had to content himself with the purchase of Keokuk's reserve at bargain rates. Another opportunity was to present itself with an outburst of fighting between the Sacs and Foxes and the Sioux. After a Sioux party lifted twenty Sac and Fox scalps, those tribes invited the Potawatomis, Iowas, and Otos to join them in a coalition against the Sioux. In the hope of heading off a war which would be detrimental to their business interests, associates of the American Fur Company contacted the Secretary of War in Washington.[12] They suggested a general peace council to be held in Washington early in the fall of 1837. The administration agreed, and word went out for the agents to issue invitations to the Sacs, Foxes, Winnebagos, Sioux, and Iowas. In councils the Sacs and Foxes expressed pleasure at the prospect of a Washington excursion. As Agent Street expressed it, they would agree willingly to anything "except to *love a Sioux*, or spare his life if they meet him in the wild prairies and have an opportunity to scalp him."

That summer such an occasion presented itself, the Foxes thought. Finding a Sioux encampment in Sac and Fox territory, a Fox hunting party left noncombatants behind and launched a predawn attack. The battle was a tragic series of errors for the Foxes. Their advantage of surprise was lost when, with bloodcurdling whoops, they sent a volley thudding into some small mounds which in the darkness had been mistaken for lodges. Leaping in with tomahawks and knives to try to salvage some of their advantage they were driven off. Then

12 S. C. Stambaugh to the Secretary of War, March 14, 1837, S–F File, NA.

the Foxes turned to perforating the Sioux lodges until, after a considerable expenditure of ammunition, they realized the Sioux were entrenched and unscathed by the hail of lead. Leaving eleven dead warriors behind and fortunate to be able to remove their wounded, the Foxes, considerably chastened, retreated.[13] They had suffered a severe setback in this encounter, but their representatives in Washington were to score a moral victory.

The large Sac and Fox delegation which was headed by Keokuk and included the principal tribal leaders reached Washington early in October, 1837. Secretary of War Joel R. Poinsett hastened to arrange a conference between them and the Sioux. The tense, colorful affair was staged in a church.[14]

On the Secretary's right sat the Sioux, who were outfitted with uniforms presented them by the Americans. Facing them were the Sacs and Foxes, in native dress and painted as if for battle. One Fox brave taunted the Sioux by conspicuously flaunting a headdress of buffalo horns and skull which he had removed from a Sioux corpse. Neither party was prepared to engage seriously in negotiations leading toward peace, and that portion of the meeting was a flat failure.

Hoping to accomplish something toward peace on the frontier, the Americans came up with a bizarre plan to remove the Winnebagos from Wisconsin and locate them on the neutral ground as a buffer between the Sioux and the Sacs and Foxes. Although the Winnebago delegation agreed to it in Washington, the program was never successfully implemented. The Winnebagos demonstrated an understandable reluctance to be placed in such a meat grinder.

Apparently, the American genius lay more in securing land cessions. The treaty signed by the Sacs and Foxes in Washington October 21, 1837, provided for the cession by those tribes

---

[13] Joseph M. Street to Henry Dodge, August 27, 1837, S–F File, NA.

[14] Thomas L. McKenney and James Hall, *The Indian Tribes of North America*, II, 99–103, 115–49.

of one and one-quarter million acres directly west of the cession made in 1832. As compensation, Commissioner of Indian Affairs Carey A. Harris, representing the United States, agreed to pay $100,000 of Sac and Fox debts and expend about $67,000 more for mills, farming assistance, and presents. This was topped off with an annuity of $10,000, part of which could be spent on education at the president's discretion.

The provision for $4,500 in presents and horses to be delivered to the delegation when it reached St. Louis was an obvious incentive for the Indians to sign. Keokuk's co-operation occasioned a clause providing that while an eight months' deadline was imposed for removal from the ceded land, as an exception Keokuk's village might be retained for two years. The tactic previously resorted to of conducting the delegation on a guided tour of some of the metropolitan areas was also employed. The Sacs and Foxes had the opportunity of comparing the merits of equestrianship in Philadelphia, Governor Edward Everett's oratory in Boston, and Catlin's Indian art in his gallery in New York. In Washington they were even exposed to the lure of the theater, although that staunch Presbyterian Joseph M. Street resisted this temptation. Disposing of choice real estate to the United States could be an educational if sometimes expensive and frustrating experience.

If Carey A. Harris believed that the Washington conference had improved relations between the Sacs and Foxes and their enemies, he was badly mistaken. The Sacs and Foxes left the East with their hatred of the Sioux simply intensified by contact with them, as was reflected by a continuing series of clashes on the prairies. Again, blood flowed on a small scale tolerably fast.

Also, the trouble over the style of annuity payment and Keokuk's role in the confederation became more serious after the 1837 treaty. These disputes manifested themselves in some surprising ways as the whites were drawn in and the power of the press was recognized. A Burlington newspaper in 1840 carried "A Notice to the Public" signed by about fifty of "the Chiefs and Representatives of the Sac and Fox tribes," warning against dealing with Keokuk as the authorized representative of the Sacs and Foxes.[15] The Iowa Legislative Assembly also got in the act with a request to President Van Buren that Sac and Fox annuities be paid to individuals instead of to the chiefs. When three hundred Sacs and Foxes signed a petition calling for the relief of agent John Beach, Governor Lucas passed it on to Washington with his approval, and for a few months it was Keokuk and Beach vs. Lucas and Hardfish. The replacement of Lucas by John Chambers ended this impasse and unified the white officials behind Keokuk, although the latter was forced to make some concessions on the payment issue.

Although perhaps a majority of the Sacs and Foxes challenged Keokuk's handling of the annuities, no one appeared to contest his role as the spokesman for the tribes during land negotiations. The 1837 cession had only momentarily halted the fog of white men engulfing Keokuk and his silver saddle. Even as the Sacs and Foxes had negotiated in Washington, Governor Dodge had recommended a panacea for their ills— purchase of all their holdings in Iowa and their transfer south of the Missouri River.[16] This would remove them from contact with the whites and also separate them from the Sioux.

Others were more plain-spoken. One representative in Congress spoke of the injury to his constituents that would be inflicted by permanent residence of the Indians in Iowa and was reassured that there was no policy to that end.[17] Newspapermen added their bit, and when another representative made the same complaint two years later, the official machinery

15 *Iowa Territorial Gazette*, February 29, 1840.

16 Annual Report of the Superintendent of Wisconsin Territory, 1837, 25 Cong., 2 sess., *House Ex. Docs.*, serial 321, pp. 574–78.

17 W. W. Chapman to T. Hartley Crawford, January 15, 1839, S–F File, NA; Crawford to Chapman, January 22, 1839, Office of Indian Affairs, Letters Sent, NA.

was set in motion to secure another cession. No sooner was the rumor out that another cession was pending than squatters appeared on Sac and Fox land and had to be evicted by dragoons.

When Commissioners John Chambers, T. Hartley Crawford, and James Duane Doty assembled the Indians in October, 1841, they proposed that the Sacs and Foxes sell all their land in Iowa and move into the southwest corner of what would someday become Minnesota.[18] The argument for sending the tribes north instead of south of the Missouri was that their chances of becoming civilized were better than if they were placed among the thousands of Indians already located to the south. To forestall obvious Sac and Fox distress at being placed so close to the Sioux, the commissioners promised to build three forts for their protection.

The Indians flatly refused to sell on these terms. Keokuk described the country as "a country of distress," and other Indians deplored the lack of timber. Wapello, the principal Fox chief, spoke bitterly of the land they once owned around Rock River and Dubuque. Appanoose, a Sac chief, claimed that at Washington in 1837 they had been assured they would not be asked to sell any more land. The commissioners explained that the Indians, having just received their annuities and fresh credit from the traders, were not ripe for an offer.

Although fruitless, the negotiations were carried on in a friendly atmosphere. Keokuk apparently seized the opportunity to try to rebuild some of his political fences. He arranged for Poweshiek's band of Foxes to receive their annuities before his own followers and then staged a "Smoking for Horses" with the same band. This involved Poweshiek's people seating themselves and then being approached by individual Sacs carrying pipes and leading horses. If the Fox ap-

---

18 Minutes of a Treaty held at the Sac and Fox Agency, October 15, 1841, 27 Cong., 2 sess., *Senate Docs.*, serial 395, pp. 270–75; *Burlington Hawk-Eye and Iowa Patriot*, October 21, and 28, 1841.

proached accepted the pipe, he was also presented the horse, and thirteen changed hands in this fashion. However, horses were not the only gifts; blankets and every article of dress were tendered in a burst of generosity. One brave, perhaps spurred on by the applause that greeted the gifts, stripped himself to his breechcloth and leggings. Not to be outdone, the dragoons wheeled and galloped in an impressive mounted drill for the assembled Indians and whites.

During the negotiations the Sacs and Foxes were united. Hardfish's followers saw eye to eye with Keokuk's on the issue of selling land. Black Hawk was no longer around to stand on the sidelines in silent rebuke to Keokuk. The old warrior had died in 1838, and less than a year later his grave was opened by a white man and his bones stolen, later to be destroyed in a fire which swept a museum. Even in death Black Hawk would not be permitted to rest in the land of his forefathers.

During the 1841 negotiations one government official, remembering the powerful tribes he had seen in 1832, commented thoughtfully, "What a melancholy difference nine years have made among them."

Indian extravagance and white pressure made it unlikely that Black Hawk's survivors would long enjoy residence in Iowa. Four months was a sufficient period for the Indians to run through the annuities and credit, and in February, 1842, their spokesmen broached the idea of selling half their remaining Iowa holdings. Approved, it was passed up through channels by Beach and Governor Chambers, with the qualification that the plan to remove them north would be abandoned and the original idea of location south of the Missouri be revived.[19]

As the rumors of a pending treaty circulated, the Indians were deluged by another wave of squatters. Some of these had to be removed by force, and they retaliated by burning mills constructed by the government for the convenience of the In-

[19] John Beach to John Chambers, February 26, 1842, Beach Letter Book; Chambers to T. Hartley Crawford, March 12, 1842, S-F File, NA.

dians. But all this was forgotten in the preparation for a buffalo hunt.

In June, 1842, a party of about eight hundred Indians left Hardfish's village on the Des Moines for a six weeks' buffalo hunt. The party, which included three hundred warriors, was larger than usual in anticipation of a possible clash with the Sioux. Accompanied by thousands of dogs and horses the party moved slowly across the prairies, stopping late every afternoon. After a supper of meat and corn boiled in large kettles, the Indians would sit around smoking and exchanging experiences and a crier would circulate giving the marching orders for the next day. Up at daybreak the party would be on its way early.

Within a week the first buffalo signs were discovered, but already the Sacs and Foxes were dangerously near Sioux territory. Several days of hunting followed, during which time the Indians implored the spirits to assist them, but only poor success greeted their efforts. Those buffalo that were downed were butchered immediately, and the tongues, choice morsels, were delivered to the chiefs. Everyone gorged himself on the fresh meat, and the seven or eight dogs accompanying each family scavenged until they were so bloated that they had to drag themselves around like tadpoles.

Although more buffalo were in the offing, the strain of hunting with one eye constantly on the lookout for Sioux was too much. The chiefs, headed by Keokuk and Hardfish, determined to cure what meat they had and return to their own country. With another treaty upcoming they figured they should be able to live well through the winter anyway, and that was about as far ahead as the Indians would look.

Early in October, 1842, the Sacs and Foxes gathered at the agency to negotiate with Governor John Chambers. This time the cession was contracted, despite the reluctance of the Foxes and some of the Sacs to sell.[20] The half-bloods, traders, and

20 Annual Report of T. Hartley Crawford, November 25, 1843, 28 Cong., 1 sess., *House Ex. Docs.*, serial 439, pp. 271; John Chambers to J. C. Spencer,

squaw men created a little friction, as usual, but the Indians were learning how to cope with them. The chiefs publicly supported grants of land to two squaw men and privately opposed them. The Indians adamantly refused to approve any expenditures for agriculture or education but did approve the creation of a fund which would provide salaries for the chiefs and a fund for them to disperse in the tribal interest. This strengthening of the position of the chiefs was endorsed by Governor Chambers, who feared that unless something were done the chiefs would sink into insignificance and lose all influence (an end striven for by American officials years later). Chambers had reason to appreciate the influence of the chiefs. Keokuk apparently labored long to overcome resistance to the cession by Fox chiefs and braves of both tribes and was finally successful only after a judicious distribution of gifts.

For the promise of a 5 per cent annual return on $800,000 and the payment of $258,566.34 of their debts, the Sacs and Foxes sold all their holdings in Iowa, which included about ten million acres gleefully described by the Commissioner of Indian Affairs as "as fine land, probably, as the world can produce." The eastern half of the cession the Indians would have to evacuate by May 1, 1843; the western half they might occupy for three years, and then they would move to a tract on the Missouri River or its tributaries to be furnished by the United States.

The Street family did well by the negotiations. The Indians presented the General's widow with a section of land and the agency house, for which they paid the government $1,000. Perhaps with Black Hawk's fate in mind, the Indians insisted that their former chief Wapello continue to rest in his grave near that of General Street, whom Wapello had admired and by whom he asked to be buried. The excellent agency farm,

October 13, 1842, S–F File, NA; *Burlington Hawk-Eye and Iowa Patriot,* October 20, 1842.

located on the undulating prairie and including some fine groves of timber and a never failing stream, was made available through a pre-emption claim to a Street son-in-law who had served for a short period as agency farmer.[21]

The winter of 1842–43 was a bad one, and about half of the Indian ponies died. On schedule nevertheless, the Sacs and Foxes evacuated the eastern half of the recently ceded area and moved to new village sites where they would await completion of plans for removal south of the Missouri. Their temporary home in western Iowa represented an entirely new habitat for the tribesmen. The Sac and Fox women had difficulty finding good soil for their garden patches; timber was scarce, which made it difficult to find sheltered locations for their winter lodges, and the presence of lakes and marshes betrayed the prevalence of malaria in the country. Game was so scant that the Indians were fast becoming dependent on their annuities.

For three miserable years the Sacs and Foxes lingered on in western Iowa. Poweshiek's band of Foxes, which had never been happy about the Treaty of 1842, twice returned to their old villages on the Iowa River. Prompt eviction by dragoons the first time they returned in the winter of 1843–44 did not prevent their returning the following winter. Hardfish's Sac band also spent one winter among the whites on the Missouri frontier. Some of the settlers did not object, as they profited by trading whiskey to the wandering tribesmen for anything of value the Indians might possess. Demoralized by these forays, the Sacs and Foxes also suffered badly from malarial fevers, smallpox, and sometimes actual want of food.

Dissatisfaction was rampant with regard to the location of their new home south of the Missouri. The Foxes were generally unco-operative about attending councils to discuss re-

21 Ruth A. Gallaher, "Indian Agents in Iowa," in *The Iowa Journal of History and Politics*, Vol. XIV, p. 384.

moval plans, and even Keokuk refused to accept the first tract assigned.[22] When removal did get underway in the fall of 1845, precisely where their new home was to be was undecided. With a minimum of discomfort, Keokuk led his followers directly to the vicinity of two tracts, one of which was to be their new home. Other bands reluctantly followed and suffered in some instances considerable discomfort. By the spring of 1846 the Sacs and Foxes were gathered around the headwaters of the Osage River.

The Sac and Fox tenure in Iowa had come to an end, with the exception of one band which would return later. The removal from Iowa signaled the end of an era for the tribes. Even more than the Black Hawk War it demonstrated their rapid decline. The Mississippi and its wooded, fertile banks had been their home as far back as Indian memory went, but now they had been uprooted and relocated in a new land. Perhaps, Black Hawk was fortunate he did not live to see the change.

[22] John Beach to John Chambers, May 29, 1845, Beach Letter Book.

17. Aborted Acculturation in Kansas

THE AREA in Kansas which the Sacs and Foxes were to occupy for the next twenty-three years was a far cry from their ancestral home. Located on the headwaters of the Osage River, it consisted of 435,200 acres, mostly prairie intersected by a few good timbered streams. Being very sandy and not well adapted to the Indian's primitive methods of agriculture, these acres occupied by the Sacs and Foxes were the poorest on the large reservation they shared with the Ottawas, Chippewas, and Kansas.

At their Osage River agency the Sacs and Foxes made an earnest attempt to pursue life as they had for generations. Although they became increasingly dependent upon their annuities, they continued to hunt, primarily buffalo out on the great plain, since the immediate area was nearly denuded of wild life. Small parties occasionally hunted southeast into Indian Territory seeking deer and other game. Toward the end of their stay on Osage River such hunting parties were more frequent, as the Sacs and Foxes found the plains closed to them by troops pursuing hostile tribes or by the hostile tribes themselves.

There is no better index to the decline of the Sacs and Foxes than their relations with the southern Plains tribes, the Comanches, Kiowas, and Arapahoes. These tribes rightfully resented the intrusion on their hunting grounds of red men from farther east, red men whom the proud Plains Indians regarded as wards of the United States.

In the 1820's, at the peak of their power, the Sacs and Foxes had fought the Sioux to a standstill whenever the tribesmen clashed among the buffalo herds on the plains west of the Missouri, and they had terrorized at will the neighboring Menominees and Winnebagos. The Sacs and Foxes could muster one thousand eager warriors to oppose their enemies in those days. In the early 1850's, when a brave or war chief consulted the Great Spirit and called on the Sacs and Foxes to demonstrate their courage by seeking out the Comanches or the Arapahoes, the Sac and Fox numbers were still such that a few hundred warriors might take up the challenge.

During the early years in Kansas the Sacs and Foxes did well in their battles with the plains tribes. The Pawnees incurred their hostility first and furnished scalps to be danced in the Osage River villages. But the battle which became a part of frontier folklore took place about one hundred miles west of Fort Riley in 1854 between one hundred Sacs and Foxes and a combined force of about one thousand Comanches, Kiowas, Cheyennes, and Osages.[1] The Plains Indians had joined forces to wipe out any "frontier" Indians found buffalo hunting, and the Sac and Fox party was doing just that. Assuming, as one Plains chief phrased it, that they could "eat up" such a small force with ease, they attacked after attempting to gain tactical surprise by offering to smoke. Hurriedly dismounting to take shelter in a convenient ravine, the Sacs and Foxes met the initial charge with a volley which killed many ponies and emptied some saddles. Although outnumbered ten to one, the

---

[1] B. A. James to George W. Manypenny, August 2, 1854, S–F File, NA; J. W. Whitfield to A. Cumming, September 27, 1854, 33 Cong., 2 sess., *Senate Ex. Docs.*, serial 746, pp. 297–304; A. Cumming to Charles E. Mix, September 30, 1854, in *ibid.*, 284–86.

Sacs and Foxes had rifles while the great majority of the Plains Indians had only their bows. After a series of charges which only cost them more ponies and more casualties, the Plains Indians withdrew to the accompaniment of jeers and taunts from the entrenched Sacs and Foxes. The latter tribesmen had lost a half-dozen warriors but had killed at least twenty-six of their enemy and wounded many more. By leaving some of their dead on the field to be scalped and mutilated, something seldom done by Plains Indians, the Comanches and their allies demonstrated the completeness of their defeat.

The Sacs and Foxes had shown that they had not lost the fighting prowess that had once made them the most feared tribes on the upper Mississippi. Nor did they choose to rest on their laurels. Around their council fires their war chiefs urged that the battle be carried to the enemy, particularly the Osages, who were presumably the only Indians in the combined force who had been armed with rifles and were therefore charged with the Sac and Fox casualties.

One warrior whose brother had been killed revenged him in approved Indian fashion. Alone, he approached within four hundred yards of an Osage camp and surprised two warriors. One of these he killed and scalped; the other he permitted to carry the news to the village. Tarrying long enough to drink in the piercing cries and wailing with which the women greeted the shocking report, the daring Sac raced for home with his trophy. Elated, his fellow tribesmen moved to within a mile of the agency's safety to dance the scalp.

Other skirmishes followed, but none to compare with the rout of the Plains Indians west of Fort Riley. This was not due to a slackening of Sac and Fox belligerency. In the summer of 1856 practically every warrior who could straddle a horse left in search of Comanche scalps. Locating a party on the Arkansas River the Sacs and Foxes killed twenty-one and took two prisoners at a loss of only two killed. In his annual report that year the superintendent of the central division of the Indian Bu-

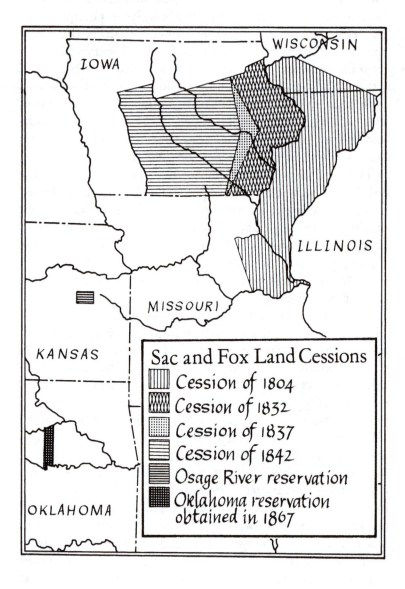

Sac and Fox Land Cessions
 Cession of 1804
 Cession of 1832
 Cession of 1837
 Cession of 1842
 Osage River reservation
 Oklahoma reservation
 obtained in 1867

reau stated that the Sacs and Foxes, "By their adventurous courage have so often defeated the Comanches in the open prairies, though greatly outnumbered by the latter, that the very sound of the name of Sacs caused a panic among those very bands of Comanches long considered so terrible upon the frontiers of Texas."[2] The Sacs and Foxes had amply demonstrated that eastern tribes still imbued with their native fighting spirit were able to cope with Plains bands who terrorized white plowmen and Indians enervated by contact with the white culture.

In the mid-1850's the numerical inferiority of the two tribes had been balanced by their superiority in weapons. However, by the 1860's their numbers had declined so rapidly that a war chief would do well to inspire fifty young men to follow him into battle. Such a war party could not hope to hold its own among the hostile Indians competing for the ever decreasing buffalo.

More than 2,400 of the confederated tribesmen had settled on the Osage River Agency, but by the time they were removed to Indian Territory they numbered less than 700. Allowing for the approximately 300 Indians who returned to Iowa, that still presents a tragic picture. Annually the death rate exceeded the birth rate, as cholera, smallpox, measles, and other diseases introduced among them by the whites took their toll. One agent reported that in the three years he had held office, deaths exceeded births by 300.

During one smallpox epidemic one band refused inoculation on account of the influence of "an old Winnebago prophet"—Black Hawk's nemesis? The old villain had dropped from sight after 1836, but it is not inconceivable that he was the author of this mischief in 1851.

The high mortality rate from disease was occasionally explained by white observers in terms of the dissipated condition

---

2 A. Cumming to George W. Manypenny, September 25, 1856, 34 Cong., 3 sess., *House Ex. Docs.*, serial 893, pp. 616–25.

of the Sacs and Foxes. Drunkenness became even more prevalent than in Iowa, as the warriors, with hunting and fighting no longer absorbing their time and energies, lolled around the villages and proved easy targets for unscrupulous whites.

The agents who served at the Sac and Fox reservation, thirteen in all in the twenty-three-year period, were usually in office too short a time to understand their charges or conduct any coherent civilization program. At least two of the agents were relieved for misconduct, and one individual, who served as an agent himself and was instrumental in securing appointment for another, was quoted as saying that while he might have cheated the Indians on occasion he had not done any more than anyone else had done. Still another agent was so high-handed that even Keokuk, notorious among the Indians for his complaisance, rebelled and had a brush with the law as a result. Such an administration of Indian affairs could have been disastrous for neighboring whites in an earlier period.

In view of their long history of belligerency it is rather surprising that the Sacs and Foxes did not participate more actively in the Civil War. Although several volunteered for service with the Union Army on an individual basis, the tribes did not participate as a unit. Not that their loyalty, with the exception of a few, was open to serious question. In 1864 when a Confederate thrust north was coupled with a rebel Indian invitation to join them in exterminating all whites east of the Missouri River, the Sacs and Foxes took their stand with the United States. Of the ten tribes reaffirming their allegiance in council, the Sacs and Foxes furnished the largest delegation.[3] But certainly some of the aged warriors, fired by the memory of their victories over the Long Knives and embittered by the patronizing, dictatorial attitude of recent agents, must have longed to seize this opportunity to even old scores.

[3] H. W. Martin to W. P. Dole, September 11, 1864, S–F File, NA; Report of Council at Sac and Fox Agency, October 5–9, 1864, 38 Cong., 2 sess., *House Ex. Docs.*, serial 1220, pp. 506–509.

Loyalty to the United States definitely had its disadvantages. Refugee Creeks and Cherokees from Indian Territory were located temporarily on the Sac and Fox Reservation and inflicted considerable damage to their hosts' property.

Part of the bill assessed the refugees related to their occupation of houses built for the Sacs and Foxes at the Osage River Agency. These houses were the most spectacular aspect of an ill-conceived and thoroughly botched attempt to acculturate the tribesmen. Assignment of blame, however, is not an easy task. Although the implementation was in the hands of the agents and their assistants, they could always point to specific requests made by the Indians for agricultural instruction, construction of homes, and other aids to civilization.

As previously noted, when the Sacs and Foxes removed from Iowa to the Osage River Agency, they attempted to pursue their traditional way of life. By the period of the Civil War this was obviously impractical, due to the virtual extermination on their reservation of the animal life which had been the basis of the Indian economy. The Sacs and Foxes had become annuity Indians, although they might occasionally brave the overwhelming strength of the Plains Indians and kill a few buffalo.

Like most tribes caught in similar circumstances, the Sacs and Foxes were split into progressive and conservative factions, which were just continuations of the split which had been dramatized at Rock River by Keokuk and Black Hawk. Keokuk continued to lead the progressives, but Black Hawk had been succeeded by a series of warriors and chiefs who also protested any compromise and envisioned a return to the good, old days when the Great Spirit smiled on his red children and the prairies and woods, freed of whites, swarmed with buffalo, deer, and muskrats. The conservatives were strengthened in their opposition by the belief that the adoption by the Sacs and Foxes of the white man's ways would mean their annihilation as a people. Increasing friction between the tribesmen seemed to portend just that.

Apparently, a majority of the Foxes had left Iowa under protest and were never reconciled to life in Kansas. Poweshiek, brilliant in war and wise in council, led the opposition and was supported by two of his headmen, Crow and Wolfskin. They had opposed the 1842 treaty and continued to object to its provisions. Also, they believed agent Beach to be favoring Keokuk's faction in matters such as the annuities, although Beach himself explained their intransigence in terms of the selfish machinations of whites who hoped to keep the annuities within their reach.

In the winter of 1851–52 about one hundred Indians, principally Foxes, returned to Iowa and located themselves among sympathetic settlers.[4] The reason for this completely unprecedented attitude by whites must have been the government payments. As the tribesmen had once enriched men like Davenport by their hunting, now their $51,000 annuity attracted exploiters. Indians who brought thousands of dollars annually into a community were too valuable to merchants and whiskey sellers to be permitted to escape. Subsequently, they were to furnish a source of cheap labor during harvest season.

The Iowa Foxes, as the band would become known, justified their action by critical references to the Kansas country and swore they would rather die than leave Iowa again. Over the years they were reinforced by additional malcontents such as Mowmenwahnecah, a Fox chief who in 1862 was degraded for opposition to the mode of annuity payment. He promptly led five or six lodges back to Iowa, where the state legislature encouraged the federal government to appoint a special agent for the Iowa Foxes and give them a share of the tribal annuities. When the Indian Office reversed itself and eliminated the payment, Congress, probably spurred on by Iowa legislators, restored the cut. Although the united Sacs and Foxes protested for years, this arrangement continues uninterrupted to the

---

[4] Major L. A. Armistead to Captain Irwin McDowell, February 29, 1852, S-F File, NA.

present. The move to Oklahoma in 1869 only provided more recruits for the Iowa Foxes, bringing their total to about three hundred.

To compensate for those Sacs and Foxes who deserted the main body to return to Iowa, the tribes recruited about one hundred Missouri Sacs, members of that band which had maintained a separate identity since the War of 1812. White officials tried to promote the total merger of the Missouri Sacs with their parent tribe, and on several occasions such a union was apparently about to be consummated. The principal inducement to the Missouri Sacs was the larger annuity enjoyed by their kinsmen.

The division of annuities continued to cause trouble in Kansas, as it had in Iowa. Mokohoko, Hardfish's successor as the leader of the conservatives, amounting to about one half the Sacs and Foxes in the 1860's, seized on this as one of his issues. His opposition was now led by Moses Keokuk, son of Black Hawk's old rival and generally referred to simply as Keokuk. Like his father, who had died in 1848 "of dysentery brought on by a drunken frolic," Moses Keokuk stood for compromise and accommodation. Like his father he was accused of intemperance and a selfish neglect of tribal welfare.

Mokohoko, however, was no Black Hawk. Where the latter had sulked in his wickiup or stolen away to consult with the British or the Winnebago Prophet, Mokohoko headed an unauthorized delegation to Washington in the spring of 1866 and hired an attorney to represent his band before the white officials. Back on the reservation in July, Mokohoko switched character and, painted for war, led his band to the agency to receive their annuities. Although they insisted on staging a war dance, the "Wildband" had not decided to appeal their case to the god of battles. When a special investigator was dispatched to check their complaints against the current agent, Mokohoko's people were once again represented by an attorney. The tomahawk had been displaced by the legal brief, the war chief by the student of law. The new medicine was effective; Mokohoko was restored to the full power and prestige of a blood chief, a position from which he had been arbitrarily removed by the agent for failure to co-operate.[5]

Although he was willing to employ the legal weapons developed over the centuries by the white man, Mokohoko represented a majority of the Sacs and Foxes in his refusal to avail himself of the white man's developments in religion, education, and agriculture. Not until the 1860's did the Sacs and Foxes demonstrate the slightest willingness to exchange the magic of their medicine bags for the magic of the white man's Bible. Indeed, proposals to introduce missionaries and schools "excited them almost to hostilities," and one agent described them as "more opposed to schools, missionaries, and to building houses, than any other tribe on the northwestern frontier."[6] Although Keokuk, shortly before his death, had confided privately to the agent that he was finally prepared to work toward that end, not until 1860 did the chiefs and headmen of the Sacs and Foxes indicate any desire in council for the introduction of teachers or missionaries among them.

A year earlier their agent had invited a Quaker couple to move to the agency, the husband to help in agricultural instruction, the wife to open a school for Indian children. After contact with the whites dating back to the seventeenth century, a school had at last appeared among the Sacs and Foxes. Less than ten Indian children were in attendance eighteen months later, but the sight of Indians in open council approving and even requesting the erection of a building for a school and mission was as encouraging as it was unprecedented.

[5] H. W. Martin to D. N. Cooley, May 18, 1866, S–F File, NA; Martin to Cooley, May 23, 1866, 39 Cong., 2 sess., *House Ex. Docs.*, serial 1284, p. 271; Thomas Murphy to Cooley, July 21, 1866, in *ibid.*, 273–74; W. R. Irwin to Cooley, October 9, 1866, in *ibid.*, 269–70; Statement, October 7, 1866, S–F File, NA.

[6] Annual Report of Charles N. Handy, September 6, 1850, 31 Cong., 2 sess., *Senate Ex. Docs.*, serial 587, pp. 56–59; John R. Chennault to Luke Lea, September 17, 1851, 32 Cong., 1 sess., *Senate Ex. Docs.*, serial 611, pp. 326–31.

Presumably, this should have been the prelude to a rapid conversion to education, but such was not the case. Any vision of little Indians trooping into the classroom to become experts in orthography, mental arithmetic, reading, and writing quickly vanished. During the remainder of the Sac and Fox stay in Kansas painfully little progress was made in this area. The Quaker school seems to have had a brief existence, and one established in 1863 under Methodist sponsorship did only relatively better. It struggled along with fewer than twenty students under a succession of instructors, was involved in tribal politics, and was affected adversely by controversies over such unrelated matters as trading franchises.

Fond hopes of converting the Indians to farming likewise proved unrealistic, despite fine oratory in council which on several occasions represented the Indians to be clamoring for aid in getting their land broken and fences built. Although Moses Keokuk and a few half-bloods made earnest efforts, farms in the white man's sense never appeared among the Sacs and Foxes while they were in Kansas. The incentive was certainly there, as game had all but disappeared, and instruction was available from farmers hired with tribal funds by the government, but the genuine desire was absent. The Sacs and Foxes continued to raise their corn, beans, pumpkins, and squashes as they had on the banks of the Rock, but in their new home on the Osage drouth conditions, particularly in the decade from 1855 to 1865, cut production. When grasshoppers united with the drouth, the Indians went hungry. Obviously, life on the Osage could not be exactly like what it had been on the Rock, but the Sacs and Foxes would try.

Living in villages, the Indians cultivated their vegetable patches in common fields which were divided into lots and assigned by the chiefs and braves, with favoritism not an unknown factor. Late in the summer the women would dry the corn and pumpkins and beans, storing some in rawhide sacks which they would either take with them on the winter hunt

or bury as Sac and Fox women had done since time immemorial. The three hundred odd acres tilled in this fashion
hardly constituted intensive use of their land resources, and
this waste provided ammunition for those who would be happy
to displace them.

A quarter century elapsed between the Treaty of 1804 and
the appearance of concerted pressure to remove the Sacs and
Foxes from the Rock River area. In Iowa their tenure had
been exposed to attack almost immediately, and the same
was to be true of their residence in Kansas. "The Year of Decision," 1846, saw the United States reach a settlement with
England on the Oregon question and enter a war which would
detach California and the Southwest from Mexican allegiance.
Mokohoko probably never heard of Dr. Marcus Whitman or
the Treaty of Guadalupe Hidalgo, but both were factors in
his removal from Kansas. Within four years the pressure for
securing railroad routes to the burgeoning Pacific settlements,
coupled with the growth of population in Missouri, brought
demands for the removal of the Sacs and Foxes to Indian Territory.

Allied with white pressure was Indian discontent. Disappointed in their new home and dismayed at the mortality rate
on the Osage River reservation, the Sacs and Foxes had begun
as early as 1852 to think in terms of another treaty and removal.[7] Some Indians advocated a location farther west, where
they would be nearer the buffalo herds which, in the early
1850's, were still so important to them. When Commissioner of
Indian Affairs George W. Manypenny visited Kansas and Nebraska in the winter of 1853–54, he met the Sacs and Foxes
in council. His mission was to prepare the tribes for subsequent
treaties which would open Kansas to white settlers. The current Sac and Fox agent reported that they would be ripe for
a treaty the following summer, and they were already dis-

[7] John R. Chennault to Luke Lea, November 21, 1852, S–F File, NA.

cussing an expedition to the big bend of the Arkansas River to find a new home.

In Congress, the debate over the Kansas-Nebraska Bill produced a few vehement protests against the proposed removal of the Indians from their "permanent" home. Senator Edward Everett, who was to share a platform with Abraham Lincoln one memorable day at Gettysburg, beseeched his colleagues, "If we must use the tyrant's plea of necessity, and invade the 'permanent home' of these children of sorrow and oppression, I hope that we shall treat them with more than justice, with more than equity, with the utmost kindness and tenderness." In the House, a representative protested that the Indians of Kansas had already been torn away "from all that was delightful in the present, and sacred and glorious in the recollections of the past." Still another member of Congress compared the "stirring appeals upon the wrongs of the African" with the silence on the subject of the wrongs of the Indian. Senators from Massachusetts might beseech and representatives from Vermont protest, but congressmen from the frontier states were unmoved; the Sacs and Foxes and their neighboring red men would have their land holdings pared and would ultimately be removed.

All of this, of course, was to be done with the Indians' welfare in mind; securing additional land for white settlers was of secondary interest—or so the official line ran. The Osage River agent in 1855 insisted that the tribes under his jurisdiction all had more land than they needed or would need under any circumstances. And he sounded a note that would swell to crescendo in the next thirty years: "Large annuities—in money, and property held in common . . . are drawbacks upon their advancement in civilization."[8] The Commissioner of Indian Affairs agreed and proposed to remedy the fault through additional treaties.

8 B. A. James to George W. Manypenny, September 1, 1855, 34 Cong., 1 sess., *House Ex. Docs.*, serial 840, pp. 425–26.

The Indians themselves acknowledged that they possessed a surplus of land. Failing to consider the influx of whites that would inevitably follow a cession of some of their land, the Sacs and Foxes apparently only went so far as to mentally translate the idle land into large annuities, which were necessary now that their income from hunting was declining rapidly. Repeatedly, they proposed cessions to their agents.[9]

As the official machinery in Washington slowly adjusted itself to this new situation, the citizens on the frontier covetously surveyed the Sac and Fox lands, two-thirds to three-quarters of which lay idle. They agreed with the Scotch-Irish who had bedevilled William Penn's agents in colonial Pennsylvania that "it was against the laws of God and Nature that so much land should remain idle while so many Christians wanted it to labor on." A people who had brushed aside royal proclamations, proprietary edicts, and state and national laws to squat on land would not long be restrained by respect for a confederation of red men well past its prime. Osage River agents doubted that the settlers could be restrained much longer from forcibly evicting the Indians, as already the whites were cutting timber and stealing ponies.

By 1859 authorities in Washington were ready to act. On receiving a report from a special commissioner who had held a council with the Sacs and Foxes because they had requested a treaty to provide for allotment of land to individual Indians and sale of the surplus, Commissioner of Indian Affairs Alfred B. Greenwood decided to negotiate with the tribes during a projected visit to Kansas.

Late in September, 1859, Commissioner Greenwood met the Sacs and Foxes in council, with Moses Keokuk playing for the Indians that role his father had previously performed competently—or disastrously, depending upon one's point of view.

9 For example, see B. A. James to George W. Manypenny, October 13, 1855; B. A. James to J. M. Denver, May 9, 1857; Perry Fuller to A. B. Greenwood, June 22, 1859; Proceeding of Council at Sac and Fox Agency, July 16, 1859; all in S–F File, NA.

By the terms of the treaty, similar to those negotiated with several other tribes in this period, enough land was to be retained by the Sacs and Foxes to provide every Indian, irrespective of age or sex, eighty acres. With the exception of generous grants to half-bloods and Indian women who had married whites and 160 acre tracts for the use of the agency and the school, the remainder of the reservation, about 300,000 acres, was to be sold by sealed bid. Additional articles cleared the way for the construction of railroads through Sac and Fox land and attempted to pressure absent Sacs and Foxes by giving them one year to rejoin their fellows or lose their share of the treaty income.

The tracts assigned in severalty to the Indians could not be sold by them except to Sacs and Foxes or to the government. The proceeds from the sale of the surplus land were to be used to assist the Sacs and Foxes in adapting themselves to the agricultural life. Houses were to be built, livestock and tools purchased, land plowed, and fences erected. This provision occasioned one of the most flagrant examples of exploitation of an unsophisticated Indian community.

Within a year of the negotiation of the treaty, some Sacs and Foxes were demanding that the clauses involving allotments and construction of houses be implemented.[10] And log houses would not do; they were insisting upon "comfortable houses framed lathed and plastered with good stone or brick chimneys." Moving with remarkable, almost suspicious celerity, the government contracted with one Robert S. Stevens to construct 353 houses and plow and fence 100 acres for a mission farm. To undertake such a project when the Indians had not voluntarily abandoned their traditional housing was sheer madness.

Work was no sooner underway than protests about the

10 Perry Fuller to Charles E. Mix, September 6, 1860, 36 Cong., 2 sess., *Senate Ex. Docs.*, serial 1078, pp. 333–36; Fuller to A. B. Greenwood, September 29, 1860, Sac and Fox Letter Book, Oklahoma Historical Society (hereafter cited as S–F Ltr. Bk., OHS).

quality of the construction reached Washington. Green, rough lumber was being used, and the workmanship was shoddy. Moreover, the building costs were exorbitant. Commissioner of Indian Affairs William P. Dole inspected the project after about one-third of the houses had been completed and found the criticisms justified. Reasoning that the prices were excessive and that the Indians should display enough initiative to build their own homes, Dole terminated the contract. But then the Indians protested; so after renegotiating the contract to lower the cost somewhat, he permitted building to be resumed.

The entire project represented a loss of about $200,000 to the Sacs and Foxes. Very few Indians chose to reside in the houses, although some quartered their livestock there. Others removed doors and window frames and traded them for something valuable like whiskey or split them up to feed their fires. And the fires were probably not built in the houses, which had fireplaces so shallow as to be fire hazards. The houses also featured cellars which would not drain and foundations which settled badly.

As has been suggested earlier, Stevens must have had good political contacts to enable him to reap such a harvest. The government, for its role in the tawdry affair, merits the blackest mark since Governor Harrison negotiated his treaty in 1804. If this represented the best program which could be evolved for civilizing the Indians, it is not strange that they chose to remain innocent of the culture which could produce such a fraud.[11]

During the construction of the houses which were supposed to attract the Indians from their primitive way of life and establish them as permanent residents of Kansas, a memorial appeared in Washington which requested the removal of all

[11] C. C. Hutchinson to W. P. Dole, May 25, 1861, December 18, 1861, July 24, 1862, all in S–F File, NA; Annual Report of W. P. Dole, November 27, 1861, 37 Cong., 2 sess., *Senate Ex. Docs.*, serial 1117, pp. 626–47; Vital Jarrot, H. W. Farnsworth, and Joseph Bogy to L. V. Bogy, February 2, 1867, Central Superintendency File, NA.

Indians in Kansas to Indian Territory. Submitted by a Kansas citizen, it contained the usual observations of the extent to which the Indians' welfare would be furthered if they were removed once more—to even more undesirable surroundings. What is significant about the memorial is the reception accorded it. The Commissioner of Indian Affairs expressed general approval, with the qualification, "I take it for granted that the removal of the Indians will not be attempted without their voluntary assent." The Secretary of the Interior agreed and proposed that only those Indians who could subsist by agriculture should remain.[12] Practically no Sac or Fox would fall into this category.

In September, 1863, Dole negotiated a treaty with the Sacs and Foxes which provided for their removal to Indian Territory. However, the Senate attached some amendments unsatisfactory to the tribesmen, and the treaty did not go into effect.

This initial failure did not discourage those anxious for a treaty, although they did have to wait until the Civil War drew to a close. The Indians themselves requested another negotiation, as they had realized very little from the sale of lands under the 1859 treaty after their debts were paid, principally to Robert Stevens.[13] Kansans also stepped up the pressure and demanded that more land ceded in 1859 be put up for sale. An official in Washington described the situation succinctly: "The State of Kansas is fast being filled by an energetic population who appreciate good land. . . . *But one result can be expected to follow.*" And certainly that was true in view of his recommendation to Congress, which described the Indian situation in Kansas as being "of very great injury to the white race, and also . . . very bad for the Indians."

One novel argument employed was that the lands occupied

12 Annual Report of Caleb B. Smith, November 29, 1862, 37 Cong., 3 sess., *House Ex. Docs.*, serial 1157, pp. 3–28.

13 H. W. Martin to W. P. Dole, December 8, 1864; Kansas Congressional Delegation to W. P. Dole, February 23, 1865; both in S–F File, NA.

by the Indians had become valuable only as a result of the labor of the white men. In a sense that might have been true, but Commissioner of Indian Affairs Lewis V. Bogy, who employed the argument in 1867, probably did not subsequently become a follower of Henry George. Bogy's jocular attempt to ingratiate himself with the tribesmen by recalling his participation in the Black Hawk War and his youthful ambition to scalp old Keokuk—his memory failed him at this point as Keokuk was not then opposing the whites—must have grated on Indian ears.[14]

The occasion for this reminiscing was a meeting in Washington attended by representatives of the Kansas tribes. Drawn there like the others for the purpose of negotiating treaties for their removal, the Sacs and Foxes soon had their turn. The document to which they affixed their X's on February 18, 1867, provided for the cession of all land in Kansas and removal to Indian Territory. The United States, through Commissioner Bogy, agreed to purchase all Sac and Fox land not included in the 1859 cession, as well as any of that land which remained unsold, for a price in excess of one dollar per acre and other considerations. To compensate the Indians for the improvements made on their lands, the government agreed to secure for them a tract of not more than 750 square miles in Indian Territory. Signing the treaty were five chiefs, representing each of the five Sac and Fox bands in Kansas.

Mokohoko, leader of the conservative faction, did not sign, but one of his headmen did. Mokohoko's absence was explained by his being incapacitated by an ulcer which prevented him from leaving his hunting camp far out on the Arkansas.[15] However, the special commissioners who had done the preliminary work on the treaty assured Washington that

[14] Report of an Interview between Indian Tribes of the State of Kansas and the Commissioner of Indian Affairs, January 30, 1867, in Toner Collection, Library of Congress.

[15] Vital Jarrot and H. M. Farnsworth to L. V. Bogy, February 26, 1867, S–F File, NA.

during two visits to the Sac and Fox reservation they had secured the consent of the Indians to every clause of the treaty. Almost two years elapsed between the signing of the treaty and the Sac and Fox removal from Kansas. The interim was a period made hectic by the persistent maneuverings of land-hungry Americans. Squatters swarmed onto the reservation and began parcelling out land among themselves and drawing up squatter agreements to protect their ill-gotten gains. Some of the elderly Indian women, seeing settlers' cattle pouring through their flimsy fences to devour or trample their garden patches, must have been reminded of comparable scenes when they lived around Saukenuk many years earlier. "They [the whites] have taken possession of this reservation," the Sac and Fox agent stormed," and have held it against President, Secretary of the Interior, Commissioner of Indian Affairs, superintendents, agents, and the soldiers who have been sent here."[16] Protests were in vain, and the tribes could no longer produce a Black Hawk to evict forcibly obstreperous squatters. Had such an attempt been made, Governor Crawford of Kansas would obviously have been happy to have filled the role once played by the Old Ranger, Governor John Reynolds of Illinois.

The delay in removal, which permitted much confused scrambling for the best land to be evacuated by the Sacs and Foxes, was occasioned by the failure of Congress to appropriate money for the immediate transportation of the Indians. It was perhaps just as well that the delay ensued, as the tribesmen were unable to come to a decision on a choice for their new home and Mokohoko's Band declined even to discuss leaving Kansas. When the removal finally got underway in December, 1869, Mokohoko and over two hundred of his followers remained behind, some of the dissidents joining their friends and relatives in Iowa, others joined the Missouri Sacs in Nebraska.

[16] Albert Wiley to Enoch Hoag, August 10, 1869, 41 Cong., 2 sess., *House Ex. Docs.*, serial 1414, pp. 804–806.

The nineteen-day trip was accomplished with relatively little discomfort. Wagons were provided for the young, aged, and infirm, and the baggage and tools had been sent on ahead to await the arrival of the Indians. Some of the Sacs and Foxes went directly to Indian Territory from the plains, where they had been hunting buffalo with an eye out for hostile Indians. The weather during the nineteen days was good, but a snow-storm greeted the tribesmen when they arrived in Indian Territory.

This dismal introduction to their new home was also a fitting conclusion to their twenty-three-year residence on the Osage River reservation. That one-generation span had seen a tragic decline in the Sac and Fox population and the end of a way of life they had followed since time immemorial. The only question remaining was how long Black Hawk's people could withstand the continuing assaults on their native culture.

18. The End of the Trail

N EARLY A CENTURY has come and gone since the snow-shrouded arrival of the Sacs and Foxes at their new reservation in Indian Territory. In that time the United States has emerged from the frontier stage and has taken its place as the greatest industrial power in the world. Tucked away in a corner of what is now Oklahoma is the largest remnant of the once great Sac and Fox confederation. Slowly, painfully, and usually reluctantly the Indians have accommodated themselves to a rapidly changing white man's world. Three distinct periods are apparent in the story of the Oklahoma Sacs and Foxes. The first covers the events leading to the allotment in 1891, the second carries the story to the 1920's, and the third brings it down to the present.

Between 1869 and 1891 the Sacs and Foxes in Oklahoma adjusted themselves to their new home, their fourth in a period of about two generations. Early reports on the reservation purchased from the Creeks had described it effusively as "a very rich country," "a beautiful tract of 480,000 acres, well supplied with clear, living streams" and an abundance of wild game. The author of these reports was Enoch Hoag, in charge of the central superintendency. One of the Quakers appointed to

245

office by President Grant, Hoag must have lacked a firsthand knowledge of the country. Rich and productive bottom land the reservations did have, but outside the bottoms the soil was generally thin and sandy, and any significant decrease in rainfall produced drouth conditions, which were frequent during the 1870's and 1880's. In consequence, less than 10 per cent of the reservation could be classified as good arable land. This was a poor place to locate tribesmen originally from the rich and well-watered lands of Iowa and Illinois, if any enthusiasm for agriculture was expected.

Although little progress had been made in Kansas in acculturating the Sacs and Foxes, the government was still committed to a policy of converting them into self-sustaining farmers, and efforts to that end were accelerated. The Indians themselves were content to fall into their familiar routine. They hunted as long as buffalo and other game were available and, when not, sat around the fires in the winter or in the shade in the summer heat and discussed Sac and Fox exploits against the Sioux and the Comanches.

Between 1869 and 1891, the Sacs and Foxes changed little outwardly. Although the trend was toward the white man's way, at the end of the period a majority of the Indians still wore part of their old native costume, painted when the occasion demanded it, and permitted their hair to grow long.[1] In preference to log or frame structures, these Sacs and Foxes resided in the traditional bark houses or winter lodges. As late as 1876 a large Sac and Fox hunting party sought out the buffalo, but the southern herd had virtually ceased to exist; gone was the Indian's traditional source of meat and hides to help feed him through the winter and shelter him from winter winds. The Indians would continue to adhere to the cycle of hunts, but the return was more and more disappointing and each hunt attracted fewer warriors than the previous one.

[1]Annual Report of Moses Neal, August 20, 1888, 50 Cong., 2 sess., *House Ex. Docs.*, serial 2637, pp. 110–13; Annual Report of Samuel L. Patrick, September 1, 1890, 51 Cong., 2 sess., *House Ex. Docs.*, serial 2841, pp. 103–106.

War parties which had once spread terror among neighboring tribes and whites no longer sallied from Sac and Fox villages at the slightest pretext. Fighting the white man was out of the question, and forays against the Comanches became less likely as the buffalo ceased to attract rival hunting parties.

The energy once expended in these pursuits might have been channeled into agriculture, and this was a prime objective of government policy makers. Undoubtedly, agriculture was gaining ascendancy, but at a rate which disappointed members of the Indian service. Sac and Fox males understandably preferred gambling, ceremonial dancing, feasting, racing horses, and visiting friends to close contact with a hoe or plow. Such activities could monopolize a young brave's time and help him forget momentarily that the hunting and fighting for which his culture had prepared him were no longer feasible.

Naturally, the Sac and Fox agents disapproved of these activities. They forbade horse racing and gambling on the reservation and expelled white men who corrupted the Indians. Nevertheless, the practices continued, and apparently the Indians were not the easy marks some whites envisioned them. Frequently, the white gamblers descending on the agency at annuity payment time went away poorer but wiser.

The visiting, feasting, and dancing were likewise denounced as barriers to Indian progress. But the Indian who had participated in a dog feast like that Black Hawk prepared for the Potawatomis before Stillman's Run, or sensed the excitement of the war party or the buffalo hunt as he shuffled and stamped around the big drums, was not easily dissuaded. Agriculture held few thrills for him.

Even before the allotment took place in 1891, the Indians were concluding arrangements with white farmers to till some of the better land on the reservation and more was cultivated in this fashion than by the Indians themselves. One rationalization advanced by the tribesmen to justify this was that their ponies were incapable of breaking the sod and they lacked the proper farm implements. Undoubtedly, another factor was the small but steady income they derived from their tribal funds. Why should a young Sac or Fox take up the hoe when his wife's labors, supplemented by his annuity, would provide his minimum needs? In the twenty years after removal to Oklahoma the per capita annual income of the Sacs and Foxes averaged about $60. This relatively large sum placed these Indians in a more independent position than their Shawnee, Potawatomi, and Mexican Kickapoo neighbors.

The division of annuities was not the cause for factionalism in Oklahoma that it had been in Kansas, but factions continued to exist. The principal irritants now were varying attitudes toward the 1867 treaty providing for removal from Kansas. Of the five chiefs heading bands in 1867, only Mokohoko had failed to sign the treaty. Those responsible for laying the groundwork for the negotiation insisted that his failure to sign was not evidence of a rejection of the treaty but was due rather to his inability to attend. However, Mokohoko and his band did not remove on schedule, and the chief claimed he was not a party to the treaty and asked to be permitted to go to Washington and personally investigate the situation.

In the ensuing months some of the band did remove to Oklahoma, some returned to Iowa to join the Indians there, and a few merged with the remnant of Missouri Sacs in Nebraska. To offset these losses, Mokohoko received a few reinforcements from Oklahoma. Finally, in December, 1874, the Oklahoma Sacs and Foxes approved the expenditure of $1,000 to finance a visit by Mokohoko to Washington. The following February the chief and his delegation met with President Grant in the White House, and the Indians learned directly from their Father that they would have to leave Kansas.[2] With that formality out of the way, government agents removed Mokohoko's band to Oklahoma, only to have nearly all promptly return

[2] Mokohoko Band's Council with President Grant, February 4, 1875, S–F File, NA.

to Kansas. Undoubtedly, they were encouraged by the success of the other Sacs and Foxes in remaining in Iowa. Unfortunately, the reception accorded the recalcitrant Sacs and Foxes in Kansas did not equal that enjoyed by their wayward brothers in Iowa. The Kansas citizenry resented the intrusion and expressed their feeling by beating Indians and destroying their property. Even after Mokohoko's death in 1878 the dilapidated band lingered on, wandering through the countryside, sometimes dependent on charity.

In May, 1886, a delegation of Oklahoma Sacs and Foxes visited Kansas but failed to persuade the Mokohoko Band, as it continued to be known, to return with them. Then complaints from Kansas citizens had their effect. The following November a detachment of cavalry conducted the tattered Indians south to the Sac and Fox agency. Even this did not lead to a peaceful reunion of the bands. Mokohoko's successor, Pawshepawho, and two of his headmen refused to sign the tribal rolls to receive their share of the annuities. Denying that they had sold their lands in Kansas, they co-operated only after having spent several days in custody and receiving assurances that they could send a delegation to Washington. They wished to check the validity of the belief among the Indians that Mokohoko in 1875 had secured permission for them to remain in Kansas. When officials in Washington denounced this as a rumor, the disillusioned delegation returned to their band. With the exception of a few who drifted back north, they settled down in a village in the northern part of the reservation.[3] Mokohoko's band became the backbone of the conservatives' opposition to acculturation.

That the opposition was not more intense can perhaps be explained in part by the steady trickle back to Iowa of Sacs and Foxes during the Kansas period and apparently in the

3 Moses Neal to C. D. Bannister, December 24, 1886, S–F Ltr. Bk., OHS; Annual Report of Moses Neal, August 25, 1887, 50 Cong., 1 sess., *House Ex. Docs.*, serial 2542, pp. 176–79.

early 1880's. The settlement at Tama, Iowa, in effect acted as a safety valve by attracting those most determined to resist acculturation. Certainly, the Sacs and Foxes around Tama were the most reactionary of the old confederation.

Religion and the cause of education made little more progress among the Oklahoma Sacs and Foxes than it did at Tama. Throughout the period from 1869 to 1891, a manual labor school was maintained at the agency, and a few youths were sent to schools like Chilocco and Hampton. Although there was a gradual improvement in school attendance, it was slow and begrudged. Indian parents had no compunction about withdrawing children for days on end or enrolling them late if a hunt were protracted. In 1892 the Commissioner of Indian Affairs classified the Sacs and Foxes with the Apaches, Cheyennes, and a few other tribes as those most resistant to education. The Indian police were kept busy returning runaways.

Considering the Sac and Fox social organization and the actual administration of the school, the lack of sensational progress is understandable. The Sac and Fox people still prized most prowess in war. Educated Indian youths found themselves scorned or ridiculed as always. Frequently they reverted to the blanket or, not completely acceptable in either of the two societies, lapsed into idleness and dissipation. An example would be a young Indian who attended Hampton Institute in Virginia and later taught in the agency school. He was ultimately removed after contracting a venereal disease and heading Indian opposition to the administration of the school, the latter apparently being considered the greater crime.

During most of these years, the Indians bore the brunt of the expenses of the school themselves. Their $5,000 annual appropriation and the $13,000 allotted for a new school building in 1891, however, reflect more their complaisance than their genuine approval. The tribesmen objected to the regimented manual labor school, which emphasized tasks for the boys such as milking cows, building fences, and hoeing corn, and for the girls, cooking, sewing, and scrubbing. Nor were they always happy with the school administrators, chosen for them by religious denominations. They naturally resented the occasional transfer of children from the agency school to schools off the reservation without consultation with parents. This intolerable practice once led to a "raid" on the Chilocco school and the "liberation" of Sac and Fox children in attendance there.[4]

Signs of adjustment in religion were even less evident than in education. Perhaps half of the eligible school children were in regular attendance in 1891, but relatively little progress had been made by the missionaries. Sunday school and church services were held regularly, but the harvest of souls was unimpressive. Only the conversion of Moses Keokuk in 1876 was a cause for elation. Reverend William Hurr, an Ottawa Indian representing the Baptists on the Sac and Fox reservation for several years, can be credited with this coup. But Keokuk did not lead a mass movement into the Christian ranks. The average Sac or Fox still preferred his medicine bundle to Holy Writ as a guide in supernatural matters.

Perhaps Keokuk's marital difficulties stemming from his conversion also discouraged his fellow polygamists. His second wife, who had also become a Baptist, was convinced by her good church sisters that her position in a polygamous household was immoral, and she left Keokuk. He then remarried his first wife in a church ceremony and left his second wife in indigence.[5]

The adherence to the native religion not only was an embarrassment to the missionaries, it also handicapped other civilization efforts. In Oklahoma in 1882, Sacs and Foxes were listening attentively to an aged Shawnee woman who had had a vision in which the Great Spirit advised the Indians to revert

4 Samuel L. Patrick to T. J. Morgan, February 25, 1890, S-F Ltr. Bk., OHS.
5 John S. Shorb to E. A. Hayt, October 16, 1879, S-F File, NA.

to their old ways, much as Tecumseh's brother the Prophet had preached.[6] A decade earlier in Iowa, Sacs and Foxes had solemnly informed their agent that they had received a revelation from the Great Spirit directing the men to resume hunting, trapping, and fishing and permit their women to do the work. The agent tried to put an end to this foolishness by issuing a proclamation against revelations that might interfere with the work habits of his charges.[7]

There were several factors which help explain the near failure of the civilization programs. Geographic and economic factors were not the least important. President Cleveland pointed out in 1894, "In these days when white agriculturists and stock raisers of experience and intelligence find their lot a hard one, we ought not to expect Indians, unless far advanced in civilization and habits of industry, to support themselves on the small tracts of land usually allotted to them." And the Oklahoma site for the Sac and Fox experiment was certainly not ideal in terms of rainfall and soil fertility.

The implementation of the program was not always entrusted to the best of hands. Nepotism was common; one agent included six of his relatives among his twenty subordinates. Another in the 1870's signed false vouchers, made false certificates to pay rolls, misappropriated public property, and loaned tribal annuities to a fellow conspirator, a licensed trader. An inspector in the Indian service described the agent's successor in office as "the typical village politician, oblivious, self asserting and mendacious. . . . utterly unfit for such a charge as an Indian Agency. His manners and bearing are in marked contrast to the quiet self possession and dignified bearing of the better class of Indians." And the subject of this diatribe himself described the Sac and Fox agency, when he took it over, as

[6] William Hurr to J. V. Carter, August 13, 1879, in Annual Report of J. V. Carter, 1883 (Report of the Secretary of the Interior for 1883, serial 1291, pp. 144–45).

[7] Annual Report of A. R. Hombert, September 1, 1873, 43 Cong., 1 sess., *House Ex. Docs.*, serial 1601, pp. 550–51.

"the most demoralized, scandalous, infamous place I ever had the misfortune to get into in my Indian experience." It is small wonder that the Indians distrusted the enlightened policies advanced by such administrators. Finally, when the Indians displayed some interest in managing their own affairs—the Indian school—for example—they were slapped down. Indian initiative which might conflict with established policy was not welcomed.

The Sac and Fox experience during the wave of leasing arrangements which made grazing land available to cattle companies in the 1880's was not calculated to inspire more faith in the white officials. There is no evidence that the leases of Sac and Fox land were more objectionable than those negotiated with other tribes. Nevertheless, the picture of an inspector in the Indian service using his position to negotiate Sac and Fox leases for himself is not a pleasant one. The inspector subsequently denied having bribed Moses Keokuk, who acted as his intermediary, and charged his detractors with having grazed cattle on the reservation for five years without paying a cent.[8] The general comment of Cleveland's secretary of the interior, L. Q. C. Lamar, on arrangement of such leases is appropriate: "Not the least among such influences were the encouragements and persuasions of the respective Indian agents or some of them at least; and in many instances I fear they have shared in the profits of these speculative transactions."

Grazing leases were defended as affording a fair compensation for land which might otherwise be grazed illegally. Moreover, leasing brought the Indian in contact with the livestock industry, which was the one best suited to the area. Thus, as if guided by an unseen hand, these cattlemen would be furthering the civilization of the red men while they themselves profited.

8 Testimony of E. B. Townshend before Senate Indian Affairs Committee, January 22, 1885, 49 Cong., 1 sess., *Report of Committees of the Senate*, serial 2362, pp. 198–230.

By 1891 two other means to this end were being emphasized, allotment and the dissolution of the tribal form of government. During the Iowa interlude the official policy had been to strengthen the chiefs in order to afford means of controlling the tribe. Not long after their arrival in Oklahoma the agents of the Sacs and Foxes began relaying to Washington unfavorable comments on the tribal form of government, comments which coincided with administration views. The principal chiefs, who received $500 annually as compensation for the services they performed, were described as reactionary, with the possible exception of Moses Keokuk, and even he had his critics among the whites. When, in 1885, the Sacs and Foxes met in council and adopted a constitution based on that formulated by the Osages a few years earlier, their action was prompted by their agent.[9] He was not completely satisfied with it, but he regarded it as an encouraging start toward "a complete overthrow of their old Indian form of government," as the progressive element among the Indians would probably secure control of the new machinery. The agent guaranteed this by stripping Chief Waucomo of his title and income for opposition to the adoption of the constitution.

That a government imposed on the Indians in this fashion could have been effective in representing them or commanding their respect was unlikely. In operation it performed too few functions to justify the expenditure of more than $3,000 annually. The council, the representative body under the new constitution, did emerge as the sounding board for tribal opinion and involved itself particularly in the controversy over white control of the schools around 1889. The multiple executive, consisting of four chiefs, and the supreme court, which had civil jurisdiction, were not notably active. Using economy and the general inaction of the tribal government as excuses, in November, 1891, authorities in Washington

[9] Isaac A. Taylor to the Commissioner of Indian Affairs, April 1, 1885, S–F Ltr. Bk., OHS.

concluded that the Indians should disband their government.[10]
The Sacs and Foxes complied by abolishing their constitution
and supreme court. They retained a numerically smaller council and the chiefs, but even the necessity for these was questioned, and more demands would be made upon them later.
Thus, Washington's policy on tribal government during the
first two decades of the Sac and Fox residence in Oklahoma was
to first force on the Indians a governmental system for which
they had no preparation and then to destroy that system. The
net effect of the policy was the achievement of its principle
objective—the weakening of tribal organization.

Allotment was also designed to accomplish that end. The
principles of the Dawes Severalty Act of 1887 were not applied
to the Sacs and Foxes until 1891, and then through the agency
of the Cherokee Commission, which rendered the same service—or disservice, as many Indians saw it—to other tribes in
Oklahoma. Within the Indian service there seems to have been
near unanimity on the virtue of allotment. So long as the Indians held land in common, they would lack the incentive to
apply themselves to agriculture. White friends of the Indian,
represented by such organizations as the Indian Rights Association, agreed with this concept. Americans who wanted to
separate the Indians from their land were also happy to co-
operate.

Among the Sacs and Foxes probably only a small minority
supported the allotment policy, but the hostile majority was
not effective in opposition. The national council did send a
delegation to Washington, including Charles Keokuk, the son
of old Moses Keokuk. Temporarily, at least, the third of the
Keokuk line was to represent his people; but the delegation
accomplished nothing. The time had passed when the threat
of the scalping knife could force the president of the United
States to interrupt his routine to listen to a Sac and Fox dele-

[10] T. J. Morgan to Samuel L. Patrick, August 2, 1892, S–F Councils File,
OHS.

gation or alter the course of government policy. Nor was any attempt made to justify current policy on the grounds that the majority of the Sacs and Foxes wanted it. This also was no longer necessary, and the Indians submitted fatalistically, "knowing their weakness and that they were children," as one Indian petition phrased it.

By August, 1891, 549 allotments of 160 acres each had been made to individual Indians and about $250 had been given to each Indian as his immediate share of the proceeds of the sale of unallotted lands. Only Mokohoko's band offered even passive resistance, but they included about one-quarter of the tribe. This band denied having shared in the negotiation with the Cherokee Commission the year before and required some persuasion. Most of the Indians who were absent when allotments were made were from this group. The selections made for absentees occasionally were very poorly chosen, but the Indians had no recourse.

Apparently, some of the Indians appreciated the situation well enough to litigate over the custody of children. One couple had separated to the accompaniment of the husband's charges of infidelity, and after the negotiation with the Cherokee Commission he tried to claim the baby, but his wife denied his paternity and won custody of the child and the allotment.

One agent observed at the time of allotment that "many of this tribe look forward to the settlement of this reservation by the whites as a new era in their method of living, and expect themselves to settle down upon their allotments, profiting from the knowledge their white neighbors will introduce in the arts and methods of agriculture, and become prosperous and industrious citizens." Undoubtedly, there were some in this category, but that there were many is not substantiated by the evidence. Approved or not, allotment had been accomplished, and its effect would show up markedly on the generation maturing after World War I.

Between 1891 and the end of World War I, many Sacs and

Foxes passively resisted acculturation rather successfully. The Secretary of the Interior in 1892 might declare generally that "the reservation system and the continuance of tribal relations have been broken to such a degree that what remains of these obstacles to the Indian's progress is light and easily removed," but such was certainly not always the case. Although the Sacs and Foxes no longer occupied a closed reservation and the fog of white men had finally engulfed them, they were not giving up easily.

The effects of allotment were apparent, but they were not always salutary. The Mokohoko band received contiguous allotments and fenced them in, with the result that their land was for several years still held in common. More than a decade after allotment the official report on the Oklahoma Sacs and Foxes was that "not a single full-blood Indian family is now sufficiently advanced to be self-supporting on a farm, all other aids removed."[11]

This was not due alone to the Indian allergy to plows and hoes; those anxious to become farmers lacked the capital to buy the equipment and the stock necessary. With the passage of the years and the death of original allottees, the problem of fractional ownership aggravated the situation. The usual answer to what could be done with an allotment with its ownership divided among ten or more people was to lease it. The practice was defended on grounds that the Indians would receive some income from it this way and they would gain from contact with the whites. Critics of the policy suggested that the white lessee would be concerned only with extracting a quick profit from the soil and would impoverish it, while the Indian lessor would be incapable of protecting his interest. Apparently, most of the Sacs and Foxes themselves, with the exception of Mokohoko's band, were anxious to lease. Official policy was at first to discourage it but later to accept it for

11 Annual Report of Ross Guffin, August 27, 1903, 58 Cong., 2 sess., *House Docs.*, serial 4645, pp. 276–79.

the reasons cited above and to prescribe a particular form to be followed. The whites resisted this interference with the free play of the market place which permitted them to fleece the unsophisticated Indians, and in 1895 and 1896 dishonest lessees banded together and threatened to defend their ill-gotten gains by force of arms. By 1920, however, illegal leasing was virtually a thing of the past and over half of the original allotments remaining in Indian hands were being farmed by whites with the approval of the Bureau of Indian Affairs.

The original agreement reached by the Sacs and Foxes with the Cherokee Commission had provided that of the 160-acre allotments, 80 acres would be in trust and exempt from taxation for a period of twenty-five years; the other 80 acres would be in trust for a five-year period with the possibility of extension. This latter clause was invoked and the trust period extended so that both would expire in 1916. Congress, however, did make it possible in 1902 for heirs of deceased allottees to sell their land if their agents approved. Anticipating a bonanza, speculators flooded in and "held high carnival in the saloons and gambling dens" until they learned the restrictions hedging such transactions.[12] By 1919, 345 titles in fee simple had been granted Indians, and these had usually been promptly sold to whites.

The exemption from taxes for trust lands was generally respected by county authorities in the years immediately following allotment, but Indian personal property was heavily assessed, as were plowed land, buildings, and wells. This practice, in the opinion of one agent, "has prevented them from making improvements, has caused many to scatter and leave the Reservations, prevented others that were away from returning, demoralized and discouraged them from trying to advance in civilization."[13] If ever a levy could be charged with taxing

[12] Annual Report of Ross Guffin, August 27, 1902, 57 Cong., 2 sess., *House Ex. Docs.,* serial 4458, pp. 304–305.

[13] Samuel L. Patrick to the Commissioner of Indian Affairs, March 2, 1893, S-F Ltr. Bk., OHS.

the life out of thrift and industry this was it.

In 1912 one additional source of income for the Sacs and Foxes materialized in oil and gas leases, as company representatives rushed in hoping to find wealth beneath Indian lands. Wealth there was, as travelers today passing the site of the old agency can observe in wells within one hundred yards of the ruins of buildings once the headquarters of the reservation. By 1917 the tribe was dividing about $25,000 annually from this source. However, very few individual Sacs and Foxes accumulated substantial incomes from gas and oil comparable to those enjoyed by the Osages.

A half century earlier the division of this additional income would have precipitated an acrid controversy in the tribe, and the chiefs and headmen would have been split into bitterly opposing factions. By 1920, however, tribal government was so inconsequential that even if factions did exist there was little tangible power for which to struggle.

As of 1891 the Sac and Fox government had been reduced to two chiefs who received $500 per year and eight councilmen who received $300 per year. The impressive façade of a national constitution and a supreme court had collapsed. Within a few years Indian service personnel were questioning the wisdom of paying the chiefs' and councilmen's salaries. In 1909 word came from Washington that a council should be called to discuss abolishing the present body and substituting for it a business committee. Of 135 Indians eligible to vote, 80 presented themselves. When only 10 of these voted to abolish the council and 49 to retain it, a number abstaining, the Secretary of the Interior ignored this expression of tribal sentiment and abolished the council. As had been demonstrated in the school incident, the policy of the Bureau of Indian Affairs was to encourage self-determination only as long as it was confined to innocuous matters. This was further illustrated when the superintendent, as the head of the agency was now called, broke a deadlock by personally selecting the new three-man business committee which replaced the old council and chiefs.[14] Given no real function by the government and distrusted for obvious reasons by the Indians, in 1914 the business committee lost what prestige it had had when the salaries of its members were eliminated. By 1920 it existed in theory only.

The long-time objective of eliminating tribal government had apparently been achieved, but otherwise the Sacs and Foxes by 1920 were a source of both pride and disappointment to their guardians. Only occasionally did one see a Sac or Fox with long hair, and blankets and paint had gone out of style. However, Indians continued to consume much time visiting, feasting, and dancing.

More of the Indians were farming their own tracts now or doing casual farm labor, but they were still regarded as shiftless and lazy by their white neighbors. As one tribesman explained it in 1912, Indians can't work because they want to sleep all the time, and white men can't sleep because they are thinking about making money all the time. "We can't work," he continued, "we try to work but we can't, the great spirit don't want us to work, it is for another thing he put us here, that is to hunt. Now the game is all gone to the west and they forbid us to go hunting."[15]

The Great Spirit to whom he referred was still not necessarily that deity the white man envisaged. By 1920 probably one-half of the Indians were actively pagan, and the Peyote cult had also secured a foothold among them. The record in education was more impressive as attendance at schools improved. With the merger of the Sac and Fox agency with the Shawnee agency, the Sac and Fox school closed and more young Indians entered the public school system, a move in line with government policy. However, educated Sacs and Foxes still were a problem, particularly the young men. Caught midway

[14] Copy of Sac and Fox Superintendent to the Commissioner of Indian Affairs, September 11, 1912, S-F Councils File, OHS.

[15] Meeting of Sacs and Foxes with Superintendent Horace J. Johnson, July 17, 1912, S-F File, NA.

between two cultures, they too frequently adopted the less socially acceptable traits of both. The one American institution they wholeheartedly adopted was baseball, but then the government officials complained of their concentration on the sport at the expense of normal employment. More young graduates of Indian schools chose to emulate Jim Thorpe, one of the greatest athletes America ever saw, than William Jones, who earned a Ph.D. at Columbia University.

Even baseball seems to have held no allure for the Iowa branch of the confederated tribes. They retained their reputation as conservatives by holding their land in common, wearing long hair, and painting long after the typical Oklahoma Sacs and Foxes had abandoned these customs of their forefathers. By 1920, relations between the Iowa and Oklahoma factions were improving, but only after negotiations which had strained their connection to the breaking point. In 1891 Congress approved payment by the Oklahoma Sacs and Foxes of $100,000 to the Iowa Indians in full satisfaction of any claims they might have. Nevertheless, the latter sought additional compensation, only to have the Supreme Court finally disallow a $450,000 claim in 1911.

About 1906 the old Mokohoko Band considered once again the possibility of emulating their kinsmen in Iowa by breaking away from the main body and returning to Kansas, where they would purchase a tract of land and return to the old customs.[16] But only a remnant of the band was around to consider this project. In 1899 smallpox had taken a heavy toll, and as part of the quarantine the village had been evacuated and burned. Even the sacred bundles which had been cherished by generations of Sacs and Foxes were destroyed. In 1956 Indians recalled that the officials crowned this indignity by forcing on them teams, wagons, and other equipment which they did not necessarily want but were a means by which traders extracted

[16] Annual Report of W. C. Kohlenberg, August 6, 1906, 58 Cong., 3 sess., *House Docs.*, serial 4798, pp. 306–309.

an additional $50,000 from them. Smallpox was at once a source of profit for some and an accessory to the civilization program; although stricken Sacs and Foxes might be only rolled in a blanket for interment, their estates were charged with caskets.

By 1920 it could be maintained that the Sacs and Foxes had moved a long way down the trail of acculturation. Officials happily pointed out the agricultural fair that was becoming an annual event, the organization of 4H Clubs, and the social amenities learned by teenage boys and girls at school functions featuring checkers, crokinole, and dominoes. They chose to ignore the Indians still stubbornly resisting the white man's way, and annually there were fewer of these.

After 1920 much of the old will to resist seems to have collapsed. The generation maturing in the twenties took less interest in the tribal ceremonies which had been preserved since the days on Rock River. Outnumbered one hundred to one by whites on what had once been their reservation, the Sacs and Foxes, now citizens by act of Congress, lost all semblance of tribal unity. By the end of World War II a full blood Sac or Fox was a rarity. Of the few full blood Indians on the tribal rolls, most were products of intermarriages between Sacs and Foxes and Kickapoos, Iowas, or members of other neighboring tribes. And no longer was there any attempt at distinction between Sacs and Foxes. The popular belief now was that all the Sacs lived in Oklahoma and all the Foxes in Iowa, although the term Sac and Fox Tribe was used to describe those Indians in Oklahoma.

Gradually, the Indians drifted from the reservation; by 1956, of about fifteen hundred Oklahoma Sacs and Foxes on the tribal rolls, there were approximately sixty families residing within the limits of the old agency. Various motives led to this dispersion, most of them economic. Although a few Sacs and Foxes rose in the world financially, many eked out an existence on the fringes of the white economy. With 60 per cent of the Indian land in complex multiple ownership, lease money had to be divided many ways. As has been the case since allotment, the Indian farmer was handicapped by a lack of capital necessary to procure equipment to expand operations. The period since World War I has seen the government policy toward the Indian go full cycle. In the twenties the government continued to urge the Indian to move out on his own and completely shed his Indian culture; Indian religion and customs were discouraged. The business committee, the remnant of the old tribal government, was consulted from time to time to "secure their co-operation and good will," but for all practical purposes was ignored.[17] Indeed, when the committee attempted occasionally to interfere in the conduct of official affairs, it was speedily put in its place.

With the passage of the Oklahoma Indian Welfare Act in 1936 came a new deal for the Sacs and Foxes. Over the vociferous protests of a minority of the tribe, the Indians reorganized their tribal government under a new constitution. Although the 1936 legislation was in line with the new policies exemplified by John Collier and designed to rehabilitate the Indian and save what was best in his culture, its practical effect on the Sacs and Foxes seems to have been little.

Currently, the Sacs and Foxes have a chief, but he receives no salary and exercises no real authority. The tribal council furnishes a forum for debate, but a lack of interest in it is manifested by the difficulty of obtaining a quorum of one hundred to conduct business. There is no evidence of any effective opposition to the trend underway since about 1950 to disassociate the federal government from Indian affairs. One by one, federal services to the Indian are either being terminated or transferred to the state.

Socially, the Sacs and Foxes are slowly merging with their white neighbors. Each decade since 1920 has seen the rate of acculturation accelerated. True, there are today tribesmen

[17] Shawnee Agency Narrative Report, 1927, Narrative Report File, NA.

who do not speak English, at least one still wears his hair long, the Peyote cult has a few adherents, and a number of Sacs and Foxes are still pagans. Also, without a doubt, there is a sizable minority within the tribe which would like to cling to the old ways, as is evidenced by the respect which it accords the memory of Black Hawk and the low esteem in which it holds old Keokuk and his son Moses. But the dances, which are the principal manifestation of their conservatism, are a far cry from those Thomas Forsyth saw in Saukenuk before Black Hawk went on the warpath. The costumes of the dancers, the songs, the dances themselves, as a result of borrowings from other tribes, retain little of the old flavor. And old Black Hawk would turn over in his grave at the thought of the Sacs and Foxes staging a war dance under the sponsorship of the local Chamber of Commerce.

Obviously, the process of acculturation is practically complete among the Oklahoma Sacs and Foxes. In 1954, the most recent government study reported 90 per cent of those under sixty as acculturated.[18] Among the old Missouri Sacs the process is regarded as complete, but the Tama Indians are classified as a group as incompetent, due to their poor progress in assimilating white culture.

Although the goal of complete acculturation of the Oklahoma Sacs and Foxes is finally in sight, there is little in the record of a century and a half of United States dealings with these Indians to inspire pride in an American. All the Oklahoma Indians have left of their once great landholdings are a few acres and a per capita annual income of about $40 from interest on tribal funds and oil leases. Left to their own devices the tribesmen would certainly never have deserted Illinois, Wisconsin, and Iowa and today would retain much of their old culture. But they were not allowed the freedom of choice. From Harrison's treaty in 1804 to the recent trend toward

[18] Investigation of Bureau of Indian Affairs, 83 Cong., 2 sess., *House Report No. 2680*, serial 11747, p. 84.

cutting the tribesmen adrift from the government, white officials have had the determining voice in Sac and Fox affairs, and they had to work for the welfare of the Indians with one eye on what would be the most satisfactory solution to white voters.

The dependence of the tribes was obvious to all by the end of the Black Hawk War, which acts as a great dividing point in the history of the Sacs and Foxes. Before 1832 the confederated tribes were a potent force on the frontier. In the War of 1812 they had thrown the balance to the British in the upper Mississippi Valley. Following 1832 they were a beaten people, to be shuttled from one reservation to another as the white man's greed for land dictated. It is a depressing story and not one that attracts the historian or the general reader like the tales of the thrilling days when Sac and Fox warriors proudly patrolled the Mississippi and Colonel Zachary Taylor, Lieutenant Zebulon Montgomery Pike, and sundry Sioux, Menominees, and Winnebagos took heed.

The trail down which General Harrison directed Black Hawk's people in 1804 was a long and thorny one. Ironically, the chairman of the Congressional Committee which signalled the arrival of the Oklahoma Sacs and Foxes at the end of that trail was William Henry Harrison, a great great grandson of the original architect of their downfall.

Bibliography

I. Manuscripts

1. National Archives
   Adjutant General's Office Files, 1830–33.
   Black Hawk War Miscellaneous Papers.
   Central Superintendency File.
   Inspectors File.
   Letter Books of the Commander-in-Chief, 1831–33.
   Letter Books of the Commander of the Eastern Department, 1831–33.
   Letter Books of the Commander of the Western Department, 1831–33.
   Narrative Report File.
   Quartermaster Historical File, 1831–32.
   Sac and Fox Agency File.
   Secretary of War, Letters Received, 1803–33.
   Secretary of War, Letters Sent, 1803–33.
   Secretary of War, Letters Sent, Indian Affairs, 1803–33.
   Unratified Treaty File.
2. Illinois Historical Library
   Black Hawk War Papers. They include Atkinson's Letter Book and Order Book, Albert Sidney Johnston's Journal, and many other valuable items.

Frank E. Stevens Papers.
3. Kansas Historical Society
   William Clark Papers.
4. Missouri Historical Society
   Thomas Forsyth Papers.
   P. Chouteau-Maffitt Collection. This contains some correspondence of the traders at Rock Island.
5. North Texas State College Library
   Microfilm copy of John Beach's Letter Book.
6. Oklahoma Historical Society
   Sac and Fox Agency Records. They include agency letter books, incoming correspondence, and an abundance of other indispensable items for the period following the Sac and Fox removal from Iowa.
7. State Historical Society of Wisconsin
   Nicholas Boilvin Letters, 1811–23. Ed. by Marian Scanlan. Transcripts and translations of letters in the National Archives.
   George Boyd Papers. Boyd was Indian agent at Mackinac and and Green Bay during much of this period.
   Thomas P. Burnett Papers. Burnett was Indian sub-agent at Prairie du Chien, 1829–34.
   Cass Letters Received, 1819–31. Photostats of records in the National Archives.
   Draper MSS. The Thomas Forsyth Papers were the principal item used in this collection.
   Joseph Steele Gallagher Papers. Extracts from letters and other accounts of Gallagher.
   Nathan Goodell Papers. Goodell was a resident at Fort Winnebago during the Black Hawk War.
   William Henry Papers. Henry was an early resident of northern Illinois and southern Wisconsin.
   House Files. Photostats of records in the National Archives.
   Indian Office Files, 1803–33. Photostats of records in the National Archives.
   Indian Office Letter Books, 1824–33. Photostats of records in the National Archives.

Bibliography

Parkinson, Peter Jr. "Henry Dodge in the Black Hawk War." A manuscript memoir.

Prairie du Chien MSS.

L. F. Stock Transcripts. Typed copies of manuscript notes of a survey of archival material made in Washington about 1910 by Stock.

Joseph M. Street Papers.

United States Miscellaneous Archives.

8. University of Illinois Library

Harper, Josephine Louise. "John Reynolds, 'The Old Ranger' of Illinois, 1788–1865." Unpublished Ph.D. Dissertation, 1949.

II. Government Documents

Annual reports of the Sac and Fox agents, the Commissioner of Indian Affairs, the Secretary of War, and the Secretary of Interior.

Indian Affairs (American State Papers, Vols. VII and VIII), Washington, 1832–34.

Investigation of Bureau of Indian Affairs, 82 Cong., 2 sess., House Report No. 2503, serial 11583.

Investigation of Bureau of Indian Affairs, 83 Cong., 2 sess., House Report No. 2680, serial 11747.

III. Newspapers

The Burlington Hawk Eye and Iowa Patriot, 1839–43.

The Cincinnati Chronicle, 1831–32.

The Detroit Democratic Free Press and Michigan Intelligencer, scattered numbers, 1831–32.

The Eastern Argus (Portland, Maine), scattered numbers, 1812.

The Galenian (Galena, Illinois), 1832.

The Globe (Washington, D. C.), 1831–32.

The Indiana Journal (Indianapolis), scattered numbers, 1832.

The Intelligencer (Vandalia, Illinois), scattered numbers, 1832.

The Iowa Territorial Gazette (Burlington), 1839–41.

The Michigan Herald (Detroit), scattered numbers, 1825–28.

The Missouri Republican (St. Louis), 1831–32.

The Sac and Fox Indians

The National Intelligencer (Washington, D. C.), scattered numbers, 1815–32.

The New York Mercury, 1831–32.

The New York Observer, 1832.

The New York Sentinel, scattered numbers, 1832.

Niles Weekly Register (Baltimore), 1811–33.

The Ohio State Journal (Columbus), scattered copies, 1827.

Oklahoma Historical Society newspaper holdings. I have used extensively the subject index but did not search entire files on particular newspapers.

The Sangamo Journal (Springfield, Illinois), 1831–32.

The Scioto Gazette (Chillicothe, Ohio), scattered numbers, 1832–33.

The St. Louis Beacon, scattered copies, 1831–32.

The Weekly Kansas Herald (Leavenworth), 1859.

The Wisconsin Territorial Gazette (Burlington), 1838.

IV. Other Printed Sources

Abel, Annie Heloise. "Indian Reservations in Kansas and the Extinguishment of their Title," *Transactions of the Kansas State Historical Society,* Vol. VIII, 72–109.

Anderson, Captain T. G. "Capt. T. G. Anderson's Journal, 1814," *Wisconsin Historical Collections,* Vol. IX (1882), 207–61.

Armstrong, Perry A. *The Sauks and the Black Hawk War with Biographical Sketches, Etc.* Springfield, Illinois, 1887.

Atwater, Caleb. *The Writings of Caleb Atwater.* Columbus, Ohio, 1833.

Black Hawk. *Life of Black Hawk: Ma-Ka-Tai-Me-She-Kia-Kiak.* Ed. by Milo Milton Quaife. Chicago, 1916. Purportedly the memoirs of Black Hawk as dictated by him to Antoine LeClaire, an interpreter, and subsequently edited by J. P. Patterson. This volume must be used with care. This writer is certain that Black Hawk did contribute to the production of this work, but he is also certain that LeClaire and Patterson left their imprint as well. It is particularly weak on chronology.

Bibliography

Boilvin, Nicholas. "Prairie du Chien in 1811," *Wisconsin Historical Collections,* Vol. XI (1888), 247–53.

Bracken, Charles. "Further Strictures on Ford's Black Hawk War," *Wisconsin Historical Collections,* Vol. II (1903), 402–14.

Bryant, William Cullen. *Prose Writings of William Cullen Bryant.* Ed. by Parke Godwin. 2 vols. New York, 1901.

Brymner, Douglas. "Capture of Fort M'Kay, Prairie du Chien, In 1814," *Wisconsin Historical Collections,* Vol. XI (1888), 257–70.

Bulger, Alfred Edward. "Events At Prairie du Chien Previous to American Occupation, 1814," *Wisconsin Historical Collections,* Vol. XIII (1895), 1–9.

–––. "Last Days of the British at Prairie du Chien," *Wisconsin Historical Collections,* Vol. XIII (1895), 154–62.

"The Bulger Papers," *Wisconsin Historical Collections,* Vol. XIII (1895), 10–153.

Catlin, George. *North American Indians.* 2 vols. Philadelphia, 1857.

Cleaves, Freeman. *Old Tippecanoe: William Henry Harrison and His Times.* New York, 1939.

Cole, Cyrenus. *I Am A Man: The Indian Black Hawk.* Iowa City, 1938.

Collections and Researches Made by the Michigan Pioneer and Historical Society, Vol. XV. Lansing, 1909.

Carter, Clarence Edwin, ed. *The Territorial Papers of the United States.* 18 vols. Washington, 1934–52.

Cooke, Phillip St. George. *Scenes and Adventures in the Army.* Philadelphia, 1857. Cooke participated in the campaign in 1832.

Cruikshank, Ernest. "The Employment of Indians in the War of 1812," *American Historical Association Annual Report for 1895,* 321–35.

–––. "Robert Dickson, The Indian Trader," *Wisconsin Historical Collections,* Vol. XII (1892), 133–53.

Dawson, Moses. *A Historical Narrative of the Civil and Military Service of Major General William H. Harrison, and a Vindication of his Character and Conduct as a Statesman, a Citizen, and a Soldier.* Cincinnati, 1824.

The Sac and Fox Indians

Drake, Benjamin. *The Great Indian Chief of the West or, Life and Adventures of Black Hawk.* Cincinnati, 1858.

Dyer, Brainerd. *Zachary Taylor.* Baton Rouge, 1946.

Edwards, Ninian W. *History of Illinois from 1778 to 1833 and Life and Times of Ninian Edwards.* Springfield, 1870.

Elliott, Charles Winslow. *Winfield Scott: The Soldier and the Man.* New York, 1937.

Ferris, Ida M. "The Sauks and Foxes in Franklin and Osage Counties, Kansas," *Collections of the Kansas State Historical Society, 1909–1910,* Vol. XI, 333–95.

Ford ,Thomas. *A History of Illinois from Its Commencement as a State in 1818 to 1847.* Chicago, 1854.

Foreman, Grant. *The Last Trek of the Indians.* Chicago, 1946.

Fulton, A. R. *The Red Men of Iowa.* Des Moines, 1882.

Gallaher, Ruth A. "Indian Agents in Iowa," *Iowa Journal of History and Politics,* Vol. XIV, 348–94, 559–96.

———. "The Tama Indians," *The Palimpset,* Vol. XXXI, 249–59.

Gates, Paul Wallace. *Fifty Million Acres: Conflicts Over Kansas Land Policy, 1854–1890.* Ithaca, 1954.

Gittinger, Roy. "The Separation of Nebraska and Kansas From the Indian Territory," *The Mississippi Valley Historical Review,* Vol. III, 442–61.

Glimpses of the Past. Publications of the Missouri Historical Society, Vol. II. (1935).

Greene, Evarts Boutell, and Clarence Walworth Alvord, eds. *The Governors' Letter Books. Collections of the Illinois State Historical Library,* Vol. IV (1909).

Gregg, Kate L. "The War of 1812 on the Missouri Frontier," *The Missouri Historical Review,* Vol. XXXIII (1939), 3–22, 184–202, 326–48. An able account which makes particularly good use of local newspapers.

Hamilton, Holman. *Zachary Taylor: Soldier of the Republic.* Indianapolis, 1941.

Harmon, George Dewey. *Sixty Years of Indian Affairs.* Chapel Hill, 1941.

Harrington, M. R. "Sacred Bundles of the Sac and Fox Indians," *University of Pennsylvania Anthropological Publications,* Vol. IV, No. 2 (1914).

Bibliography

Harrison, William Henry. *Messages and Papers*. Ed. by Logan Esarey. 2 vols. Indianapolis, 1922.

Hodge, Frederick Webb, ed. *Handbook of American Indians North of Mexico*. Bureau of American Ethnology, *Bulletin No. 30*. 2 vols. Washington, 1907.

Iles, Major Elijah. *Sketches of Early Life and Times in Kentucky, Missouri and Illinois*. Springfield, Illinois, 1883. Iles was Lincoln's commanding officer for a brief period during the campaign of 1832.

Joffe, Natalie F. "The Foxes of Iowa," in Ralph Linton, ed., *Acculturation In Seven American Indian Tribes*. New York, 1940.

Johnston, William Preston. *The Life of General Albert Sidney Johnston*. New York, 1879.

Jones, William. *Ethnography of the Fox Indians*. Bureau of American Ethnology, *Bulletin No. 125*. Washington, 1939.

Kappler, Charles J., ed. *Indian Affairs: Laws and Treaties*. Washington, 1904.

Lambert, Joseph I. "The Black Hawk War, A Military Analysis," *Journal of the Illinois Historical Society*, Vol. XXXII (December, 1939), 442–73.

Lewis, Meriwether, and William Clark. *Original Journals of the Lewis and Clark Expedition 1804–1806*. Ed. by Reuben Gold Thwaites. 7 vols. New York, 1905.

Lindley, Harlow. "William Clark: The Indian Agent," *Proceedings of the Mississippi Valley Historical Association for 1908–1909*, 63–75.

McCall, George A. *Letters From the Frontiers, Written During a Period of Thirty Years' Service In the Army of the United States*. Philadelphia, 1868. McCall was aide to General Gaines during the campaigns of 1831 and 1832.

McKenney, Thomas L., and James Hall. *The Indian Tribes of North America*. Ed. by Frederick Webb Hodge. 3 vols. Edinburg, 1933.

McKinley, S. B., and Silas Bent. *Old Rough and Ready*. New York, 1946.

Malin, James C. "Indian Policy and Westward Expansion," *Bul-*

letin of the University of Kansas, Humanistic Studies, Vol.
II, No. 3 (1921).

Maximilian, Prince of Wied. *Travels in the Interior of North America, 1832–1834.* Vols. XXII, XXIII, and XXIV in R. G. Thwaites, ed., *Early Western Travels 1748–1846.* Cleveland, 1904–1907.

Mahan, Bruce E. *Old Fort Crawford and the Frontier.* Iowa City, 1926.

Manypenny, George W. *Our Indian Wards.* Cincinnati, 1880.

Meese, William A. *Early Rock Island.* Moline, Illinois, 1905.

"Papers from the Canadian Archives 1767–1814," *Wisconsin Historical Collections,* Vol. XII (1892), 23–132.

"Papers of Thomas G. Anderson, British Indian Agent, 1814–21," *Wisconsin Historical Collections,* Vol. X, 142–49.

Parkinson, Daniel M. "Pioneer Life in Wisconsin," *Wisconsin Historical Collections,* Vol. II (1903), 326–64.

Pelzer, Louis. *Henry Dodge.* Iowa City, 1911.

Pike, Zebulon Montgomery. *The Expeditions of Zebulon Montgomery Pike to Headwaters of the Mississippi River, Through Louisiana Territory, and in New Spain, During the Years 1805–6–7.* Ed. by Elliot Coues. 3 vols. New York, 1895.

"Prairie Du Chien Documents, 1814–15," *Wisconsin Historical Collections,* Vol. IX (1882), 263–81.

Pratt, Harry E. *Lincoln 1809–1839: Being the Day-by-Day Activities of Abraham Lincoln from February 12, 1809 to December 13, 1839.* Springfield, Illinois, 1941.

Priest, Loring Benson. *Uncle Sam's Stepchildren.* New Brunswick, 1942.

Ragland, Hobart D. "Missions of the Society of Friends Among the Tribes of the Sac and Fox Agency," *The Chronicles of Oklahoma,* Vol. XXXIII, 169–82.

Reynolds, John. *My Own Times: Embracing Also the History of My Life.* Chicago, 1879.

Salter, William. *The Life of Henry Dodge from 1782 to 1833.* Burlington, Iowa, 1890.

Scanlan, Charles M. *Indian Creek Massacre and Captivity of Hall Girls.* Milwaukee, 1915.

Bibliography

Scanlan, Peter Lawerence. "Nicholas Boilvin, Indian Agent," *Wisconsin Magazine of History*, Vol. XXVII (December, 1943), 145–69.

———. *Prairie du Chien: French, British, American*. Menasha, Wisconsin, 1937.

Schoolcraft, Henry R. *Historical and Statistical Information Respecting the History, Condition, and Prospects of the Indian Tribes of the United States*. 6 vols. Philadelphia, 1827.

———. *Personal Memoirs of a Residence of Thirty Years With the Indian Tribes on the American Frontier: with Brief Notices of Passing Events, Facts, and Opinions, A.D. 1812 to A.D. 1842*. Philadelphia, 1851.

Silver, James Wesley. *Edmund Pendleton Gaines: Frontier General*. Baton Rouge, 1949.

Smith, Captain Henry. "Indian Campaign of 1832," *Wisconsin Historical Collections*. Vol. X (1909), 150–66. A reprint of an article which first appeared in the *Military and Naval Magazine* in August, 1833. During 1832, Smith served as a company commander under Atkinson.

Smith, William R. *The History of Wisconsin In Three Parts, Historical, Documentary, and Descriptive*. 3 vols. Madison, 1854.

Snyder, J. F. "The Burial of Black Hawk," *Magazine of American History*, Vol. XV (May, 1886), 494–99.

Spencer, J. W., and J. M. D. Burrows. *The Early Day of Rock Island and Davenport*. Ed. by Milo Milton Quaife. Chicago, 1942.

Stevens, Frank E. *The Black Hawk War Including a Review of Black Hawk's Life*. Chicago, 1903. Stevens devoted many years to collecting material relating to the war and wrote a history which is remarkably full in some details. Unfortunately, it is marred by a strong prejudice against the Indians.

———. "Illinois in the War of 1812–1814," *Transactions of the Illinois State Historical Society for 1904*, 62–197.

———. "Stillman's Defeat," *Transactions of the Illinois State Historical Society for 1902*, 170–79.

Tax, Sol. "The Social Organization of the Fox Indians," in Fred Eggan, ed., *Social Anthropology of North American Tribes,* 243–84. Chicago. 1937.

Thwaites, Reuben Gold. *The Story of the Black Hawk War.* Madison, Wisconsin, 1892.

"Voyage on the Upper Mississippi," *The Military and Naval Magazine of the United States,* Vol. III (1834), 245–52, 349–57. From similarities between this article and the accounts of George A. McCall I have concluded that McCall was the author of this one as well.

Wakefield, John A. *History of the War Between the United States and the Sac and Fox Nation of Indians, and Parts of other Disaffected Tribes of Indians in the Years 1827–31–32.* Jacksonville, Illinois, 1834. Wakefield was a participant in the campaigns of 1831 and 1832. With the exception of chronology in a few instances, his account is relatively dependable.

Washburne, E. B., ed. *The Edwards Papers. Chicago Historical Society Collections,* Vol. III (1884).

Wesley, Edgar B. "James Callaway in the War of 1812," *Missouri Historical Society Collections,* Vol. V (1927–28), 38–81.

Whittlesey, Colonel Charles. "Recollections of a Tour Through Wisconsin in 1832," *Wisconsin Historical Collections,* Vol. I (1903), 64–85.

Index

Index

Index

281

Index

The Sac and Fox Indians

has been planned for maximum comfort in reading and handling. The type is eleven point Baskerville, set on the Linotype with two points of spacing between the lines. This face is the first of the transitional romans in English printing, and was developed about 1750 by John Baskerville. Based on Caslon, it is the link between tradition and revolution in printing types.

 UNIVERSITY OF OKLAHOMA PRESS : NORMAN

H 7/19